TEACHING READING
USING
MICROCOMPUTERS

TEACHING READING USING MICROCOMPUTERS

Robert T. Rude

Rhode Island College
Providence, Rhode Island

Prentice-Hall, Inc., Englewood Cliffs, New Jersey 07632

Library of Congress Cataloging in Publication Data

Rude, Robert T. (date)
  Teaching reading using microcomputers.

  Includes bibliographies and index.
  1. Reading—Computer-assisted instruction.   2. Reading
—Computer programs.   I. Title.
LB1050.37.R83   1985   428.4'07'8   85-6427

Cover photo courtesy of
Commodore Electronics Limited

Editorial/production supervision and
    interior design: Marianne Peters
Cover design: Diane Saxe
Manufacturing buyer: Barbara Kelly Kittle

Printed in the United States of America

10   9   8   7   6   5   4   3   2   1

ISBN   0-13-895285-X   01

Prentice-Hall International (UK) Limited, *London*
Prentice-Hall of Australia Pty. Limited, *Sydney*
Prentice-Hall Canada Inc., *Toronto*
Prentice-Hall Hispanoamericana, S.A., *Mexico*
Prentice-Hall of India Private Limited, *New Delhi*
Prentice-Hall of Japan, Inc., *Tokyo*
Prentice-Hall of Southeast Asia Pte. Ltd., *Singapore*
Editora Prentice-Hall do Brasil, Ltda., *Rio de Janeiro*
Whitehall Books Limited, *Wellington, New Zealand*

This book is dedicated to those who keep me going . . .

Pat

Tracy

Laura

Pepper

White Lightning

CONTENTS

PREFACE

Who would have thought a decade ago that a computer could be purchased at a discount department store? Who even envisioned that stores specializing in the sale of microcomputers would sprout up across the country? Certainly few of us had the insight to foresee that microcomputers would be as popular as hand-held calculators. The 1980s has launched us full-bore into what has been called the computer revolution. At this point, the future of educational computing is still unclear. What is clear, however, is that the influx of microcomputers into all segments of our society has changed the way we live and think. This book explores some of the ways computers have affected the way teachers of reading carry out instruction. In some areas of instruction, microcomputing is already widely used. In other instances, however, we are only beginning to tap the potential uses of these machines.

The volatility of the microcomputer market makes it impossible to envision clearly the classroom of the 1990s. Nevertheless, the technology will inevitably affect our teaching strategies. Educational computing, being the new field that it is, lacks the solid research base that supports much of what we know about the teaching of reading. Perhaps it is most pertinent at this time, then, to examine how computers can complement what we know to be effective strategies for teaching reading. Only time will permit us to evaluate whether microcomputers and their accompanying software have made our students better readers. This book tries to meld what we know about the teaching of reading with an examination of computer hardware and software.

Chapter 1 provides a short history of school uses of microcomputers. Specifically, it looks at the growth of microcomputers in education and earlier attempts to integrate computer-assisted instruction into school settings.

Chapter 2, *Microcomputer Systems*, is intended to acquaint the computing neophyte with the terminology of the field. Many readers already know much about microcomputer systems and their operation. For those individuals, I have attempted to provide more detailed information than would typically be found in an Introduction to Microcomputers text. Additionally, projections regarding future hardware trends are presented. Chapter 2, however, is primarily for the new computer user.

Classroom Applications, Chapter 3, is a discussion of the various categories of educational software. Overviews of how drill-and-practice, tutorial, gaming, simulations, and materials generation software relate to reading are provided.

Chapter 4, *Software for Reading*, specifically addresses the availability of software for teaching decoding, comprehension, and study skills. Issues such as the possible interaction of the reluctant reader and the microcomputer are also discussed. Theories of the reading process and their relationship (or lack of) to available software are also presented.

Chapter 5, *Word Processing and Related Software*, is the most comprehensive chapter in the book. Word processing has the potential to become the most powerful application available to teachers of reading and the language arts. This chapter raises some of the issues teachers must address when attempting to use word processors with students. The chapter also introduces the reader to two related applications – electronic dictionaries and thesauruses.

Chapter 6, *Specialized Classroom Applications*, examines readability analyses, speedreading programs, authoring systems, spelling programs, and administrative software. As in the previous chapters, this chapter attempts to link our theoretical understanding of the reading process with available software.

The last chapter, Chapter 7, *Selecting Software*, discusses the software selection process. Of special importance is the explanation and discussion of why the typical software reviewing process and the published reviews of reading and language arts software is usually found wanting. A special form is provided to help teachers of reading better evaluate the instructional merit of reading software.

Readers desiring more information about microcomputer software are referred to the Appendices and Indices. The first appendix includes a list of computer-related books that are suitable for students. Appendix B lists the software described in this book. Appendix C provides the reader with a list of the software publishers' addresses. There are also two indices in the book – the conventional author listing and the subject index.

Teaching Reading Using Microcomputers is an attempt to integrate what is known about reading instruction with the software that is available to teach reading and the language arts. Each chapter follows a similar format. First, the objectives of the chapter are identified. These objectives should help the reader focus his/her attention on the content to be presented. Extensive use of center heads and sub-heads have been included to lend a sense of organization and coherence. The reader will find that end of chapter summaries provide a capsule review of the chapter. For individuals desiring to go beyond the information presented in the text, a list of recommended readings are suggested. These readings cut across the disciplines of reading and computer-assisted instruction.

Finally, each chapter concludes with a list of references that are used throughout the chapter.

Throughout this book I have attempted to present an up-to-date picture of reading-related software tied to a consistent theory of reading. When appropriate, statements are supported with bibliographic entries. Some books and articles that discuss reading software do so in a light, chatty style that lacks the authoritative references needed to support pedagogical recommendations. Other publications present extensive bibliographic information but fail to discuss the existing software market. *Teaching Reading Using Microcomputers* attempts to take the best of these two worlds and synthesize them into a handy paperback text that can be used as a supplement to reading methods courses or that can serve as a stand-alone text for a special issues course or workshop that specifically focuses on microcomputers and reading instruction.

ACKNOWLEDGMENTS

Any book is the combined effort of a host of individuals, each contributing in their own special way to the final product. Some people offer suggestions relating to the overall organization of chapters. Others provide a detailed critique of the mechanics of writing. Still others raise questions that are overlooked by the author in earlier drafts of the manuscript. I have been fortunate to have many friends, coworkers, students, and reviewers who have provided these services and furnished the necessary feedback as this text evolved from an idea to the printed page. Among the host of "assistants," a number have been especially helpful. The individuals noted below are deserving of my special thanks.

Susan Willig, Education Editor at Prentice-Hall, for her willingness to undertake this project in light of our earlier association in the production of a reading methods textbook. Susan and her trusty associate, Shirley Chlopak, were always there when questions needed to be answered. A special thank you also goes to my friendly production editor, Marianne Peters. Marianne performed yeoman's duty as she shepherded this text through its various stages of production.

Bill Oehlkers, a coauthor on another Prentice-Hall textbook, was most helpful in providing feedback regarding the underlying reading methods described in this text. I have enjoyed ten years of Bill's friendship; over half of this time has been as a coauthor or an astute reviewer of published works. Thanks, Bill.

Rita Wilson, on location in Nova Scotia, reacted to the manuscript with the eagle eye of an English teacher. I am especially grateful to her for her insights. In the midst of pregnancy, childrearing, and blizzards, Rita provided fresh perspectives that I frequently overlooked.

I am indebted also to Maureen Lapan, Director of the Rhode Island College Curriculum Resources Center, for her willingness to order and share much of the software listed in this text as well as hundreds of other software programs that are not discussed herein. Maureen was always ready to make special provisions to enable software to be evaluated.

Also deserving of mention is a cadre of graduate students who enrolled in a Reading and Microcomputers workshop. These students used a draft of the manuscript as a text and offered innumerable recommendations for improvement. Among those who always came through for me were Mary Cerullo, Kay Liptak, Mary Lowe, Arlene Millitello, Lois Oehlkers, Arlene Sequin, and Celia Stabile. I hope they learned as much from me as I learned from them.

I am also indebted to my family who never complained about my 5:00 AM escapades on the keyboard and printer or my reluctance to give up some weekends to join them on their "outings." Hopefully, it was worth it.

Many individuals and companies supplied complimentary copies of software for review purposes as this text evolved. Some of the programs were especially pertinent for inclusion, others were fine products but for one reason or another were inappropriate. I am especially appreciative to all those who supplied software for examination whether it was used as examples in this text or not.

Finally, an author's best friends are his/her reviewers. I am especially grateful to Professor Donna Alverman of the University of Georgia, Dr. David Pearson of the University of Illinois, Dr. Peggy Ransom of Ball State University, Mr. Bruce Reynolds of Torrey Pines High School, Dr. Timothy Shanahan of the University of Illinois, and Professor Dixie Lee Spiegel of the University of North Carolina.

TEACHING READING USING MICROCOMPUTERS

ONE

INTRODUCTION

Upon completing this chapter, you will be able to

— 1. Describe the rapid growth of microcomputers in our society.
— 2. Articulate some of the patterns of microcomputer use throughout the United States.
— 3. Describe research on the effectiveness of computer-assisted instruction.
— 4. List the advantages of using microcomputers for reading instruction.

AN OVERVIEW OF MICROCOMPUTERS

"Microcomputer" is the buzzword of the 1980s. Virtually everywhere you turn, this term appears. Newspapers in metropolitan areas regularly carry columns devoted to microcomputer use or sales. Newspaper ads for microcomputers proliferate. Even popular weekly magazines such as *Time, Newsweek,* and *U.S. News & World Report* carry feature stories about how microcomputers and related high-technology hardware are affecting our daily lives.

The business and scientific communities, while among the first to benefit

1

from the microcomputer revolution, are not the only areas of our society to feel the impact of this new technology. Microcomputing is a "grass-roots" movement. According to at least one source (Bell, 1983), the home market is perhaps the fastest-growing segment of the microcomputer movement. By the end of 1983, 6.2 million computers had been purchased for use in American homes (Shea, 1984). This means that 7.5 percent of American homeowners owned a microcomputer. Programs designed to operate on home computers are being sold at a phenomenal 71 percent increase per year (p. 63). While during the 1950s parents pondered over which television set to purchase, today's parents are faced with deciding which microcomputer and what kind of software to buy.

Purchasing computers is only one facet of a greater parental concern. In addition to worrying about their childrens' mastery of basic reading, writing, and arithmetic skills, the parents of the 1980s are now raising youngsters who need to become computer literate. Not only must Johnny read; now he must compute!

Schools have been quick to respond to parental and societal pressures to introduce microcomputers into the curriculum. It is difficult, though, to know exactly how many microcomputers are available in our nation's schools. By the time a nationwide study is undertaken, the number of machines has increased so dramatically that the data collected are hopelessly out of date. Nevertheless, several efforts have been made to understand the dimensions of this groundswell.

According to the National Center for Educational Statistics, in 1981, about half of the school districts in the United States owned one or more microcomputers (Spencer and Baskin, 1983). By 1982, this number increased by 60 percent. According to Ingersoll, Smith, and Elliot (1983), however, by the 1981–82 school year, microcomputers were located in nearly one-third of the nation's public schools. A 1981 *EPIE Report* (EPIE Institute, 1981) documented that approximately one out of every four public schools had at least one microcomputer or computer terminal that was used for instructional purposes. A Lou Harris poll conducted at the end of 1983 found that children in 40 percent of the households with school-aged children used a computer at school (*Report on Educational Research*, 1983). When administrators were asked, in 1983, whether they would be purchasing additional microcomputers for their schools, almost 60 percent responded that they expected to purchase at least one additional microcomputer for their school within that academic year (Ingersoll, Smith, and Elliot, 1983). Between the 1981–82 and 1982–83 school years, a 290.4 percent increase in microcomputer purchases was reported, bringing the total number of microcomputers in our nation's schools to 55,175 (*Report on Educational Research*, 1984). The growth trend in educational computing should continue during the 1980s and possibly into the 1990s. In a few years, virtually every school will have at least one microcomputer. It is difficult, however, to predict what impact microcomputers will ultimately have on the education of today's youngsters. One thing is clear, though. Manufacturers will continue to sell these machines at a blistering speed.

Hofmeister (1982) contends that the three top manufacturers of microcomputers produced a million micros during 1982 and that a 40 percent growth rate will continue into 1985. That translates into 3.7 million microcomputers worth roughly $3.9 billion. After reviewing the data of a New England research group, Hamilton (1983) discovered that microcomputer sales have soared from $1.0 billion in 1981 to $1.5 billion in 1982 with more than $2.0 billion in sales recorded by year-end 1983. Sales during the early 1980s were so good, in fact, that the opening of new computer stores increased more than 50 percent—during the worst economic slump in almost half a century!

These phenomenal sales have had an impact on almost every educator. Apple Computer, one of the largest producers of computers for the home and school market, has already donated thousands of microcomputers to California schools (Merton, 1983). Conceivably, the passing of state and federal legislation will make it even more enticing for manufacturers to make donations of microcomputers to public and private educational institutions. Perhaps, before 1987, the prediction of an average of thirty-five microcomputers in every high school will be a reality (Bell, 1983).

Approximately 15 percent of the nation's elementary and secondary schools are using computers as teaching tools (Zeiser and Hoffman, 1983). Their use, however, varies by grade level as well as by region of the country. In a survey of 1,082 microcomputer-using schools, the Center for Social Organization of Schools at the Johns Hopkins University (1983) described the following profile of school use of computers.

1. In about half of the surveyed schools, one or two teachers were the primary microcomputer users.
2. At the elementary school level, the average school had two microcomputers. Each was used about eleven hours per week under the direction of a teacher or staff member. Forty percent of the activities were of the drill-and-practice variety. A typical student used a micro for less than thirty minutes during the week.
3. At the secondary level, a typical high school had five microcomputers, each of which was used for a total of thirteen hours per week. Sixty-six percent of the time these machines were used for programming or similar types of activities. There was some use of microcomputers for word processing, but much less time was spent on writing than was devoted to programming. A typical student used a microcomputer for slightly more than forty-five minutes per week.

According to the Center, though,

microcomputers in elementary schools do not function as major ingredients in the teaching of principles and techniques of verbal and mathematical operations, as do other media such as books, chalkboards, and worksheets. Most students do not get a sufficient amount of time for any appreciable skill building to take place. (p.8)

The average secondary school student, on the other hand, received about twice as much access time during a typical week according to the Center (1983).

Interestingly, computers are used in varying degrees and for different purposes based on where they are found in the United States. Elementary schools in the northeastern United States, for instance, use their computers less extensively than do elementary schools in other parts of the country. Fewer students in this region have access to micros as well. Elementary schools in the southern United States spend more time using microcomputers for drill-and-practice applications than they do for teaching programming. The opposite is true in western U.S. schools, however. In the West, they use their machines primarily to teach programming to above-average students. Computer users in midwestern schools report about an equal distribution of drill-and-practice and programming activities. Because microcomputer use varies dramatically not only by grade level (i.e., elementary versus secondary) but also by geographic region, there is probably no single "best" way in which to use these machines effectively. Use will vary depending upon the teacher's perception of what will most benefit students. And, since we are only in the early phases of using this technology, the verdict is still out on the long-range implications of computer-related instruction.

Related to the educational use of microcomputers is the training of teachers. For the most part, teacher training has not kept pace with the introduction of microcomputers. This is not because there is a lack of interest on the part of educators. Anyone who has attended an educational conference in the past five years can attest to the popularity of computer-related sessions. Teachers are not only interested in microcomputers but they also have positive feelings toward them (Ingersoll, Smith, and Elliot, 1983). A facet that teachers find especially attractive is the enthusiasm and motivation that students demonstrate when using the computer. In addition, most teachers believe that the computer is an excellent tool to drill students on curriculum-related subjects.

With the field of educational computing rapidly changing, it is difficult to predict what innovations will occur in hardware or software. What is clear, though, is that in this decade microcomputer use should have a profound impact on our schools and the manner in which students receive instruction. While the specific outcomes of this effort are impossible to foresee, it is sure that microcomputers will continue to play an important role in the education of students.

RESEARCH ON THE EFFECTIVENESS
OF COMPUTER-ASSISTED INSTRUCTION

In examining the research in the field of computer-assisted instruction (CAI), it is clear that few investigations are directly related to the use of microcomputers and instruction. Instead, most CAI-related studies have used large mainframe computers in an attempt to improve student achievement. According to Spencer and Baskin (1983), instructional uses of microcomputers are so new that little formal research has been conducted. Nevertheless, there is probably a close relationship between learning from mainframe CAI programs and learning from microcomputer CAI materials.

A review of past CAI investigations reveals a number of important findings. Among them are the following:

1. CAI has been shown to be most effective in the areas of science, math, and foreign languages. Because of the nature of the subject matter, it has been less effective in reading and the language arts (Fisher, 1983; Merton, 1983).

2. CAI is at least as effective as traditional instruction and may actually lead to significant improvements in some subject areas (Holmes, 1982).

3. Children are highly enthusiastic about working with computers and academic motivation usually improves (Spencer and Baskin, 1983; Merton, 1983; Fisher, 1983).

4. Students learn instructional materials at a faster rate—in some cases up to 40 percent faster—when computers are used (Fisher, 1983; Gleason, 1981; Hofmeister, 1982; Orlansky, 1983).

5. CAI appears most effective when used with either low-achieving or high-achieving groups rather than with entire student populations (Fisher, 1983).

One reason for the effectiveness of CAI may lie in the fact that the computer is able to deliver focused instruction at a level of student need. According to Mason (1982), between 75 and 80 percent of a reading teacher's instructional time is spent giving directions and supervising students as they complete worksheets in noncomputer environments. Durkin (1978) has also found that in many classrooms, only a small amount of time is actually devoted to teaching reading comprehension skills. Whether this lack of focused instruction is the result of insufficient instructional materials or is due to inappropriate teacher planning is unclear at this time. What is known, however, is that a computer is frequently able to provide additional drill and practice that cannot be provided personally by the teacher. Microcomputers permit students to spend more time on instructional tasks. One hour per day with a microcomputer can theoretically provide a student with more interaction than he or she would receive in a day in a regular classroom (Holmes, 1982).

A potential danger of CAI, however, is the reduction of fruitful communication among students (Deford, 1981; Rubin, 1983). As teachers of the communication arts, we know that social-interpersonal relationships play an important part in learning. Microcomputers have the potential for reducing the interactions among individuals and, at an extreme, could have a deleterious effect on the social environment of the classroom. As more and more machines are introduced into schools, educators need to monitor how they are being used.

Watchdogs of CAI continually remind us that the long-term effects of instruction via computers are still unclear. One interesting question that remains is, "Does the role of the teacher change substantially in a CAI environment?" As students become more responsible for their own learning and as computers play a greater role in instruction, "Will teachers need to alter their teaching behaviors?" Answers to these questions are unavailable at this time.

Ultimately, of course, the issue of improved performance must be addressed. Roblyer (1981) and Steffin (1983) both argue that the final consideration in any experiment is whether measurable changes in student achievement or behavior can be identified. Unless student performance improves, the millions of dollars invested in microcomputer hardware and software may be for naught. At least one critic (Eisele, 1981) has suggested that a common practice when introducing a new technology in education is to take action first without examining the long-term instructional effects. This frequently leads to a waning interest in the innovation and eventually results in an abandonment of a potentially useful aid to teaching. Let us hope that this is not the case with microcomputers and education.

THE ADVANTAGES OF USING MICROCOMPUTERS FOR READING INSTRUCTION

Picture if you will how a classroom of middle school students receiving reading instruction might appear in the foreseeable future. As you enter the room, you notice that five microcomputers have been placed in key locations and are being used by the students. You begin to walk around the room and peer over the shoulders of students busily engaged at the keyboards of their microcomputers.

Here's Ann Smith, working on a drill-and-practice activity. Ann needs to develop a basic sight vocabulary of high-frequency words. Her teacher has selected several programs that permit the instructor to "customize" the words that need to be learned. The words all appear in a sentence context. As Ann identifies the words, the computer automatically advances to a randomly selected word from the preprogrammed list of words. At the conclusion of the lesson, Ann will raise her hand, signaling that she has finished her assignment. Her teacher will then command the computer to print a list of words Ann missed on the first trial. These words will form the basis for Ann's future lesson.

In another section of the room, Sean McDonald is reviewing a lesson on synonyms and antonyms. This computer program is a tutorial that defines both synonyms and antonyms, provides examples of each, and then presents an arcade-type lesson in which Sean must select the appropriate antonym from a given list by using the computer keyboard as a laser to "shoot" the correct answer. Should he miss more than three consecutive items, the computer reviews the meaning of antonyms and then returns to the game format.

Arthur Freidman has a problem. Arthur is so advanced for his age that he has little patience for the humdrum of basal reader stories. Arthur wants action!!! To challenge him, the teacher has assigned an interactive novel to be read on the computer screen. Arthur carries on a running conversation with the computer, asking questions, seeking clues, and trying to outwit the author of the novel. Arthur is in seventh heaven.

Josh Anderson is yet another interesting study. He is so timid he seldom volunteers information in front of his peers. To help Josh, the teacher has assigned some lessons that will help assess whether he is comprehending his reading assignments yet don't force him to perform in a large-group situation. In time, Josh's confidence will develop to the point that he will no longer need to work extensively on the computer.

Finally, huddled around the fifth microcomputer is a group of students. What can this be? Aren't computers designed for one-to-one instruction? A closer inspection reveals that these students are busily engaged in writing the "Riddle Page" for the class newspaper. Using an inexpensive word processor, they are typing riddles submitted by other members of the student body. At this point, they are rearranging text to group the riddles into logical categories. Once finished, they will submit a draft of the paper to their teacher for final editing.

As you can see, the computers in this room are used in a variety of ways to help improve students' reading ability. Of course, this classroom may have more microcomputers than most, but the computers can be used to enhance reading instruction in a variety of ways.

This is not to imply that microcomputer instruction is not without its problems. Indeed, the development of software programs has not kept pace with hardware developments, and as a result, most of the educational software that does exist has not been validated (Hofmeister, 1982). The software is also narrow in scope (Hannaford and Taber, 1982), and educators have not been sufficiently instructed in the use of microcomputers as an adjunct to increasing their teaching effectiveness.

Even with these limitations, though, the picture is becoming brighter. Today, relatively inexpensive CAI is available for a large percentage of our students. Access to this technology should provide a number of benefits according to Steffin (1983). For one thing, the computer is able to generate problems in a random order, thereby assuring that students will encounter a fresh sequence of problems each time they use the machine. Second, unlike some earlier instructional tools, the computer forces learners to take an active role in their learning. Another desirable feature is that through continuous feedback, students are kept abreast of their progress in learning new materials. Finally, the computer can provide individuals with an opportunity for learning in an almost private environment. This can be especially beneficial for students who are anxious about teacher or peer approval. Through patient drill, the computer can encourage even the most timid learner.

Contrary to what some individuals may believe, computer-assisted instruction in reading is not a new technology. One of the earliest attempts to use computers to teach reading was the Stanford Projects (Fletcher, 1979). These efforts, like many CAI projects of the 1960s, were plagued by several shortcomings. It was expensive to connect terminals via telephone lines to large mainframe computers, the computers were relatively slow by today's standards, software material was primarily text oriented, and many of the computers were unreliable (Wagner, 1983).

But things are changing—rapidly changing. Microcomputers appear everywhere in schools. In the chapters that follow, we will explore where this technology is leading us (or should we say where we are leading it?) and what challenges it presents for teachers of reading. There are many Anns, Seans, Arthurs, and Joshes in the classrooms of the world. This book explores what can be done to help these students become even better readers.

SUMMARY

Adoption of the technology of microcomputers has been a grass-roots movement that has swept our country by storm during the past decade. Many families now own a personal computer. The influx of microcomputers in schools has also mushroomed beyond all expectations.

While computer-assisted instruction is not a new technology, the use of microcomputers in schools is. Since schools have not had sufficient time to assess the value of these machines, their long-range impact on education is unknown. Nevertheless, microcomputers do possess several apparent advantages for teachers such as being able to assign students independent work on tailor-made lessons, being able to provide immediate feedback to the user, and having the capability to store test results, thereby providing information to the teacher that can result in more personalized instruction.

While some questions concerning their use remain unanswered, it appears as if microcomputers can help the teacher of reading in a number of ways. The purpose of this book is to explore those applications.

RELATED READINGS

HAWKRIDGE, DAVID. *New Information Technology in Education.* Baltimore, Md.: Johns Hopkins University Press, 1983.

TAYLOR, ROBERT P. (ed.). *The Computer in the School: Tutor, Tool, Tutee.* New York: Teachers College Press, 1980.

REFERENCES

BELL, TRUDY, "Computer Literacy: The Fourth R," *Personal Computing,* Vol. 7, no. 5 (May 1983), 63–69.

CENTER FOR SOCIAL ORGANIZATION OF SCHOOLS, "School Uses of Microcomputers," Baltimore, Md.: Johns Hopkins University Press, Issue No. 3, October 1983.

DEFORD, DIANE E., "Literacy: Reading, Writing, and Other Essentials," *Language Arts,* Vol. 58, no. 6 (September 1981), 652–658.

DURKIN, DOLORES, *What Classroom Observation Reveals About Reading Comprehension Instruction,* Technical Report No. 106, Champaign: Center for the Study of Reading, University of Illinois, October 1978.

EISELE, JAMES E., "Computers in the Schools: Now That We Have Them...?" *Educational Technology,* Vol. 21, no. 10 (October 1981), 24–27.

EPIE INSTITUTE, "Materials—Microcomputer Courseware/Microprocessor Games," *EPIE Report*, Vol. 15, no. 1/2M (Fall–Winter 1981), 1–11, 16–19.

FISHER, GLENN, "Where CAI Is Effective: A Summary of the Research," *Electronic Learning*, Vol. 3, no. 3 (November–December 1983), 82, 84.

FLETCHER, J. D., "Computer-Assisted Instruction in Beginning Reading: The Stanford Projects," in *Theory and Practice of Early Reading*, Lauren B. Resnick and Phyllis A. Weaver, eds., Hillsdale, N.J.: Lawrence Erlbaum Associates, 1979.

GLEASON, GERALD T., "Microcomputers in Education: The State of the Art," *Educational Technology*, Vol. 21, no. 3 (March 1981), 7–18.

HAMILTON, ALLEN, "Computers Come Home—Via the Corner Store," *The Providence Sunday Journal*, (May 8, 1983), F1–F2.

HANNAFORD, ALONZO, and FLORENCE M. TABER, "Microcomputer Software for the Handicapped: Development and Evaluation," *Exceptional Children*, Vol. 49, no. 2 (October 1982), 137–142.

HOFMEISTER, ALAN M., "Microcomputers in Perspective," *Exceptional Children*, Vol. 49, no. 2 (October 1982), 115–121.

HOLMES, GLYN, "Computer-Assisted Instruction: A Discussion of Some of the Issues for Would-be Implementors," *Educational Technology*, Vol. 22, no. 9 (September 1982), 7–13.

INGERSOLL, GARY M., CARL B. SMITH, and PEGGY ELLIOT, "Microcomputers in American Public Schools: A National Survey," *Educational Computer*, Vol. 3, no. 6 (October 1983), 28, 30–31.

MASON, JANA, *A Description of Reading Instruction: The Tail Is Wagging The Dog*, Reading Education Report No. 35, Urbana: The University of Illinois at Urbana—Center for the Study of Reading, (August 1982), 1–30.

MERTON, ANDREW, "Computers in the Classroom," *Technology in the Classroom*, Vol. 3, no. 9 (September 1983), 39–42, 44, 46.

ORLANSKY, JESSE, "Effectiveness of CAI: A Different Finding," *Electronic Learning*, Vol. 3, no. 1 (September 1983), 58, 60.

Report on Education Research, Vol. 15, no. 26 (December 21, 1983), 2, Arlington, Va: Capital Publications, Inc.

Report on Education Research, Vol. 16, no. 8 (April 11, 1984), 3, Arlington, Va: Capital Publications, Inc.

ROBLYER, M. D., "When Is It 'Good Courseware'? Problems in Developing Standards for Microcomputer Courseware," *Educational Technology*, Vol. 21, no. 10 (October 1981), 47–54.

RUBIN, ANDEE, "The Computer Confronts Language Arts: Cans and Shoulds for Education," *Teaching Writing Through Technology*, Chelmsford, Mass.: Northeast Regional Exchange, 1983, 15–40.

SHEA, TOM, "News Briefs," *InfoWorld*, Vol. 6, no. 18 (April 30, 1984), 15.

SPENCER, MIMA, and LINDA BASKIN, "Computers in the Classroom," *Childhood Education*, Vol. 59, no. 4 (March–April 1983), 293–296.

STEFFIN, SHERWIN A., "A Suggested Model for Establishing the Validity of Computer-Assisted Instructional Materials," *Educational Technology*, Vol. 23, no. 1 (January 1983), 20–22.

WAGNER, WALTER, "Microcomputers and the Management of Instruction," *Educational Computer*, Vol. 3, no. 6 (October 1983), 46–47, 71.

ZEISER, EDWARD L., and STEVIE HOFFMAN, "Computers: Tools for Thinking," *Childhood Education*, Vol. 59, no. 4 (March–April 1983), 251–254.

TWO

MICROCOMPUTER SYSTEMS

Upon completing this chapter, you will be able to

— 1. Identify a number of popular microcomputers and discern their basic differences.
— 2. Describe the differences between monitors and television sets used with microcomputers.
— 3. Explain the operation, benefits and limitations of using cassette operating systems for software and data storage.
— 4. Summarize the operation, benefits, and limitations of using disk drives for software and data storage.
— 5. Compare different types of printers.
— 6. Explain the use of modems, hard disk drives, and optical mark readers.

Achieving a comprehension of the wide variety of microcomputers and their accompanying components (usually referred to as peripherals) is an overwhelming task. Not only is the market flooded with many types of microcomputers but changes occur so frequently that it is difficult to keep abreast of new developments. While it is impossible to keep track of every new piece of hardware, it is possible to highlight several distinctive trends.

First, as microcomputers have become more common, prices have tended to decline. This price reduction has resulted in lower profit margins for many companies, which, in turn, has driven them from the school and home marketplace. Second, rapid technological developments have produced more powerful computers than their earlier counterparts at no significant increase in price. In fact, many machines are actually cheaper today than when they were first introduced. Third, the educational computing market has become less volatile than the home market, with three or four major microcomputer companies dominating the field. As of the mid-1980s, roughly half of the microcomputers owned by schools were manufactured by Apple Computer while the combined sales of Apple, Radio Shack, and Commodore Computers accounted for over three quarters of the educational market ("Two New Studies," 1983). As IBM continues to move into the school market, however, more and more schools may opt to purchase machines developed by this blue-chip company.

Teachers of reading who are unfamiliar with microcomputers should not be frightened by the barrage of microcomputers that exists in today's marketplace. In all probability, the shakeout in this industry is likely to continue, and before long, publishers of educational programs for microcomputers will no doubt develop materials to run on only the more popular school microcomputers.

Educators new to the field of educational computing should understand several important terms and be aware of the equipment that is available for school use. Readers who consider themselves well versed in computer jargon and operation might want to skip the following section and move directly to Chapter 3, Classroom Applications.

MICROCOMPUTERS FOR TODAY'S SCHOOLS

If the present trend in educational microcomputing continues, four companies will continue to dominate the school market: Apple, Radio Shack, Commodore, and IBM. Each of these manufacturers, however, has a number of computers in its product line. With so many new products from which to choose, selecting a microcomputer system may seem a formidable task. Williams and Shrage (1983) said it well:

> The variety of microcomputer systems in schools makes the decision to purchase any particular unit both exciting and frustrating. Exciting because the flexibility of the different units and number of available alternatives gives purchasers a variety of systems that will meet their needs. Frustrating because any purchase involves compromise between the costs and features of the different systems. (p. 12)

To gain a better understanding of the options available, a general intro-duction to microcomputers and their special features is in order.

Portable Microcomputers

A number of self-contained, portable microcomputers have been recently introduced for those individuals who need a compact machine that can be easily moved from one location to another. These machines vary in size from

FIGURE 2.1   Radio Shack Model 100 Portable Microcomputer (Courtesy of Radio Shack, a division of Tandy Corporation.)

FIGURE 2.2   Compaq Portable Microcomputer (Courtesy of Compaq® Computer Corporation.)

FIGURE 2.3   Apple® Macintosh Microcomputer (Courtesy of Apple® Computer, Inc.)

approximately 1 × 4 × 10 inches and weighing less than 5 pounds to portables measuring 20 × 9 × 16 and weighing roughly 26 pounds. Each machine has a keyboard, screen, and a system to load or save programs. Radio Shack's Model 100 (Figure 2.1) and the Compaq microcomputer (Figure 2.2) are two such machines. To date, though, both of these machines have found only limited use in schools. The importance of these microcomputers is that they are probably the progenitors of what is to follow within the next decade. Apple Computer, for instance, introduced its Macintosh microcomputer in January 1984 (Figure 2.3). While slightly larger than the Radio Shack Model 100, it is substantially smaller and lighter than the Compaq portable. The Macintosh also has a number of innovative features such as extremely high-resolution graphics and heretofore unheard of user-friendliness. These two features could make it one of the most popular microcomputers ever built. Just as calculators decreased in size over the years, so too will the size of microcomputers continue to shrink. Full-sized keyboards and viewing screens will probably keep micros from being placed on wristwatches, but powerful microcomputers already exist that are no larger than an average-sized textbook.

In the future, portable computers will be common in schools. Conceivably, students will carry and use microcomputers with the same nonchalance that they do calculators.

Semiportable Microcomputers

Most of the microcomputers found in schools can be categorized as semiportable machines. Some individuals have dubbed these microcomputers as "transportable." In general, they are light enough that they can be carried or wheeled on carts from room to room. Some manufacturers have designed their microcomputers to be self-contained. That is, keyboard, monitor, and memory devices are mounted in an integral, one-piece housing. Other manufacturers have opted for a more modular approach with each of these components existing as separate units, interconnected with cables.

There are advantages and disadvantages to each system. The self-contained units are easy to move and generally require less space. The disadvantage of these systems is that if any part should malfunction, the entire unit must be returned for repairs, thus disabling the whole computer system. The modular system has the advantage that components from various manufacturers may be intermixed, thereby creating a "customized" computer. Moreover, if any of the parts malfunction, they can be replaced while the defective item is brought in for repairs. Usually, this permits the computer to stay in operation. The disadvantages of the modular system are that they are more cumbersome to move, components may be inadvertently dropped or damaged, and the system has a less "streamlined" appearance.

More important than the physical appearance of microcomputers, however, are the distinctive characteristics of the various machines. Let us now turn our attention to some of the features teachers should consider when selecting a machine to help teach reading.

Special Features

There are a number of facets that may affect the ultimate utilization of microcomputers. Memory size, color capability, sound generation, keyboard layout, and compatibility with other machines are just five factors that should be considered when selecting a school computer.

Memory Size.   For the most part, computer users are most concerned with the random access memory, or RAM, of a microcomputer. RAM is the amount of internal storage that a computer contains. Whenever a key is depressed on the keyboard, one piece of information (or byte) is stored in the RAM. Random access memory is usually available in increments of a thousand bytes. One thousand bytes constitutes 1K of memory. (Technically, 1K is 1,028 bytes, but for most purposes it is sufficient to think of it as 1,000 bytes.) Most popular school computers contain 16K, 32K, 48K, 64K, or 128K of RAM.

When purchasing programs, it is important to know the RAM capacity of a machine since it is impossible to run programs that exceed the memory capabilities of the microcomputer. Purchasing a commercial reading software program that requires 64K of RAM and trying to run it on a 48K machine will usually result in an error message on the screen informing the user that the program demands more memory than is presently available. In other words, the user will be unable to load the program into the microcomputer, and, hence, the program cannot be used.

Users should also know that RAM is volatile. This means that once the computer is turned off, everything contained in RAM will be lost. This presents no problem if commercially available software is being used since the user simply reloads it into the RAM of the machine. If a letter is being composed and the operator accidentally shuts the microcomputer off before saving the information on a magnetic disk or tape before printing it, however, the treasured composition will be lost.

Occasionally, users may encounter the term read only memory, or ROM. The ROM of each machine contains the operating instructions or programming language for the microcomputer. These instructions are inscribed on the silicon ROM chips. Unlike RAM, ROM is nonvolatile. Regardless of whether the machine is turned on or off, the operating instructions remain permanently inscribed on the ROM chips. For practical purposes, users need not be concerned about the ROM unless they are interested in learning more about the inner architecture of microcomputers.

Color Capability.   Ultimately, a teacher's purpose for using a micro-computer will determine whether or not he or she needs color capability. If the machine will be used primarily to compose worksheets, record student dictation while conducting language-experience lessons, or introducing students to word processing, there is little need to purchase a computer with color capability. On the other hand, if the primary use will be to run commercially available games and drill-and-practice activities, it may be important to select a computer that has color capability. Some programs require a color computer, monitor, or other hardware such as internally installed circuit boards. This is necessary since a monochrome monitor sometimes will not permit the user to discern some features of a program, such as color-coded doors or pathways.

As with many things in life, added capabilities mean added expense. A color monitor or television set can easily add $200.00 to $500.00 to the cost of a system. It is important, therefore, to determine how a microcomputer will be used so an appropriate system can be purchased.

Sound Generation.   Many popular microcomputers have built-in speakers that enable the production of high-quality sound. Depending on the program, sounds ranging from laser blasts to sonatas are possible. For the teacher of reading, however, sound capability should only be a secondary concern. Most programs that use sound do so strictly for reinforcement purposes. The exact effect of using sound as a reinforcer has not been demonstrated to enhance performance significantly, so for the time being, educators should not let the fact that a computer lacks this capability deter them from purchasing a specific machine.

Two additional features relating to sound also deserve mention. As the technology becomes more and more sophisticated, we will no doubt witness microcomputers that have built-in speech synthesis capabilities. Some machines already support such features, but these add-on features are usually available through third-party vendors, not the manufacturer of the microcomputer. Speech synthesis promises to be an exciting development, especially for teachers who work in the communicative arts or in special education settings. To date, however, this technology is still in its infancy and has not had a major impact on schools or the teaching of reading.

Finally, at least one company has developed a piece of hardware that permits the integration of a cassette tape recorder with a microcomputer. This switch, called a cassette-control device, is an electronic box that is installed between the microcomputer and the tape recorder. Teachers can use the device when recording spelling lessons for students. The system operates by activating the tape recorder to play the dictated spelling words. After each word, the student types the word on the computer keyboard. The cassette recorder then advances the tape to the next dictated word. Students continue to type their responses on the computer until the lesson is finished. The computer maintains a record of the students' responses. By connecting headphones to the cassette recorder, students may be drilled on lessons without disturbing others in the classroom.

Keyboard.   Keyboard designs are simultaneously similar and unique. Their similarity resides in the fact that the majority of microcomputers use a standard "qwerty" keyboard. This term is derived from the fact that as one looks at the upper-most row of keyboard letters, the six left-most letters spell "qwerty." Keyboard similarities end here, however.

At one point, some microcomputer manufacturers used membrane keyboards. These keyboards resembled the control panel of some popular microwave ovens. Instead of keys, a plastic panel containing slight depressions at each key location was used. Such an arrangement assured that no foreign particles would be spilled or dropped between the keys, but it did little to enhance the speed or accuracy of touch typists.

A second development that microcomputer users have witnessed is the emergence of reduced-size keyboards that have nonstandard keys. Simply put, these keyboards do not lend themselves to standard finger-hand placement. Eventually, as the user becomes more facile, a more conventional keyboard is desired. Nonconventional keyboards of any kind, therefore, are not recommended.

Perhaps the most distinguishing features of popular school microcomputer keyboards are numeric keypads and function keys. Each can enhance ease of use depending upon the ultimate use of the machine (Figure 2.4).

Numeric keypads are calculatorlike number keys usually located on the right-hand edge of the keyboard. While not necessary for most classroom applications, they are desirable if large quantities of numerical data must be

FIGURE 2.4   Keyboard of an IBM PC Microcomputer (Courtesy of IBM.)

entered. A reading supervisor, for example, who is responsible for entering students' reading test scores into a computer management system would benefit from a numeric keypad. The device permits scores to be quickly entered. It also eases the job of entering budgetary data about reading programs.

Function keys are keys that permit the computer to perform special tasks by simply striking a single key. They are usually numbered "F1," "F2," "F3," and so on and are perhaps more important than numeric keypads for most reading teachers. This is because many word processing programs take advantage of these special keys. One program, for example, uses one function key as the "help" key. Whenever the user is unsure of how to execute a particular operation, simply pressing the "help" key brings a series of prompts to the screen. This on-screen prompting makes for a very "user-friendly" system and usually negates having to page through printed manuals.

As computer users become familiar with the power of word processing, these function keys enable more sophisticated operations to be performed with less effort. If the ultimate goal is to use word processing with middle school or older students, the user should consider a microcomputer with an advanced keyboard design.

Compatibility.   Compatibility refers to the degree to which two or more computers are able to use the same programs. As a rule, commercial programs are designed to run on only one manufacturer's machine. While there are exceptions, users shouldn't count on interchanging programs from one make or model of computer to another. This means that programs designed to run on an IBM PC, for instance, are not usable with a Radio Shack microcomputer. (It should also be noted, however, that there may be a degree of compatibility within some product lines. Most Apple II+ software, for instance, will run on a IIe or IIc, and most TRS-80 Model III software will run on the Model IV. Not all of the software for an IBM PC will run on a PC *jr*, however.)

The importance of compatibility is directly related to the microcomputers available in the school or district. If most of the computers are brand X, buyers are probably better off selecting that brand for use. Doing so means that more programs will be available for shared use—all other things being equal. On the other hand, if a school has brand Y and examination of software reveals that few reading or language arts programs are available to use with that machine, it is probably better to switch brands. While compatibility is an important consideration, even more important is the fact that a microcomputer is virtually useless if appropriate programs are unavailable. The "best" system, therefore, is the one that will help teachers do their job. Or to put it another way, the "best" microcomputer is the machine with the greatest amount of high-quality software.

Popular School Microcomputers

At the end of 1983, an estimated 325,000 microcomputers were in use in American schools ("Two New Studies," 1983). The "Big Three" manufacturers were Apple, Radio Shack, and Commodore. While IBM is the nation's foremost supplier of large computers, it was not until late 1983 that IBM entered the school and home computer market. Rather than provide an in-depth analysis of each company's products, however, only the salient features of their more popular microcomputers will be described here.

Apple Microcomputers. The three most prevalent microcomputers found in schools are the Apple II+, the Apple IIe, and the Apple IIc. The II+ machine was the forerunner of the IIe and IIc. The success of the II+ microcomputer, in both the school and the home market, is probably attributable more to the companies who developed software programs to run on the Apple than it is to the machine itself. Literally thousands of programs have been written for the Apple II+. As a result, it was inevitable that the II+ should find such favor with educators since many of these programs could be used in school settings.

The Apple II+ is characterized by its 52-key, standard qwerty keyboard. It can be connected to a television set or to a standard computer monitor. (To connect to a television set, however, a special electrical device called an RF modulator is needed.) In most schools, machines are equipped with either 48K

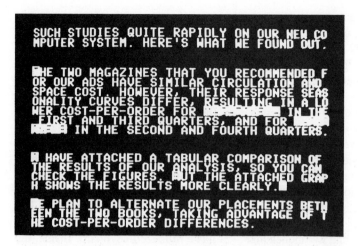

FIGURE 2.5   40-column Screen Display on an Apple® Computer (Courtesy of Apple® Computer, Inc.)

FIGURE 2.6   Apple IIe® Microcomputer (Courtesy of Apple® Computer, Inc.)

or 64K of random access memory and one or two disk drives. The display presented on the screen is 40 characters wide by 24 rows deep (Figure 2.5). The 40-column width results in printed word processing documents that are not duplicated on the printer exactly as they are seen on the monitor. This stems from the fact that printers print text that is approximately 80 characters wide rather than the Apple's 40 characters. (This topic will be discussed further in the chapter devoted to word processing, Chapter 5.)

The Apple IIe (Figure 2.6) was intended to replace the Apple II+. (The "e" stands for "enhanced".) This computer is factory equipped with 64K of RAM and can be upgraded to 128K. The screen display can be improved from 40 to 80 columns by adding an inexpensive circuit board inside the machine. (Technically, this can also be done to the Apple II+ but only at much greater expense.) The keyboard provides a number of additional keys, the most noteworthy being an upper and lowercase shift key that enables both upper and lowercase letters to be displayed on the screen, something lacking in the Apple II+. Outwardly, the IIe closely resembles the II+, but internally the former has far fewer components. Many programs written to run on the II+ can still be used on the IIe. An informal survey conducted by the author revealed that over 95 percent of the Apple II+ programs could be run on the Apple IIe with no modification to the programs.

In 1984, Apple Computer introduced the Apple IIc (Figure 2.7). (The "c" may stand for "compact" and "capable".) The machine is 12 inches long, 11¼ inches wide, and 2¼ inches high, yet has a full-sized keyboard. Inside, the IIc has 128K of RAM, the equivalent storage of 50 double-spaced typewritten pages. Other features include 16-color ultra high-resolution graphics capability, the ability to produce five octaves of sound, and a 5¼-inch built-in disk drive. The microcomputer is marketed as an easy-to-set-up machine whose operation

FIGURE 2.7   Apple IIc® Microcomputer (Courtesy of Apple® Computer, Inc.)

can be mastered in hours and whose usefulness will last for years. The IIc is especially noteworthy because it is an example of how one company has continually produced smaller but more powerful microcomputers at no substantial increase in price over earlier models.

Apple computers have an avid following of both teachers and students. The wide selection of software available coupled with the fact that many parents of students own Apple computers means that these machines should continue to be popular at all levels of education. If someone has a specific application in mind for a computer, there is probably a program written for the Apple that will allow him or her to do the job quickly and effortlessly.

Radio Shack Microcomputers.   While Apple may produce the most popular microcomputers, Radio Shack machines were the first inexpensive micros to become available to the general public and, hence, today command a large share of the home and school market. Radio Shack has produced a number of different models of microcomputers. Its first computer, the Model I, is still found in some schools. Originally, it retailed for about $1,000.00. Today, however, the Model I has been replaced by a succession of models, two of the most popular being the Model IV and the Radio Shack Color Computer. The former sells for under $1,000.00; the latter retails for about $250.00.

The Model IV is a self-contained unit that includes a monitor, keyboard, and optional disk drives (Figure 2.8). While it does not have color capability, it does offer excellent editing capabilities that are lacking on the Apple. The

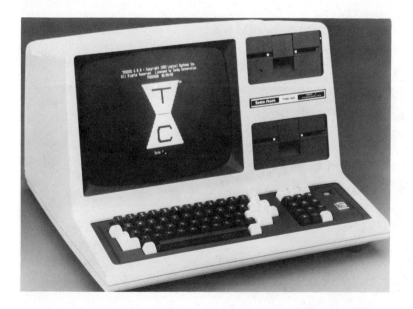

FIGURE 2.8   Radio Shack Model IV Microcomputer (Courtesy of Radio Shack, a division of Tandy Corporation.)

Model IV will also run software designed for the Model III. Overall, the Model IV is an excellent value.

Radio Shack now manufactures several color computers. Compared with the Apple micros, the former's machines lack the memory capability but they do provide an inexpensive means of enjoying the benefits of computing on a shoestring budget.

While there are many excellent science and math programs for the Radio Shack machines, the development of word processing, reading, and related language arts software has lagged behind that of the Apple microcomputers.

Commodore Microcomputers. Commodore computers are used in a number of schools throughout the country. The most inexpensive of Commodore's offerings is the VIC-20 (Figure 2.9), which sells for under $100.00 while the PET 4032 (Figure 2.10) costs substantially more. Priced between these two models is the popular and relatively inexpensive Commodore 64 (Figure 2.11).

The VIC-20 microcomputer is a keyboard with the microprocessor enclosed within the same housing. The computer can be connected to a color television set and a cassette recorder, thereby completing the entire system. One shortcoming of the VIC-20 is the limited number of educational programs available for the machine. It also has only a 22-character width screen display. Nevertheless, for individuals who want to explore what computers have to offer, and are willing to live with some limited features, the VIC-20 may be the perfect choice.

The Commodore 64 provides many advanced features for a fraction of the cost of an Apple, Radio Shack, or IBM computer. The machine resembles the VIC-20 in appearance, although the casing in which the microprocessor is housed is a different color. As its name implies, this microcomputer comes with

FIGURE 2.9   VIC-20 Microcomputer (Courtesy of Commodore Electronics Limited.)

FIGURE 2.10   PET 4032 Microcomputer (Courtesy of Commodore Electronics Limited.)

64K of RAM. The machine has a 66-key qwerty keyboard, upper- and lower-case letters, a 40-column screen format, a sound generator, and a music synthesizer. It has the capacity to produce moderately high-resolution graphics in up to 16 different colors. Furthermore, it can be programmed to run a number of different computer languages. Another feature of this machine allows the user

FIGURE 2.11   Commodore 64 Microcomputer (Courtesy of Commodore Electronics Limited.)

to connect it to a disk drive, thereby permitting access to a wide variety of educational programs. Currently, more and more publishing companies are producing software programs that will run on the Commodore 64.

One of the most popular computers of the Commodore line is the Commodore 4032 (Figure 2.10). This machine has a built-in monitor, special numeric keyboard, graphics keys, and special function keys. The machine can be connected to either a cassette recorder or disk drives, the latter being the most popular option. Just as with the Commodore 64, an increasing number of publishing companies are producing software that will run on this machine. And, like the Commodore 64, the 4032 offers a 40-column screen format.

IBM Microcomputers.   Several years ago, IBM introduced its first microcomputer, the IBM PC (Figure 2.12). Upon its introduction, many technical writers were asked to comment on the impact this machine would have on its intended market—the small business community. One said, "When a locomotive comes down the tracks, you step aside." In one year, IBM captured 30 percent of the intended market.

While the IBM PC has had a dramatic impact on the business community, its effect on the educational community has been negligible, the major reason probably being its relatively high price. While some schools have purchased the PC for word processing applications, as long as its price is approximately double that of an Apple computer, educators will continue to purchase Apple, Radio Shack, or Commodore machines at the expense of IBM PCs.

In an effort to compete with less expensive computers, IBM introduced its PC *jr* in the final quarter of 1983 (Figure 2.13). This machine is available in two

FIGURE 2.12   IBM PC Microcomputer (Courtesy of IBM.)

FIGURE 2.13   IBM PC jr Microcomputer (Courtesy of IBM.)

versions, the cheapest selling roughly in the Apple or Radio Shack price range. The PC *jr* has the capability of running programs that are available on either diskettes or cartridges. It also has an infrared beam connection that allows the keyboard to be placed apart from the actual computer. As of this writing, this machine is too new to determine its impact on the educational market.

MONITORS VERSUS TELEVISION DISPLAYS

Configuring a microcomputer system with a video display depends on the ultimate use of the machine. Once the decision is made on how the microcomputer will be used, the local computer dealer can assist in making the choice. The purpose of this discussion is to alert the reader to some of the advantages and disadvantages of selecting one type of video unit over another. Two of the first questions that must be answered are, How will the microcomputer be used? and How much money can be spent? Once these questions have been answered, the local dealer can grapple with the technical issues that are related to the matching of computer to video display.

Purchasing a microcomputer with a built-in monitor automatically eliminates the question of selecting a video unit. But most computers enable an individual to connect any one of a variety of televisions or monitors. The type of display selected, however, may determine the types of programs able to be used with the machine.

Two important factors affecting a decision relate to (1) the type of computer purchased and (2) whether the computer will be used for word processing. As mentioned earlier, some microcomputers display as few as 22 characters across the screen. The size of each character is relatively large, and, hence, the need for a high-resolution video display is minimal. Other microcomputers, however, display as many as 80 characters across the screen. For the sake of clarity, such machines require high-resolution monitors. As a rule of thumb, instructional programs that present text or word processing applications require high-resolution monitors.

According to at least one source (EPIE Institute, 1981), most video monitors for microcomputers have a 250-line resolution. This is roughly half the resolution (i.e., "sharpness") that we are accustomed to seeing when we read print material. Because the resolution of most video monitors is considerably better than that of television sets, it is easy to understand why monitors are generally preferred whenever text material is to be displayed. Eye fatigue can be reduced considerably.

Monochrome monitors are available in black and white, green, or amber. Usually the green or amber screens are recommended for word processing applications since they tend to reduce eye fatigue. Prices for monochrome monitors generally fall between $100.00 and $200.00.

Color monitors are considerably more expensive—$300.00 up to $1,000.00. These monitors provide improved resolution over color television sets, but their resolution is still unsatisfactory for word processing applications. This is because the colors tend to "bleed" around the edges of the letters, hence reducing the sharpness of the image. This can be such a problem for computers that produce an 80-column text width that the user is virtually unable to read the screen.

Teachers interested in using their microcomputers for programs not requiring text applications may find that an existing school-owned black-and-white or color television set may suit their purpose. For teachers with limited budgets, an inexpensive microcomputer connected to a television is a financially acceptable way to move into the computer era.

In summary, word processing applications usually require investing in a monochrome monitor. Educational programs that don't make use of much textual material can be used with an existing black-and-white or color television set. Experiencing educational programs in high-resolution color is available only if you invest in a color monitor.

CASSETTE RECORDERS VERSUS DISK DRIVES

Budgetary considerations will determine, to a degree, whether a cassette recorder or a disk drive will be used as a storage medium. The former is substantially cheaper; disk drives, on the other hand, are faster, more reliable, and are quickly becoming the standard of the industry.

Whatever device is selected, the underlying principles of operation are similar. In the case of the cassette recorders, cassette tapes are used to record electrical impulses that can be fed into the computer's RAM. Disk operating systems used in educational settings usually use 5¼-inch diameter metallic-coated mylar diskettes. Since the disks are somewhat flexible, they are commonly referred to as floppy disks or "floppies."

Most educational software programs are purchased like textbooks: an educational catalog is reviewed and programs that seem most adequately to fit a particular need are ordered. Frequently, a publisher will permit a thirty- or sixty-day examination of the material. If the computer has a cassette operating system, it is important to order programs on cassette tapes. If a disk operating system is used, programs are ordered on diskettes. The documentation that accompanies programs provides instructions on how to load the program. In some instances, loading is as simple as inserting the diskette into the disk drive and turning on the computer. These are called "turnkey" programs. In other instances, users may have to enter a command such as "Load" or "Run" on the computer's keyboard before the program will operate.

A major advantage of floppy diskettes over cassettes is that diskettes load information into the computer much faster than cassette tapes. Another benefit is that disks seldom fail to transfer all the information into the computer's memory. Cassette operating systems have a reputation for being difficult to load, since the settings on the volume and tone controls of the recorder can affect the transfer of data from tape to machine.

Eventually, users of disk operating systems will want to purchase blank diskettes so they can save information from the memory of the computer (e.g., when a document created with a word processing program is to be saved). Before information can be saved on a blank diskette, though, the disk needs to be "initialized" or "formatted" so it can hold data. Initializing or formatting configures the disk so it can communicate with the computer. Formatting is done by typing a special command into the computer and inserting a blank diskette into the disk drive. The computer electronically configures the disk into pie-shaped "sectors" (Peterson and K-Turkel, 1983). Then, concentric electronic circles, or "tracks," are recorded on the surface of the disk. Electronic data are stored on these tracks and sectors. Each computer manufacturer uses a different formatting system. This is why diskettes configured to run on one machine will not run on another.

Sooner or later, users of diskettes will discover that some diskettes are labeled as "hard sectored" while others are "soft sectored." Hard-sectored diskettes have the sectors manufactured into the disks at the factory whereas soft-sectored diskettes have the sectors magnetically written onto the diskette when the user initializes the disk.

Diskettes are also advertised as single density or double density. Density refers to the ability of the diskette to capture electrical signals sent from the recording head in the disk drive to the diskette. Single-density diskettes have been tested to assure that at least 40 percent of the signal on the diskette can be read by the magnetic head. Double-density diskettes have been tested to make sure that 50 percent or more of the signal can be read. Simply put, double-density diskettes are of a higher quality, as determined by tests, than are single-density diskettes. Some microcomputer programs require that double-density diskettes be used, so it's always a good idea for individuals to read the manuals that accompany the programs.

A number of microcomputers require double-sided diskettes. This is necessary because some disk drives have two magnetic heads that simultaneously read or write electrical impulses on both sides of the diskette.

Once diskettes have been formatted, users are able to save programs and documents. Depending on the type of computer, between one and fifty programs per diskette can be stored. This translates to approximately 160,000 words or roughly sixty pages of word processed text (Budoff and Hutten, 1982).

PRINTERS

Not too many years ago, selecting a printer was a relatively easy task. A person's choices were limited to only a few affordable models. Things have changed dramatically over the past five years, however, and today a buyer is confronted with a wide variety of printers whose prices range from several hundred to over a thousand dollars. For the most part, educators must choose between two major kinds of printers: dot matrix or daisy wheel.

Dot-Matrix Printers

As the name implies, dot-matrix printers create images by printing tiny dots within a specified matrix. The quality of the printed image is dependent upon the size of the matrix. A 7×7 matrix, for example, results in a better image than does a 5×7. And a 9×9 image is sharper to the eye than either the 7×7 or the 5×7. In addition to the "tightness" of the matrix, some printers are capable of making a double pass over each character, thereby rendering the image even darker and more readable. Some printers can even print in a number of different fonts (i.e., styles of printing type). As Figure 2.14 illustrates, the quality of print can vary considerably among dot-matrix printers.

An inexpensive dot-matrix printer has the capability of printing at 80 to 150 characters per second (cps). For around $500.00, one can purchase a printer that can print about 200 cps and produce a number of different fonts. (A fast typist, by the way, types at about 8 to 9 cps!)

Daisy Wheel Printers

The daisy wheel printer is also popular. The quality of print from these machines is incredibly good, usually surpassing that of most electric

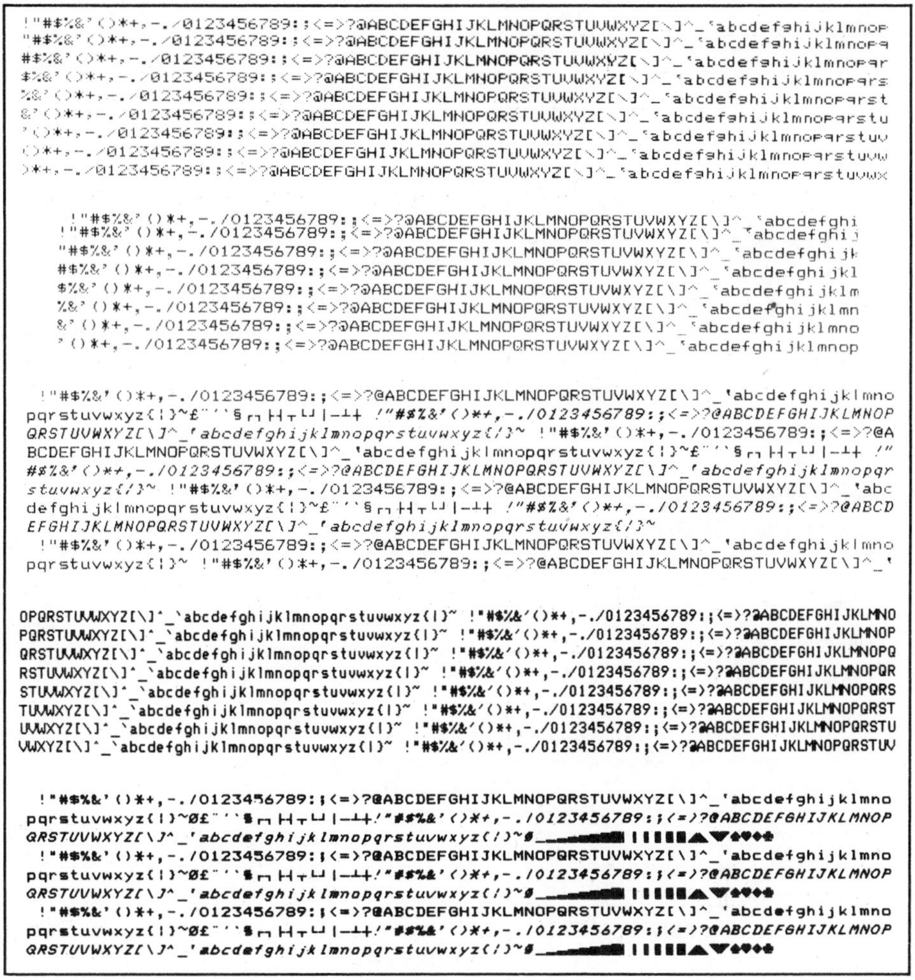

FIGURE 2.14   Print Quality from Dot-Matrix Printers

typewriters. Instead of producing dot images, these printers rely on a tiny hammerlike device that strikes a small rotating wheel that contains the keyboard letters. Daisy wheels are usually interchangeable, thereby providing the user with a variety of type styles from which to select (Figure 2.15).

While the print quality of a daisy wheel printer is superior to that of most dot-matrix models, daisy wheel printers have several shortcomings. First, they are usually more expensive than their dot-matrix counterparts. (Recently, however, several models have been introduced for around $500.00.) Second, they are considerably slower. A daisy wheel printer has a printing speed of between 20 and 50 cps.

Both types of printers handle two types of paper—fan fold or individual

APL 10	α⊥∩⌊<≤=>1234
Artisan Legal	ABCD!'"#$1234
British Pica 10	ABCD!"£$1234
Courier 10	ABCD!"#$1234
Courier 72	ABCD!"#$1234
Courier Legal 10	ABCD!"#$1234
Courier Legal 10A	ABCD!"#$1234
Dual Gothic Legal 12	ABCD!"#$1234
Elite 12	ABCD!"#$1234
Emphasis 10	**ABCD!"#$1234**
European Pica 10	ABCD!"#$1234
Forms Gothic S – 10	ABCD!"#$1234
French Pica 10	ABCD!"£$1234
French Prestige Cubic	ABCD!"£$1234
General Scientific	∇∞ψφ⌐π•{}1234
German Elite 12	ABCD!"£$1234
German Pica 10	ABCD!"§$1234
Hebrew 12	ABCD!"#$1234
Manifold 10	ABCD!"#$1234
OCR-A	ABCD$%&'1234
OCR-B	**ABCD!"#$1234**
OCR-B Kana 10	ABCD⌐з,.(@/9
Pica 10	ABCD!"#$1234
Pica Legal 10A	ABCD!"#$1234
Prestige Elite Legal 12A	ABCD!"#$1234
Spanish Elite 12	ABCD!"£$1234
UK Courier 10	ABCD!"£$1234
UK Elite 12	ABCD!"£$1234

FIGURE 2.15
Print Fonts
from Daisy Wheel Printers

sheets. To use the fan-fold paper (containing small holes on the left and right margins), a printer must have a tractor drive with sprocketed wheels that feed the paper into the machine. If individual sheets of paper are to be fed into the printer, a friction-feed model is needed. Some printers permit the option of using either tractor-fed fan-fold paper or friction-fed individual sheets. Other printers are capable of using only one type of paper.

Knowing the intended use of the computer will largely determine the type of printer needed. If corresponding with parents is the primary need and printing speed is unimportant, a daisy wheel printer would probably be a good choice. If, on the other hand, teachers are only moderately interested in high-quality type and intend to use the printer for memos or worksheet preparation, a dot-matrix printer would probably be the best choice.

Three other types of printers are also available but they are found so infrequently in schools that they deserve only passing mention. They are thermal printers (now outdated for all practical purposes), jet-spray printers (not as popular as the dot-matrix or daisy wheel models), and laser printers (so expensive that school districts seldom can afford them). In the future, we may be seeing more jet-spray and laser printers, but for the present, they are not as popular as other models.

A cable is also needed to connect the printer to the computer. The type of connection on both pieces of hardware will determine the style of cable needed. Some computers require that a special device called an interface card be installed within the machine, while others connect directly to the back of the microcomputer. Once again, a computer store technician can supply the appropriate connection.

OTHER MISCELLANEOUS DEVICES

A growing number of other peripherals such as modems, hard disk drives, and optical mark readers have begun to appear in many school districts. Each will be discussed briefly in the following sections.

Modems

Modems are devices that permit two computers to interchange information over telephone lines. Perhaps readers have seen photographs of some earlier modems. They resembled low-profiled shoe boxes with two rubber cups on top. After calling another computer user, the initiator of the call placed the telephone receiver into the rubber coupling. The coupling device was then attached to the user's computer. A second user, on the other end of the telephone line, did the same thing with his or her receiver. Through keyboard commands, it was possible to transmit data from one machine to the other.

Today's modems are much less conspicuous than the modems of yesteryear. Virtually all microcomputers built today can have the modems affixed internally. The only evidence of modem capability is usually a telephone wire and jack tailing from the back of the microcomputer. Furthermore, the operation of many modem systems is almost automatic. The author's modem, for instance, can automatically dial, redial, and answer another computer.

Modems will probably find increasing use in school settings as teachers and administrators send student records across cities and towns via telephone lines. Teachers will probably have students send correspondence to other students via electronic mail and bulletin boards. This is already being done on a limited basis in some communities. In fact, one school in California routinely corresponds with another school in Alaska via an experimental modem connection!

Hard Disk Drives

Hard disk drives serve a function similar to floppy diskettes except that hard disks are (1) considerably more expensive, (2) hold much more data, and (3) access information much faster than conventional floppy disks. Unlike floppy diskettes, hard disks are metal platters that have been magnetically coated and sealed in a protective housing. Hard disks are able to store much more information than a single floppy of comparable size. While a 5¼-inch floppy may hold between 150,000 and 360,000 characters of information, for example, a hard disk of the same size may hold between 6 million and 10 million characters. Access speeds roughly four times faster than floppy disks make hard disks highly desirable whenever information needs to be retrieved in a hurry. A small hard disk drive system sells for between $1,000 and $2,000.

Hard disk systems are most popular with administrators who have need to store large quantities of budget, payroll, personnel, or student data. Hard disks provide many administrators with the speed, ease of use, and storage capability needed (Pogrow, 1983).

A second situation where hard disk drives prove useful is when six or more microcomputers continually need to use the same program(s). Connecting all the computers to a hard disk drive usually means a cost savings to the school, since the individual floppy disk drives necessary for each machine can be eliminated. Prelle (1983) described a hard disk system consisting of eight Apple microcomputers connected to a common hard disk. The cost of this system was less than half the cost of the necessary number of floppy disk drives, while the speed at which information could be retrieved was ten times faster.

Optical Mark Readers

As teachers gain familiarity with microcomputers, we are likely to witness a growing number of optical mark readers in schools. These devices permit teachers to record student information—usually test data—from special cards that students mark. Optical mark readers permit machine scoring of teacher-designed tests. By simply passing students' marked answer sheets through a small, table-top scanner connected to a microcomputer, a teacher is able automatically to score and record student test data. Not only can the tests be scored, but test item analyses can also be performed. These readers also permit materials to be inventoried, objectives to be monitored, and library records to be maintained (Harvey, 1983).

SUMMARY

Historically, computers have continued to shrink in size while increasing in power. The first computers occupied entire rooms and had limited memories. Today, though, some computers are smaller than textbooks. This evolutionary trend will persist, and microcomputers will continue to decrease in size, become more portable, and be able to perform more functions.

Each generation of microcomputers brings added capabilities to the marketplace. Memory size is rapidly increasing at no substantial increase in price. Many microcomputers now provide both color and sound capability. Keyboards are becoming increasingly easy to use through the addition of special function keys and numeric keypads.

The three most popular microcomputers found in schools are produced by Apple, Radio Shack, and Commodore. IBM, a late arrival in the microcomputer business, is seeking to gain its share of the educational market with two relatively new microcomputers, but the other three manufacturers already have a strong foothold in educational computing.

The intended use of a microcomputer should determine the configuration of both the machine and its peripherals. Choosing a video display, a memory device, and a printer are dependent on how the computer will be used. Some individuals may need additional hardware such as modems, hard disk drives, and optical mark readers to perform some of the desired functions. Each of these devices increases the cost of the microcomputer system.

Selecting appropriate hardware is only one part of using the microcomputer as an educational tool. Selecting the appropriate software is even more important. Educational software is the focus of the remaining chapters of this book.

RELATED READINGS

Recent issues of the following magazines will provide up-to-date information on the existing technology.

Byte
70 Main Street
Peterborough, N.H. 03458

Creative Computing
Box 789-M
Morristown, N.J. 07690

80 Microcomputing
80 Pine Street
Peterborough, N.H. 03458

InfoWorld
375 Cochituate Rd.
Framingham, Mass. 01701

REFERENCES

BUDOFF, MILTON and LEAH R. HUTTEN, "Microcomputers in Special Education: Promises and Pitfalls," *Exceptional Children,* Vol. 49, no. 2 (October 1982), 123–128.

EPIE INSTITUTE, "Materials—Microcomputer Courseware/Microcomputer Games," *EPIE Report,* Vol. 15, no. 1/2M (Fall–Winter 1981), 1–11, 16–19.

HARVEY, WILLIAM J., "Optical Mark Readers: What's New?" *Electronic Learning,* Vol. 3, no. 1 (September 1983), 108, 110, 112.

PETERSON, FRANKLYNN, and JUDI K-TURKEL, "Hotline Questions About Floppy Disks," *The Providence Journal,* Business Section, May 10, 1983.

POGROW, STANLEY, "Integrated Software for Administrators," *Electronic Learning,* Vol. 3, no. 1 (September 1983), 42, 44, 46.

PRELLE, WALTER V., "Hard Disk Data Storage," *The Computing Teacher,* Vol. 11, no. 3 (October 1983), 39–40.

"Two New Studies See Major Role for Computers in Education," *Electronic Learning,* Vol. 3, no. 3 (November-December 1983), 18, 20.

WILLIAMS, WARREN S., and JULES SHRAGE, "Microcomputers and Education: An Overview of Popular Hardware and Software," *Educational Technology,* Vol. 23, no. 2 (February 1983), 7–12.

THREE

CLASSROOM APPLICATIONS

Upon completing this chapter, you will be able to

— 1. Describe what is meant by the term "drill and practice" and identify reading software programs that use this model.

— 2. Explain what is meant by tutorial software and identify reading software that can be used with this instructional mode.

— 3. Identify and discuss how educational games can be used to teach reading.

— 4. Describe what is meant by the term "educational simulations" and explain their use in reading instruction.

— 5. Explain what is meant by the term "teacher utilities" and define how these programs might be used by teachers of reading.

Reading software can be categorized under a variety of headings. Some of these headings include drill and practice, tutorial, games, simulations, and teacher utilities. While these categories may appear to be clear-cut, practitioners will soon discover that some materials seem to fit more than one category while others defy categorization. Nevertheless, for initial purposes, the examination and labeling of reading software affords teachers an opportunity to gain a better understanding of existing programs. This chapter examines five common uses of microcomputer software and identifies popular reading materials that can be used to teach skills under each of the categories.

It is impossible to identify all reading and language arts software that is available in today's market. With the information gained from this text, and by using the review form presented in the last chapter, educators should be able to do a satisfactory job of determining categories of software. Since this chapter, indeed this entire book, can only scratch the surface of the software market, the astute teacher of reading will want to examine products not identified here. There are a number of ways this can be accomplished. Many colleges and universities now have microcomputer demonstration laboratories and centers. Frequently, the software that is housed in these facilities can be examined free of charge. Another avenue for software review is nearby computer stores. Some stores even specialize in educational software. Usually, individuals in these businesses are willing to permit software to be reviewed on the premises. Another way that software can be reviewed is by requesting preview privileges from a commercial vendor. Many software distributors now permit a thirty-day examination period free of charge, providing that the software is returned in salable form. A number of publishing houses also market software. A local book representative is sometimes able to leave copies of software with a building administrator so that the teaching staff may examine the software before buying. Another way software can be reviewed firsthand is through a users' group. Users' groups are comprised of individuals with common computing interests who meet on a regular basis to discuss what is new in their respective areas. Some areas, for example, have special Logo user groups or special education user groups. Microcomputing newsletters or announcements posted at local computer stores will usually announce the next meeting of a user group.

Before delving into specific software applications, a note of caution should be sounded. The programs that are discussed in this chapter, as well as throughout the text, are used as examples to clarify points being made. No recommendation to buy or not to buy these particular programs is implied. The final judge of a program's ultimate worth is the intended user. It is hoped that the information presented here serves as a springboard to knowledgeable software purchasing.

DRILL-AND-PRACTICE SOFTWARE

Drill-and-practice programs are those pieces of software that provide practice on skills previously taught. As the name implies, the programs are designed to drill students until a skill is not only learned but is brought to a state where the response becomes automatic (Gagné, 1982). LaBerge and Samuels (1974) have discussed the importance of automaticity as it relates to decoding and reading. When decoding skills are overlearned until they become automatic, the reader is able to devote a greater portion of his or her attention to comprehending the written material.

Reading teachers frequently state that providing students with appropriate and sufficient drill activities is one of their most difficult jobs. This is so because the skill needs of a group are usually so varied that a wealth of instructional materials are needed to provide appropriate practice. Furthermore, providing repeated drilling of the same or similar material can be downright uninteresting for both the students and the teacher. Fortunately, the ability to drill students repeatedly is a strong feature of microcomputers. It is not surprising, then, that this is the most commonly used mode of instruction (Budoff and Hutten, 1982; Zeiser and Hoffman, 1983).

Drill-and-practice software offers a number of advantages over workbooks or other paper-and-pencil activities used to teach reading. For one, many software packages permit students to work at a variety of different levels. Thus, it is possible to have one student work on beginning consonants while another student works on two- or three-letter blends, both using the same software package. Another advantage of using drill-and-practice activities is that many programs permit students to receive instructional problems determined at random. This allows the same instructional unit to be presented a number of times but with each presentation occurring in a different order, thereby reducing the chance of boredom by the user.

Drill-and-practice software has received limited use with gifted and talented students, but it has been used extensively with problem learners (Bennett, 1982). Many students who eventually end up in compensatory reading programs are there because they have failed to grasp essential reading skills due to haphazard instruction. The microcomputer, coupled with drill-and-practice software, provides opportunities for these students to review skills that may have been missed in earlier instructional episodes. Moreover, the systematic design of many of these materials permits the user to proceed, step by step, through a logical instructional sequence. This highly structured learning environment is frequently enough to alleviate major skill deficiencies. Good drill-and-practice software, which complements focused teaching, is a powerful force in a teacher's instructional arsenal.

Examples of reading software that exemplify the drill-and-practice instructional mode are *Study Skills: Alphabetization Sequences* (Milliken Publishing Company) and *Homonyms* (Hartley Publishing Company).

Alphabetization Sequences is a program designed for use in grades 1–8. It provides drill-and-practice in letter recognition, alphabetical sequencing of letters, and alphabetizing by first through seventh letter. The words used in the program were taken primarily from popular word lists such as the Dolch 220 Basic Sight Words and the Spache Revised Word List. Eight different skill levels have been identified, while within each skill level there are a number of different problem levels. Each problem level generates several exercises based on the same skill. A Scope and Sequence Chart is included in the program documentation. This provides reading teachers with a readily available overview of the entire skills sequence.

At the easiest level, one of the program objectives is "Seeing likenesses and differences in lowercase letter forms that are similar." Students are asked to discern likenesses and differences in four pairs of letters (e.g., ce, rr, rn, mn).

Later in the program, students must recall the alphabetical sequence of two missing letters. When presented with the strings "ABC__E__F" and "C____ F G H" pupils are required to fill in the missing letters.

At the higher levels, students are required to determine the placement of a word in an alphabetical list by using the fourth letter. An example of a problem found at this level is

Where does beam belong in the a-b-c list? _____

1.>
    beach
2.>
    bead
3.>
    bean
4.>
    bear
5.>
    beat
6.>

Students respond by typing the numeral that corresponds to the appropriate placement. An especially noteworthy feature of this program is that the teacher may select a mastery level (i.e., percentage of items correctly identified), a failure level (i.e., the percentage of items missed, thereby terminating the program), and the minimum number of problems presented (ranging from three to twenty).

A built-in management system permits the teacher to make individual or class assignments, review individual or class performance, and receive printed records of student performance. Approximately forty pages of documentation are included with the program.

The *Homonyms* program by Hartley includes seventeen drill lessons and three review lessons, all recorded on a single diskette. Lessons are written at five different reading levels (grades 3–8).

Lessons begin with simple homonyms such as *sun/son* and increase in difficulty until, at the highest levels, word pairs such as *cereal/serial* and *sheik/chic* are introduced.

A typical lesson from *Homonyms* presents a short "tutorial" paragraph followed by a question. Students are required to type the correct response on the keyboard. Here is an example of one frame:

The sun is the star of our solar system.
A son is a boy child.

My brother is my father's

Answer:_____
            TYPE
    PRESS 'RETURN' KEY

A student planning feature monitors progress as students complete lessons. As exercises are completed, errors are recorded in the student's file. At a later time, the teacher has the option of reviewing each file to determine the exact incorrect response(s) made by each pupil. A printed copy of this profile may be requested if a printer is attached to the computer.

Another feature of *Homonyms* is that teachers have the option of adding or deleting homonyms of their choice. No technical programming ability is needed to take advantage of this feature. Directions describing how to add or delete words are found in the program documentation.

TUTORIAL SOFTWARE

Tutorial programs are designed to present small increments of information followed by questions assessing the individual's comprehension of the material. In some ways, tutorial programs are designed to teach concepts in much the same way a teacher would in a one-on-one situation (Gawronski and West, 1982). An excellent example of tutorial material in the premicrocomputer era was the programmed learning textbooks of the 1950s and 1960s. Perhaps you learned to use a slide rule, memorized history facts, or explored chemistry equations by using a programmed text. If you did, you probably recall the instructional format. First, you were presented with one or more frames of content materials. After this presentation, you were asked a question or two. If you responded correctly, the text instructed you to proceed to a new section. If you failed to answer the question correctly, you were branched to a section where the material was reviewed. Tutorial programs written for microcomputers operate in a similar manner except, of course, the student interacts with the microcomputer rather than with a text or workbook.

Tutorial software provides opportunities for students to proceed at their own pace. If the material is carefully thought out and student progress is periodically checked, rapid mastery of material can occur. Students who are able to grasp the content move ahead while those who experience difficulty are looped or branched to other learning experiences that reinforce the objectives of the lesson.

Creating high-quality tutorial software is a difficult job. This is so for a number of reasons. For one thing, to be effective, the tutorial lessons should be correlated with the existing curriculum materials. Second, the lessons must move ahead fast enough to maintain student interest but not be so rapidly paced that students have difficulty following the flow of instruction. Third, innumerable branches must be planned to enable students who experience difficulty on the first pass to have ample review lessons. Planning these learning alternatives is both difficult and time consuming. Finally, Lathrop and Goodson (1983) warn that tutorial materials need to be fully documented and self-directing and provide as complete a learning situation as possible. This means that worksheets, maps, charts, and other materials sometimes need to accompany the program. Preparing this type of package is a major undertaking. As a result, designing high-quality tutorial packages usually demands more time and effort than most teachers can afford. For this reason, most educators turn to commercial software houses for tutorial software.

One tutorial package in reading is *Word Attack (*Davidson & Associates). This program has nine levels of exercises ranging from grade 4 to grade 12. Each level includes four different activities. The first, *Word Display,* introduces the learner to new words. Each word is shown on the screen followed by its synonym or a brief definition. A sentence illustrating the usage is also given. Here is a frame from the program:

ambition

a desire to be the best

Greg has a lot of ambition. He wants to be the best architect in the United States.

Twenty-five words are presented at each level. Once students have been introduced to the new words, they may select to take a multiple-choice quiz, do a sentence completion task, or play an arcade game using the learned words. Student scores are recorded for each of the three activities, thereby providing the user with feedback regarding mastery of the lesson.

Another example of a software tutorial program for reading is the *SAT Word Attack Skills* program (Edu-Ware). This program covers topics such as word definitions, word connotations, knowledge of roots and prefixes, as well as several other skills. The 300 words included in this program were selected because they frequently appear on tests such as the PSAT and SAT. Just as with *Word Attack, SAT Word Attack Skills* presents words in contextual settings. Students have the option of seeing either the synonyms or antonyms of the target words. Students may also check their progress at any point in the lesson by simply pressing the "S" (score) key on the keyboard. Users are instructed to advance to the next level of lesson only when they have achieved an 80 percent or higher score.

Despite the advantages of tutorial programs, they should never be considered a means of eliminating teacher responsibility for learning. The teacher, unlike the computer, is able to listen and discuss topics and issues with students. Computers are unable to provide this necessary component of instruction.

EDUCATIONAL GAMING SOFTWARE

Some educators view microcomputer games and the educational process as incompatible commodities. To them, games conjure up visions of space invaders, laser beams, and pinball arcades. While such perceptions are understandable, educational games seldom resemble their arcade relatives.

Educational games are activities that are played with a prescribed set of rules and usually result in a winner at the completion of the activity. In some cases, computer games are simply popular board games that have been designed to run on the microcomputer. *Monopoly* and *Scrabble* are two board games that have made it to the microcomputer software arena.

Games involve play, an important ritual in learning. Play, according to one authority (Goles, 1982), "is preparation for more serious aspects of life. In play one practices physiological, mental and social skills that improve the fitness of the individual. It also may foster cooperation among individuals, and help one to anticipate correctly the reactions of others in the group" (p.12).

Of course, games, like all software, should be integrated into the day-to-day curriculum of the school. It does little good to play a computer game if students (and teachers) don't understand the underlying reasons for using the game in the first place. If an educational game meets a program objective, it should be considered as an appropriate educational activity. Software games that are not tied to curricular goals, however, might better be played out of school.

An excellent example of a computer game that could be used at almost any educational level is *The Game Show* (Computer Advanced Ideas). Based on a popular television show, this program uses two animated contestants and a master of ceremonies to drill students on selected facts. Students can play the game with a friend or play alone against the computer. To initiate the game, students select a topic from a given list. Examples are Animals, Computer Terms, and American History. Clues are provided to each contestant. The moderator provides feedback and keeps the game moving at a lively pace. The contestant who accrues the most points by guessing the mystery words wins the game. A commendable feature of this program is that teachers may enter their own clues and words by using the easy-to-use program editor. Reading teachers, for example, may want to create programs to drill students on topics such as prefixes or suffixes. Using the template of the existing program, they can easily design high-interest exercises. These activities can then be saved on blank diskettes, thereby permitting repeated use throughout the school year.

Another game with a totally different design is *Troll's Tale* (Sierra On-Line). Resembling a popular adventure-type board game, *Troll's Tale* offers practice in map reading and reading comprehension. The game scenario includes a wicked troll who has stolen sixteen treasures from a dwarf king. Players are to find the treasures and return them to the king. Using high-resolution graphics and an easy-to-read third-grade vocabulary, students wind their way through a labyrinth of tunnels, caves, and doors, searching for treasures at virtually every turn in the road. An accompanying map and treasure stickers help the user find his or her way through the game. Figures 3.1 and 3.2 illustrate the graphics and text used in the program.

Games can be powerful teaching tools if well-designed and used in

FIGURE 3.1   Screen Photograph from *Troll's Tale* (Sierra On-Line Inc.)

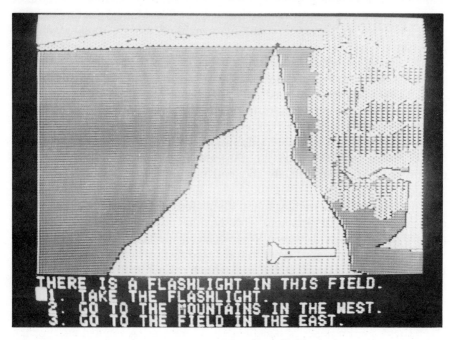

FIGURE 3.2   Screen Photograph from *Troll's Tale* (Sierra On-Line Inc.)

appropriate contexts. Since most students love to use their imaginations, games provide an excellent vehicle to impart knowledge in an enjoyable manner. Educators should continue to see more and more educational games not only for school use but also for the home market. As programmers and design specialists develop increasingly sophisticated materials and as more parents purchase microcomputers for home use, additional reading-related software will crop up in living rooms and dens throughout the country. The result should be a larger percentage of students entering school with more advanced reading ability.

SIMULATION SOFTWARE

Simulations are programs that are designed to depict real-world happenings without the danger, expense, or time needed to experience the actual event. One common use of simulations exists outside the school environment. These are the simulation devices used in pilot training. Both the military and the commercial airline industry continually use aircraft simulators to sharpen the flying skills of their pilots. Even the NASA astronauts fly specially equipped jet aircraft that have been modified to simulate the handling characteristics of the space shuttle. Now there are even microcomputer programs that simulate flying a private plane or a space shuttle! Simulations, whether educational or otherwise, require the learner to select choices that affect the outcome of the simulation. Simulations also provide continuous feedback to the user regarding the status of the event and the options available (Saltinski, 1981). Many educators feel that simulations are among some of the most creative and entertaining software available.

Teachers of reading will quickly discover that there is a dearth of simulation software available specifically to teach reading skills. Instead, most simulations have been designed to teach concepts in the social studies and sciences. There are programs to teach the dangers of fur trading as French explorers move throughout the northeastern United States during the eighteenth century, programs to depict the hardships of traveling in wagon trains across the Great Plains, and programs to illustrate the ecological food chains in midwestern lakes. Yet, virtually no simulation software exists with a specific focus on reading.

Reading teachers wanting to use simulations must be willing to look to the content areas for reading material. This shouldn't be perceived as a shortcoming of simulation software, however. When one considers that learning to read is a *process,* it only makes good sense to teach reading in meaningful contexts, such as in the content areas. Given material written at their instructional level, most students are eager consumers of social studies and science content. It is only when instruction is boring or materials are written at frustration levels that students become uninterested.

There are a number of benefits derived from using simulations. For the most part, they are highly motivating since there is continual input required of the user. Instantaneous feedback guides students as they proceed through the material. This permits them to try different approaches and to discover those that are successful. A second advantage is that simulations permit learning experiences that are simply beyond the capability of textbooks, worksheets, and the like. Simulations truly involve the learner as few other instructional activities do. Finally, simulations permit learning to be internalized through continuous practice in lifelike situations (Henney and Boysen, 1979).

Simulations are not without their shortcomings, however. Since most are written for content areas, the readability of much of the on-screen and written documentation is beyond the reading capability of some poorer readers. Trying to use a simulation with written material that is too difficult may turn students against the microcomputer as an instructional tool. Teachers, therefore, need to be especially alert to simulations written at high reading levels. When difficult reading material is encountered, teachers may want to team good and poor readers together, thereby giving comprehension and problem-solving practice to the poorer readers.

A second shortcoming of simulations is that some depict events in simplistic and unnatural ways. If a simulation is to be of value, it should closely represent a real-world event. Thus, each simulation is built upon a model. If the model fails to catch the essence of the real situation, students may develop inappropriate understandings of the event.

One software company, Strategic Simulations, Inc., specializes in the development of microcomputer simulations. One of its programs, *Geopolitique,* places the user in the seat of the president of the United States in the 1990s. A tense power struggle between the United States and the Soviet Union (the computer) ensues. The user must make decisions regarding raw materials, industrial capacity, and bargain table diplomacy. Should these decisions be inappropriate, a nonnuclear war may occur. These factors, combined with world tension levels, coups, and random events make for an exciting simulation.

Many of Strategic Simulations' other software packages focus on historical war battles. *Computer Air Combat,* for example, reenacts aerial warfare with thirty-six different planes from the United States, Germany, Britain, and Japan. *Fighter Command* is a simulation of the RAF against the Luftwaffe during the Battle of Britain. Generals Lee and Meade meet face to face in *The Road to Gettysburg,* a decisive Civil War campaign. Another Civil War battle is fought in *The Battle of Shiloh. Computer Baseball* and *Computer Quarterback* are also favorite sports simulations from the same company.

In summary, simulations usually make excellent use of the computer's capability. The dilemma facing the reading teacher is to find material that is written at an appropriate level and at the same time matches the instructional objectives of the school curriculum. While these two constraints may make this search difficult, the reward is usually highly motivated students using the computer to its utmost capability—an exciting combination.

TEACHER UTILITIES SOFTWARE

Utilities software refers to programs used to prepare instructional materials or to keep records of an individual's progress. As such, this category sometimes is thought of, and not incorrectly, as a catchall collection that includes a variety of programs such as word processing packages, data base management programs, authoring languages and systems, electronic gradebooks, classroom management systems, materials preparation programs, and readability analysis software. Since word processing, data base management, authoring languages and systems, and readability analysis programs will be examined in later chapters, their use is not covered here. Instead, we will examine the remaining applications as examples of teacher utilities.

Electronic Gradebooks

As the name implies, electronic gradebook programs are designed to keep up-to-date records of student grades. *The Apple Gradebook* (Creative Computing Software) is one such program. To use the program, teachers are required to enter a roster of student names. Thereafter, test scores and assignment grades can be entered at will. Electronic gradebooks permit the user to sort students alphabetically, rank order pupils by exam or by cumulative scores, and make simple statistical calculations such as means and standard deviations (Figure 3.3).

FIGURE 3.3   Screen Menu from an Electronic Gradebook (REPRINTED FROM Electronic Gradebook by Creative Computing Software, Copyright©1982 AHL Computing, Inc.)

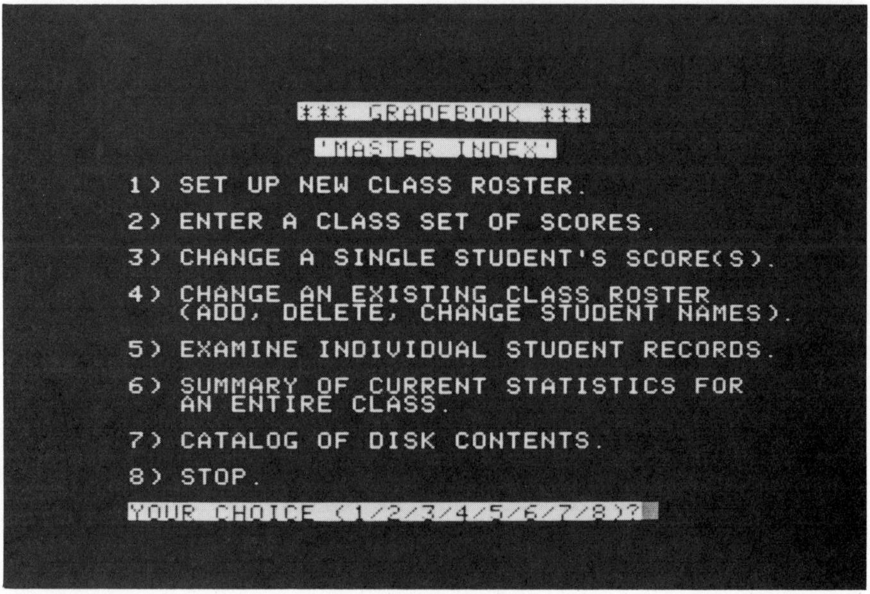

```
        *** GRADEBOOK ***
          'MASTER INDEX'
  1) SET UP NEW CLASS ROSTER.
  2) ENTER A CLASS SET OF SCORES.
  3) CHANGE A SINGLE STUDENT'S SCORE(S).
  4) CHANGE AN EXISTING CLASS ROSTER
     (ADD, DELETE, CHANGE STUDENT NAMES).
  5) EXAMINE INDIVIDUAL STUDENT RECORDS.
  6) SUMMARY OF CURRENT STATISTICS FOR
     AN ENTIRE CLASS.
  7) CATALOG OF DISK CONTENTS.
  8) STOP.
  YOUR CHOICE (1/2/3/4/5/6/7/8)?
```

A limitation of electronic gradebooks is that the user must have easy access to a microcomputer to update or add scores to the program. While this may not appear to be a shortcoming, there may be times when teachers may find themselves without access to a microcomputer (such as when working at home) and, hence, may be unable to use the gradebook. At times like these, they may wish their grades were recorded in a more convenient, nonelectronic mode.

FIGURE 3.4   Test Results—*Ginn Computer Management System* (From User's Manual, Apple II® Version of the GINN READING PROGRAM: *Computer Management System,* Copyright© 1982 by Ginn and Company (Xerox Corporation.) Used with permission.)

```
************************************************************************
*                                                                    *
*                      GINN READING PROGRAM                          *
*                         TEST RESULTS                               *
*                      LEVEL 7 -- UNIT 1 FORM A                      *
*                                                                    *
*   TEACHER:  SANDRA ORRELL              DATE:   10/07/82            *
*   CLASS:    GRADE 2                    SCHOOL:   GREENLEAF         *
*                                                                    *
************************************************************************


NAME                        VOC    COM    DEC
-----------------------------------------------------------------------


GROUP:  BUZZARDS
    BAKER,  RALPH            1 1     4     1 5
    FRANKLIN,  DIANA        1 0     3*    1 4
    GROVE,  KEITH           1 0     5     1 3
    KOWALSKI,  ANNE         1 2     4     1 3
    LING,  ANDREA           1 0     3*    1 2
    RAMOS,  TED              9*     4     1 2
    ROSEN,  GWEN            1 2     5     1 4
    YI,  DOUG               1 1     5     1 4
-----------------------------------------------------------------------
AVERAGE SCORES            10 6     4 1    13 4

SUGGESTED PASSING SCORE:   1 0     4     1 2
MAXIMUM POSSIBLE SCORE:    1 2     5     1 5


                    * BELOW SUGGESTED PASSING SCORE


VOCABULARY          WORD IDENTIFICATION
COMPREHENSION       PREDICTING OUTCOMES
DECODING            EW (CHEW/FEW) OO (WOOD) & DOUBLE CONSONANT BEFORE -ING/-ED
```

This report shows each pupil's score (number of items answered correctly) on each subtest of a Unit, Level, or Mid-Level Test. Scores below the Suggested Passing Score are marked with an asterisk.

REPORT 1

Another shortcoming of electronic gradebooks is that the time needed to enter data may not be worth the output received. While these programs are relatively simple to use, it still requires time to learn how to operate the software and enter the grades. Some individuals feel that this time could be better spent in other ways. Furthermore, many teachers aren't interested in receiving a detailed statistical analysis of individual or class performance. In short, there are times when a simple hand-held calculator or a paper-and-pencil gradebook is more convenient and appropriate than a $1,000 electronic record!

Classroom Management Systems

Classroom management systems are designed to help teachers and administrators monitor the progress of students as they move through a prescribed curriculum. In reading instruction, this implies following a hierarchical skills list, frequently taken from a publisher's list of skills found in a

FIGURE 3.5   Pupils Reading Below Suggested Passing Score—*Ginn Computer Management System* (From User's Manual, Apple II © Version of the GINN READING PROGRAM: *Computer Management System,* Copyright © 1982 by Ginn and Company (Xerox Corporation.) Used with permission.)

```
**********************************************************************************
*                                                                              *
*                          GINN READING PROGRAM                                *
*                  PUPILS BELOW SUGGESTED PASSING SCORE                         *
*                       LEVEL 7 -- UNIT 1 FORM A                               *
*                                                                              *
*   TEACHER   SANDRA ORRELL                    DATE   10/07/82                 *
*     CLASS   GRADE 2                          SCHOOL   GREENLEAF              *
*     GROUP   BUZZARDS                                                         *
*                                                                              *
**********************************************************************************

VOCABULARY     WORD IDENTIFICATION
REINFORCEMENT   BOOSTER ACTIVITIES 1A,1B,1C
                STUDYBOOK PAGES 14,16,19,21,24,27,29,31

    RAMOS, TED



COMPREHENSION   PREDICTING OUTCOMES
REINFORCEMENT   BOOSTER ACTIVITIES 2A,2B
                STUDYBOOK PAGES 20,28

    FRANKLIN, DIANA
    LING, ANDREA



DECODING    EW (CHEW/FEW) OO (WOOD) & DOUBLE CONSONANT BEFORE -ING  E:
REINFORCEMENT   BOOSTER ACTIVITIES 3,4,5A,5B
                STUDYBOOK PAGES 15,17,26

    NO PUPILS
```

This report groups pupils scoring below the Suggested Passing Score on each subtest of a Unit Test, along with appropriate Booster Activities and Studybook references.

REPORT 2

```
************************************************************************
*                                                                      *
*                        GINN READING PROGRAM                          *
*                     REINFORCEMENT ACTIVITIES                         *
*                     LEVEL 7 -- UNIT 1 FORM A                         *
*                                                                      *
*   TEACHER    SANDRA ORRELL                  DATE   10/07/82          *
*     CLASS    GRADE 2                      SCHOOL   GREENLEAF         *
*                                                                      *
************************************************************************


     NAME                         BOOSTER ACTIVITY      STUDYBOOK
    ----------------------------------------------------------------

    GROUP    BUZZARDS
      BAKER, RALPH                 NONE NEEDED
      FRANKLIN, DIANA              2A, 2B                20, 28
      GROVE, KEITH                 NONE NEEDED
      KOWALSKI, ANNE               NONE NEEDED
      LING, ANDREA                 2A, 2B                20, 28
      RAMOS, TED                   1A, 1B, 1C            14, 16, 19, 21, 24
                                                         27, 29, 31
      ROSEN, GWEN                  NONE NEEDED
      YI, DOUG                     NONE NEEDED
```

This report lists all Booster Activities and Studybook pages suggested for each pupil. The recommendations are based on pupils' Unit Test scores.

REPORT 3

FIGURE 3.6   Reinforcement Activities—*Ginn Computer Management System* (From User's Manual, Apple II® Version of the GINN READING PROGRAM: *Computer Management System,* Copyright© 1982 by Ginn and Company (Xerox Corporation.) Used with permission.)

basal reading series. For example, Ginn and Company, a publisher, has produced the Ginn *Computer Management System (CMS)*. This program permits teachers to organize, store, evaluate, and report information on pupils' achievement as they use the Ginn reading program. The software allows teachers to generate a number of reports including the following:

1. Test Results Report (Fig. 3.4)
2. Pupils Below Suggested Passing Score Report (Fig. 3.5)
3. Reinforcement Activities Report (Fig. 3.6)
4. Pupil Performance by Objective Report (Fig. 3.7)
5. Pupil Status Summary Report (Fig. 3.8)
6. Progress Report (Fig. 3.9)
7. Cumulative Record of Performance Report (Fig. 3.10)
8. Parent Report (Fig. 3.11)

Another classroom management program is the *Wisconsin Design Computer Management System* (Learning Multi-Systems, Inc.). Unlike the Ginn program, this software is intended to be used with any basal reader system that is supplemented with the Wisconsin Design for Reading Skill Development skills management system. Designed to run on an Apple microcomputer, the software is able to generate seven different types of reports in three areas of reading: word attack, comprehension, and study skills.

FIGURE 3.7   Pupil Performance by Objective—*Ginn Computer Management System* (From User's Manual, Apple II® Version of the GINN READING PROGRAM: *Computer Management System,* Copyright© 1982 by Ginn and Company (Xerox Corporation.) Used with permission.)

```
***********************************************************************
*                                                                     *
*                        GINN READING PROGRAM                         *
*                     PUPIL PERFORMANCE BY OBJECTIVE                   *
*                      LEVEL 7 -- UNIT 1 FORM A                        *
*                                                                     *
*  TEACHER   SANDRA ORRELL                    DATE    10/07/82         *
*    CLASS   GRADE 2                        SCHOOL    GREENLEAF        *
*    GROUP   BUZZARDS                                                  *
*                                                                     *
***********************************************************************


                              PUPILS   PUPILS   AVERAGE    AVERAGE
                SPS   TOTAL   TESTED   PASSED    SCORE     % CORRECT
          -----------------------------------------------------------

   VOCABULARY    10     12       8        7      10 6         88

   COMPREHENSION  4      5       8        6       4 1         82

   DECODING      12     15       8        8      13 4         89


              * AVERAGE BELOW SUGGESTED PASSING SCORE


VOCABULARY       WORD IDENTIFICATION
COMPREHENSION    PREDICTING OUTCOMES
DECODING         EW (CHEW/FEW) OO (WOOD) & DOUBLE CONSONANT BEFORE -ING/-ED
```

This report summarizes reading group or class performance on a Unit, Level, or Mid-Level Test.

REPORT 4

```
*****************************************************************************
*                                                                         *
*                       GINN READING PROGRAM                              *
*                       PUPIL STATUS SUMMARY                              *
*                                                                         *
*   TEACHER   SANDRA ORRELL                 DATE:   02 / 25 / 83          *
*   CLASS:    GRADE 2                       SCHOOL:  GREENLEAF            *
*                                                                         *
*****************************************************************************


    NAME                        ID        LEVEL  LAST TEST  DATE
    ---------------------------------------------------------------------

    GROUP:  BUZZARDS
      BAKER, RALPH             55604        8     UNIT   1    02 / 25 / 83
      FRANKLIN, DIANA          55605        8     UNIT   1    02 / 25 / 83
      GROVE, KEITH             55606        8     UNIT   1    02 / 25 / 83
      KOWALSKI, ANNE           55607        8     UNIT   1    02 / 25 / 83
      LING, ANDREA             55609        8     UNIT   1    02 / 25 / 83
      RAMOS, TED               55613        8     UNIT   1    02 / 25 / 83
      ROSEN, GWEN              55614        8     UNIT   1    02 / 25 / 83
      YI, DOUG                 55615        8     UNIT   1    02 / 25 / 83

    GROUP:  SHARKS
      ATKINS, ROGER            55603        7     UNIT   3    01 / 12 / 83
      LIEB, ROBERT             55608        7     UNIT   3    01 / 12 / 83
      MENDEZ, CARLA            55610        7     UNIT   3    01 / 12 / 83
      MILLER, SUSAN            55611        7     UNIT   3    01 / 12 / 83
      PARO, ADAM               55612        7     UNIT   3    01 / 12 / 83
```

This report shows the status of every pupil in class — the current level assignment, the test taken most recently, and the date the test was taken.

REPORT 5

FIGURE 3.8   Pupil Status Summary—*Ginn Computer Management System* (From User's Manual, Apple II® Version of the GINN READING PROGRAM: *Computer Management System*, Copyright© 1982 by Ginn and Company (Xerox Corporation.) Used with permission.)

Student Roster (Figure 3.12) is a report that provides a complete list of all students in the reading program. Students are organized by grade level or by homeroom. This report also serves as a reference for student identification.

Once students have been administered break-in tests to determine their specific skill needs, a Retest Report can be generated. This printout identifies students who did not achieve an 80 percent or higher score on specific criterion-referenced tests. (In the *Design*, tests are organized according to levels ranging

```
********************************************************************
*                                                                  *
*                    GINN READING PROGRAM                          *
*                      PROGRESS REPORT                             *
*                                                                  *
*  TEACHER:  SANDRA ORRELL                  DATE:   02/25/83       *
*    CLASS:  GRADE 2                        SCHOOL: GREENLEAF       *
*                                                                  *
********************************************************************


                                    TESTS - LEVEL 7
               ----------------------------------------------------------------
GROUP      FORM     UNIT 1    UNIT 2    UNIT 3    UNIT 4    LEVEL
           ----------------------------------------------------------------
BUZZARDS    A     10/07/82   11/12    12/15    01/21
SHARKS      A     10/21/82   11/19    01/12



                                    TESTS - LEVEL 8
               ----------------------------------------------------------------
GROUP      FORM     UNIT 1    UNIT 2    UNIT 3    UNIT 4    LEVEL
           ----------------------------------------------------------------
BUZZARDS    A     02/25/83
```

This report is a pacing map showing, for each reading group, what tests have been administered and the dates.

REPORT 6

FIGURE 3.9   Progress Report—*Ginn Computer Management System* (From User's Manual, Apple II® Version of the GINN READING PROGRAM: *Computer Management System,* Copyright© 1982 by Ginn and Company (Xerox Corporation.) Used with permission.)

from Level A through Level G. Each level is a general approximation of grade level starting at the kindergarten level.) Figure 3.13 indicates that Michael Darling mastered no skill at level D and therefore needs to be retested at Level C. Mary Jackson, on the other hand, passed three skills at Level B and is ready to be retested at the next level, Level C. Criteria for retesting at different levels is specified in the Teachers' Planning Guide, a publication included in the *Design*.

Report 2 in this program lists the skills according to the number of students who fail to demonstrate mastery (Figure 3.14). The skills at each level are listed in descending order, according to the percentage and number of students needing instruction.

Another report can be generated indicating which students need particular skills (Figure 3.15). Students are listed in rank order (highest to lowest scores). A quick perusal of this report can help the reading teacher form skill groups.

FIGURE 3.10   Cumulative Record of Performance—*Ginn Computer Management System* (From User's Manual, Apple II® Version of the GINN READING PROGRAM: *Computer Management System*, Copyright® 1982 by Ginn and Company (Xerox Corporation.) Used with permission.)

```
*****************************************************************************
*                                                                           *
*                          GINN READING PROGRAM                             *
*                        CUMULATIVE PERFORMANCE RECORD                       *
*                                                                           *
*     PUPIL    GROVE, KEITH                    ID     55606                  *
*     GROUP    BUZZARDS                        GRADE  2                      *
*   TEACHER    SANDRA ORRELL                   DATE   02/25/83               *
*     CLASS    GRADE 2                         SCHOOL GREENLEAF              *
*                                                                           *
*****************************************************************************


TESTS COMPLETED    LEVEL 7    1A, 2A, 3A, 4A
                   LEVEL 8    1A


                                                                     DATE
        UNIT   OBJECTIVE                       SCORE    % SCORE      TESTED
        ------------------------------------------------------------------

  L-7    1A    V - WORD IDENTIFICATION           10        83      10/07/82
         1A    C - PREDICTING OUTCOMES            5       100      10/07/82
         1A    D - EW (CHEW/FEW) OO (WOOD) &     13        87      10/07/82
                   DOUBLE CONSONANT BEFORE -ING
                   /-ED

  L-7    2A    V - WORD IDENTIFICATION           11        92      11/12/82
         2A    V - VOCABULARY DEVELOPMENT         3*       60      11/12/82
                   (MULTIPLE MEANINGS)
         2A    C - SEQUENCE                       5        83      11/12/82
         2A    D - I/HIGH IE/PIE O/MOTH AU(GH)/  16        89      11/12/82
                   CAUSE/CAUGHT COMPARATIVES ER
                   /EST

  L-7    3A    V - WORD IDENTIFICATION           12       100      12/15/82
         3A    V - VOCABULARY DEVELOPMENT          4        80      12/15/82
                   (SYNONYMS/ANTONYMS)
         3A    C - REALITY/FANTASY                5       100      12/15/82
         3A    D - DIGRAPH WH/WHOLE/WHAT OI/OIL  13        87      12/15/82
                   OY/BOY BLENDS SCR/SPR/STR

  L-7    4A    V - WORD IDENTIFICATION            9*       75      01/21/83
         4A    V - VOCABULARY DEVELOPMENT          4        80      01/21/83
                   (CLASSIFICATION)
         4A    C - COMPARISON                     5       100      01/21/83
         4A    D - CONSONANT BLEND SQU/SQUASH &   7        88      01/21/83
                   CONTRACTIONS WITH HAVE

  L-8    1A    V - WORD IDENTIFICATION           12       100      02/25/83
         1A    C - MAIN IDEA                       3*       60      02/25/83
         1A    D - Y TO I OR E DROPPED BEFORE    14        93      02/25/83
                   ENDING & DOUBLE MEDIAL
                   CONSONANTS


               * BELOW SUGGESTED PASSING SCORE
```

This report lists all test results for an individual pupil.

REPORT 7

Following instruction, posttests can be administered to determine the students' understanding of the specific skill. Once test scores are entered into the microcomputer, a Skill Group Test Results report can be generated (Figure 3.16). This printout gives the date, the test form, posttest scores, and the number of times the posttest was administered. Students are listed in descending order according to test score. Mastery of a skill is indicated by an asterisk in the Mastery column.

The Individual Student Profile (Figure 3.17) lists a student's progress at the level in which he or she is currently working. Each skill is listed along with

FIGURE 3.11   Parent Report—*Ginn Computer Management System* (From User's Manual, Apple II® Version of the GINN READING PROGRAM: *Computer Management System,* Copyright©1982 by Ginn and Company (Xerox Corporation.) Used with permission.)

```
******************************** PARENT REPORT ********************************

                         GROVE, KEITH

     For reading instruction in grade 2, Keith is working in the Ginn Reading
Program.  In this program Keith receives instruction in the essential reading
skills of decoding, comprehension, and vocabulary.  Specific objectives in each
of the three skill areas are included in each unit.  These objectives are
tested at the end of each unit.  This report will help you, Keith, and the
teacher to understand Keith's progress in learning to read.

     Keith is working on level 8 of the Ginn Reading Program.  There are 4
units in this level.  Keith has completed test 1A.

This report is for Keith's work on the most recent test:  1A

******************************************************************************

Keith has passed the tests on these skills:

     VOCABULARY
       100%    WORD IDENTIFICATION

     DECODING
        93%    Y TO I OR E DROPPED BEFORE ENDING & DOUBLE MEDIAL CONSONANTS

******************************************************************************

Keith will need further instruction in these skills:

     COMPREHENSION
        60%    MAIN IDEA
```

This report describes a pupil's performance on the most recent test. There is an alternate, shorter version without the introductory paragraph.

REPORT 8

```
AREA: STUDY SKILLS

                        REPORT 1--STUDENT ROSTER
                        =========================
                              11/05/84

GRADE K: MISS MARSHALL
        NAME            ID #  SPECIAL         NAME            ID #  SPECIAL
----------------------  ----  -------  --------------------  ----  -------
BROWN, GEORGE            19                    JACKSON, MARY           44
CARLTON, JIM             3                     MICHENER, EDWIN         18
DARLING, MICHAEL         4                     MILLER, MARGE           15
DOBROSKI, ANNE           46                    MILLER, PATRICK         16
DOVESTI, JERRY           42                    RICHLAND, HOWIE         45
GOSEN, MARGE             43


GRADE K: MR. EDWARDS
        NAME            ID #  SPECIAL         NAME            ID #  SPECIAL
----------------------  ----  -------  --------------------  ----  -------
ADAMS, SUZY             9                      EVERS, JOHN             21
BAILY, ELLEN            22                     FLOWERS, ROSE           24
BECK, TOM               10                     GAYNOR, MERLE           39
BILL, BRAUN             37                     HOLMES, MARK            40
BRUNER, AMY             38                     HUNT, GAYLE             25
CANTOU, SUE             17                     JAMES, GIDEON           7     ***
DIBBS, HANS             23                     ROBERTS, CHARLIE        41
DOVER, REX              20


GRADE K: MS. HOWARD
        NAME            ID #  SPECIAL         NAME            ID #  SPECIAL
----------------------  ----  -------  --------------------  ----  -------
BARTLETT, GIDEON        36                     QUINT, PAUL             30
DOVER, JANE             26                     RIDER, JAKE             31
GOOD, ANGIE             27                     SAILER, MARY            32
ICEY, KAY               28                     SMITH, JOE              34
JONES, BOB              29                     WEX, GINA               33
JONES, TOM              35


This report lists by homeroom the students included in
SkillTrac.
```

FIGURE 3.12   Student Roster—*Wisconsin Design Computer Management System (The Wisconsin Design: SkillTrac,* Learning Multi-Systems, Inc., 340 Coyier Lane, Madison, Wisconsin 53713.)

the break-in test score, the test form, the date of administration, the posttest score(s) and form(s), and the date of posttest administration. This record permits teachers to assess an individual's skill attainment and to determine how often the student has participated in group instruction.

The *Wisconsin Design Computer Management System* also permits generation of parent reports (Figure 3.18). In addition to presenting information generated in other forms, it includes a narrative explanation of the overall progress of the student.

The Class Profile (Figure 3.19) graphically depicts the overall skill attainment status for a particular group of individuals. Students are listed on one axis and skills are listed on the other. Mastery of a skill is indicated by an

```
┌─────────────────────────────────────────────────────────────────┐
│ AREA: STUDY SKILLS                                                │
│                               REPORT 2--RETESTING                 │
│                               ====================                │
│                                    11/05/84                       │
│ THIS REPORT INCLUDES THE FOLLOWING HOMEROOMS IN GRADE K:          │
│     MISS MARSHALL                                                 │
│     MR. EDWARDS                                                   │
│     MS. HOWARD                                                    │
│                          BREAK-IN                                 │
│         NAME             LEVEL     # SKILLS MASTERED  RETEST LEVEL │
│     ---------------      -------   ----------------   ------------ │
│     DARLING, MICHAEL     D-14            0                 C       │
│     MILLER, MARGE        B- 4            0                 A       │
│     MICHENER, EDWIN      B- 4            4                 C       │
│     JACKSON, MARY        B- 4            3                 C       │
│                                                                   │
│     This report shows which students need to be retested either   │
│     up or down after break-in testing.  It should be used in      │
│     conjunction with the suggestions outlined in the appropriate  │
│     Teacher's Planning Guide.  Students are grouped according to  │
│     their retest level.  Those who do not need to be retested     │
│     are not included in this report.  The information is saved    │
│     in the computer until the report is printed.                  │
│                                                                   │
│     ¹Mastery is defined as achieving a score of 80% or greater.   │
└─────────────────────────────────────────────────────────────────┘
```

FIGURE 3.13   Retesting Printout—*Wisconsin Design Computer Management System (The Wisconsin Design: SkillTrac,* Learning Multi-Systems, Inc., 340 Coyier Lane, Madison, Wisconsin 53713.)

asterisk at the intersection of the column and row. Students are rank ordered with those individuals demonstrating mastery of the most skills listed first. This profile permits teachers to see at a glance the relative skill development of their students.

A School Skill Growth Record can also be produced by this program (Figure 3.20). This printout shows, by grade level or homeroom, the average number of skills learned and the average skill growth students have made during a specified period of time. These data can be valuable to individuals who must monitor the overall school reading program.

The *Wisconsin Design Computer Management System* provides educators with a means for monitoring the reading skill development of word attack, comprehension, and study skills. While it is not a complete reading program, it has the necessary components to assure that students receive instruction in areas of demonstrated skill weaknesses. As such, teachers of reading may find it a valuable adjunct to their reading program.

The major advantage of classroom management systems is obvious. At a moment's notice, teachers can have a variety of reports at their fingertips, making ad hoc grouping and pupil analysis a relatively simple matter.

The disadvantage of classroom management systems is that tests must be administered and scored and the data entered into the computer before an analysis of student performance can be accomplished. Since data entry initially takes considerable time, some individuals may be unwilling to devote their energies to this task.

```
AREA: STUDY SKILLS

                      REPORT 3--SKILLS STUDENTS NEED
                      ===============================
                                 11/05/84
THIS REPORT INCLUDES THE FOLLOWING HOMEROOMS IN GRADE K:
    MISS MARSHALL
    MR. EDWARDS
    MS. HOWARD

                              LEVEL A
                              -------

               SKILLS          % WITHOUT MASTERY  NO. WITHOUT MASTERY
    -----------------------------  -----------------  -------------------
    A 1  PT--REPRESENTATION              100                 31
    A 3  MEASUREMENT: SIZE                97                 30
    A 2  POSITIONS OF OBJECTS             94                 29

                              LEVEL B
                              -------

               SKILLS          % WITHOUT MASTERY  NO. WITHOUT MASTERY
    -----------------------------  -----------------  -------------------
    B 4  GRAPHS: RELATIVE AMOUNTS         67                  2
    B 2  PICTURE GRIDS                    33                  1
    B 3  MEASUREMENT: DISTANCE            33                  1
    B 1  PICTURE SYMBOLS                  33                  1

                              LEVEL D
                              -------

               SKILLS          % WITHOUT MASTERY  NO. WITHOUT MASTERY
    -----------------------------  -----------------  -------------------
    D 2  PT--CARDINAL DIRECTIONS         100                  3
    D 8  PT--DICTIONARIES & GLOSSARIES   100                  3
    D 5  GRAPHS: APPROXIMATE AMOUNTS      67                  2
    D 6  TABLES: DIFFERENCES              67                  2
    D 1  POINT & LINE SYMBOLS             67                  2
    D 9  TABLES OF CONTENTS               67                  2
    D10  ALPHABETIZING                    67                  2
    D11  GUIDE WORDS                      67                  2
    D12  HEADINGS & SUBHEADINGS           67                  2
    D13  SELECTING SOURCES                67                  2
    D 3  SCALE: WHOLE UNITS               33                  1
    D 4  GRAPHS: DIFFERENCES              33                  1
    D 7  INDEXES                          33                  1
    D14  FACTS OR OPINIONS                33                  1


    This report lists the skills at each level in descending
    order, according to the percentage of students needing each
    skill.   This information is helpful when selecting skills
    for instruction.  The procedures for selecting skills are
    discussed in the appropriate Teacher's Planning Guide.

    ¹The "mastery" level is defined as 80% or greater.  Students
    without mastery achieved scores of 79% or below.
```

FIGURE 3.14   Skills Students Need—*Wisconsin Design Computer Management System (The Wisconsin Design: SkillTrac,* Learning Multi-Systems, Inc., 340 Coyier Lane, Madison, Wisconsin 53713.)

```
AREA: STUDY SKILLS

                  REPORT 4--FORMING SKILL GROUPS
                  ================================
                            11/05/84
THIS REPORT INCLUDES THE FOLLOWING HOMEROOMS IN GRADE K:
   MISS MARSHALL
   MR. EDWARDS

SKILL B2: PICTURE GRIDS

         NAME           SCORE    TEST, # TIMES TAKEN    FORM      DATE
---------------------   -----    --------------------   ----    --------
MILLER, MARGE            75            POSTTEST, 2         Q     10/20/84
JACKSON, MARY            67            BREAK-IN            P     10/10/84
MICHENER, EDWIN          40            BREAK-IN            P     10/10/84
BECK, TOM               32            POSTTEST, 1         Q     10/20/84
----------------------------------------------------------------------

    This report shows which students need a specific skill,
    whether each student has taken only a break-in test or a
    posttest, and the number of times the posttest has been
    taken, for example, twice is indicated by "Posttest, 2."
    The score, test form and date are also noted. For
    instructional purposes the students are listed in descending
    order by test scores.
```

FIGURE 3.15   Forming Skill Groups—*Wisconsin Design Computer Management System (The Wisconsin Design: SkillTrac,* Learning Multi-Systems, Inc., 340 Coyier Lane, Madison, Wisconsin 53713.)

FIGURE 3.16   Skill Group Test Results—*Wisconsin Design Computer Management System (The Wisconsin Design: SkillTrac,* Learning Multi-Systems, Inc., 340 Coyier Lane, Madison, Wisconsin 53713.)

```
AREA:  Study Skills

                  Report A--Skill Group Test Results
                  ==================================
                            10/26/84

Skill Group:  C6 Graphs:  Exact Amounts
Form: Q
GRADE 3:  MR. HARRIS

                                   Students Achieving Mastery:  33%

    Student Name        Score    Times Taken    All Group Tests    All I & PT
---------------------   -----    -----------    ---------------    ----------
MARSHALL, PAULA         100%         1              "yes"
FOX, BRAD               80%          2                                "yes"
MICHAELS, GEORGY        79%          1
SARANOVA, SYLVIA        60%          2
NUNEZ, JUANITA          40%          3
MITCHELL, RALPH         20%          4

     This report lists the students in a particular skill group and shows
their score on the posttest and number of times the posttest has been taken.
For instructional purposes students are listed in descending order by test
scores. A "yes" will appear in one of the two right columns if the student
has completed either all of the group tests and/or all of the I and PT tests.
This report is printed out immediately after the scores are entered and the
information is not saved to the disk.

----------------------------------------------------------------------------
```

FIGURE 3.17   Individual Student Profile—*Wisconsin Design Computer Management System (The Wisconsin Design: SkillTrac,* Learning Multi-Systems, Inc., 340 Coyier Lane, Madison, Wisconsin 53713.)

```
AREA: STUDY SKILLS

                    REPORT 5--INDIVIDUAL STUDENT PROFILE
                    ===================================
                             11/05/84

CARLTON, JIM
GRADE K: MISS MARSHALL
CURRENT LEVEL: D
SPECIAL:


                                        BREAK-IN            POSTTEST
                                   -------------------  -------------------
              SKILLS               SCORE  FM   DATE     SCORE  FM   DATE
--------------------------------   ------ --  --------  ------ --  --------
   D  1 POINT & LINE SYMBOLS          50   P  10/12/84   63, 1  Q 11/05/84
   D  2 PT--CARDINAL DIRECTIONS
   D  3 SCALE: WHOLE UNITS            15   P  10/12/84
   D  4 GRAPHS: DIFFERENCES           17   P  10/12/84
  *D  5 GRAPHS: APPROXIMATE AMOUNTS   17   P  10/10/84   83, 2  P 11/10/84
  *D  6 TABLES: DIFFERENCES           83   P  10/12/84
  *D  7 INDEXES                       83   P  10/12/84
   D  8 PT--DICTIONARIES & GLOSSARIES
  *D  9 TABLES OF CONTENTS            83   P  10/12/84
   D 10 ALPHABETIZING                 29   P  10/12/84
  *D 11 GUIDE WORDS                   81   P  10/12/84
  *D 12 HEADINGS & SUBHEADINGS        83   P  10/12/84
   D 13 SELECTING SOURCES             33   P  10/12/84   63, 2  Q 10/10/84
  *D 14 FACTS OR OPINIONS             91   P  10/12/84
-----------------------------------------------------------------------------




                         SKILL GROWTH CHART
                         ==================
                             11/05/84

     STARTUP PERIOD              END OF EACH QUARTER
     ---------------    -------------------------------------
     DATE     SKILLS    1ST    2ND    3RD    4TH     GROWTH
     ------   ------    ---    ---    ---    ---     ------
     10/12/81    0       1      2      2      3         3
     10/10/82    3       4      5      6      7         4
     09/30/83    7      10     12     14     18        11
     10/05/84   18      20     24     26               8
-----------------------------------------------------------------------------



     This report shows one student's skill attainment progress at
     his or her current level.  Break-in and posttest scores,
     test form and dates are noted.

     The chart shows the total number of skills attained at the
     end of each quarter and the overall skill growth for each
     year.

     ¹Stars beside skill numbers indicate mastery.
```

```
AREA: STUDY SKILLS

                         REPORT 6--PARENT REPORT
                         =========================
                               11/05/84

CARLTON, JIM
GRADE K: MISS MARSHALL
CURRENT LEVEL: D


                                      BREAK-IN              POSTTEST
                                 ------------------    ------------------
              SKILLS             SCORE  FM   DATE     SCORE  FM   DATE
    ----------------------------- ------ -- --------  ------ -- --------
    D 1 POINT & LINE SYMBOLS        50     P 10/12/84  63, 1  Q 11/05/84
    D 2 PT--CARDINAL DIRECTIONS
    D 3 SCALE: WHOLE UNITS          15     P 10/12/84
    D 4 GRAPHS: DIFFERENCES         17     P 10/12/84
   *D 5 GRAPHS: APPROXIMATE AMOUNTS 17     P 10/10/84  83, 2  P 11/10/84
   *D 6 TABLES: DIFFERENCES         83     P 10/12/84
   *D 7 INDEXES                     83     P 10/12/84
    D 8 PT--DICTIONARIES & GLOSSARIES
   *D 9 TABLES OF CONTENTS          83     P 10/12/84
    D10 ALPHABETIZING               29     P 10/12/84
   *D11 GUIDE WORDS                 81     P 10/12/84
   *D12 HEADINGS & SUBHEADINGS      83     P 10/12/84
    D13 SELECTING SOURCES           33     P 10/12/84  63, 2  Q 10/10/84
   *D14 FACTS OR OPINIONS           91     P 10/12/84
    -----------------------------------------------------------------------



                          SKILL GROWTH CHART
                          ==================
                               11/05/84

    STARTUP PERIOD                 END OF EACH QUARTER
    ---------------      ------------------------------------
    DATE      SKILLS     1ST      2ND      3RD      4TH     GROWTH
    --------  ------     ---      ---      ---      ---     ------
    10/12/81    0          1        2        2        3        3
    10/10/82    3          4        5        6        7        4
    09/30/83    7         10       12       14       18       11
    10/05/84   18         20       24       26                 8
    -----------------------------------------------------------------------


    Your child's teacher will help explain this progress report.
    Study Skills help students learn to become independent
    readers.  Jim is working at Level D.  He has mastered the
    skills that have a star beside them and needs further
    developmental instruction in the remaining skills.  When all
    of the skills at this level have been mastered, work can
    begin at the next level of skills.  When Jim completes Level
    G, he should be independent in using Study Skills and be
    ready to apply them with a variety of subject matter
    materials.
```

FIGURE 3.18   Parent Report—*Wisconsin Design Computer Management System (The Wisconsin Design: SkillTrac*, Learning Multi-Systems, Inc., 340 Coyier Lane, Madison, Wisconsin 53713.)

```
AREA: STUDY SKILLS
                          REPORT 7--GROUP PROFILE
                          =========================
                               11/05/84
THIS REPORT INCLUDES THE FOLLOWING HOMEROOMS IN GRADE K:
   MISS MARSHALL
   AAABBBBCCCCCCCCCCCDDDDDDDDDDDDDDDEEEEEEEEEEEEEEEEEEEEFFFFFFFFFFFFFGGGGGGGGGG
   12312341234567891112345678911111112345678911111111112345678911111234567891
              01        01234        01234567           012           0
------- ----------------------------------------------------------------------
CARLT J ********************************
DARLI M ***********
MICHE E *******
JACKS M ******
MILLE M *****
BROWN G  **
MILLE P **
GOSEN M
DOVES J
RICHL H
DOBRO A
      ----------------------------------------------------------------------

This report shows general progress in skill attainment for a
particular group of students. The students are listed
according to their skill attainment (highest to lowest).
Stars indicate which skills a student has mastered.
```

FIGURE 3.19   Group Profile—*Wisconsin Design Computer Management System (The Wisconsin Design: SkillTrac,* Learning Multi-Systems, Inc., 340 Coyier Lane, Madison, Wisconsin 53713.)

```
AREA: STUDY SKILLS

                    REPORT 8--GROUP SKILL GROWTH AVERAGES
                    =====================================
                               11/05/84

THIS REPORT INCLUDES THE FOLLOWING HOMEROOMS IN GRADE K:
    MRS. JONES
    MISS MARSHALL
    MR. EDWARDS
    MS. HOWARD
                        AVERAGE NUMBER OF SKILLS PER STUDENT  AVERAGE SKILL
                        ------------------------------------  GROWTH PER
   GRADE    HOMEROOM      STARTUP: 10/10/84  TODAY: 00/00/00    STUDENT
   ----- ---------------- -----------------  ---------------  -------------
   K     SELECTED HOMEROOMS      0.0              2.6             2.6
   K     MRS. JONES              0.0              2.2             2.2
   K     MISS MARSHALL           0.0              5.9             5.9
   K     MR. EDWARDS             0.0              1.5             1.5
   K     MS. HOWARD              0.0              1.0             1.0
   ----- --------------------------------------------------------- -------------


This report shows the average number of skills and the
average skill growth per student--by grade level or unit and
by homeroom--from the baseline date to the current date.
```

FIGURE 3.20   School Skill Growth Record—*Wisconsin Design Computer Management System (The Wisconsin Design: SkillTrac,* Learning Multi-Systems, Inc., 340 Coyier Lane, Madison, Wisconsin 53713.)

To ease the test scoring burden, publishers are exploring the feasibility of using a number of different scoring devices. The Ginn program, for example, can use a special graphics tablet to assist in the marking of test papers. Holt, Rinehart and Winston, another publishing company, uses an optical card reader that scores special cards marked by students. Both systems reduce time needed to score tests and contribute toward more acceptance of classroom management systems.

Materials Preparation Programs

Materials preparation software permits teachers to produce materials that might be difficult or perhaps impossible to do without the microcomputer. Some of these programs produce word searches, crossword puzzles, and banners.

Wordsearch (Hartley Publishing Company), for example, allows a teacher, or child for that matter, to enter a series of words to create a word search puzzle. Users have the option of having words overlap; spelling words forward, backward, or diagonally; or having them printed left to right or top to bottom. Words used in the puzzle are printed on the bottom of the page. To use the program, the individual simply enters the words to be used in the puzzle and selects from the printing options available. In a matter of minutes, the printer completes the word search puzzle.

Crossword puzzles are easy to produce, provided that teachers have the appropriate software. *MECC—Elementary—Language Arts,* Volume 2 (Minnesota Educational Computing Consortium) is one such program. Once loaded into the microcomputer, the user inputs the words and clues to be used in the puzzle. After these data have been entered, the computer automatically formats the crossword grid and provides the clue phrases in either the "across" or "down" categories. In a manner of minutes, an entire puzzle can be designed on the printer. Since many printers will print images on ditto masters, both crossword puzzles and word search games can be quickly reproduced.

Word searches and crossword puzzles are two ways in which to reinforce the vocabulary words typically taught in reading lessons. Furthermore, teachers at all levels who are responsible for teaching reading, science, and social studies may find teacher-generated materials an excellent means for teaching vocabulary.

SUMMARY

Software for teaching reading can be arbitrarily categorized into a number of different schemes: drill and practice, tutorial, games, simulations, and teacher utilities are but five. In reality, most educational software falls into more than a single category. For discussion purposes, however, it is usually beneficial to examine reading software by including it in one of the foregoing categories.

The intention of this chapter has been to alert users to the advantages as well as the disadvantages of using each type of software to teach reading. In addition, examples of programs that illustrate each category were presented.

Using software effectively, however, requires more than the ability to determine its category correctly. Software, like other educational materials, is only as good as the teacher who uses it. Knowledgeable and creative teachers will integrate computer programs in ways that will enhance what has already been taught in the classroom. This chapter has introduced the reader to some possible classroom applications. The remainder of this text will examine reading software from a pedagogical and theoretical perspective. Teachers of reading should then be able to determine critically the appropriateness of educational software as they attempt to improve the reading achievement of their students.

RELATED READINGS

COBURN, PETER, PETER KELMAN, NANCY ROBERTS, THOMAS F. F. SNYDER, DANIEL H. WATT, and CHERYL WEINER. *A Practical Guide to Computers in Education.* Reading, Mass.: Addison-Wesley Publishing Company, 1982.
LATHROP, ANN, and BOBBY GOODSON. *Courseware in the Classroom.* Menlo Park, Calif.: Addison-Wesley Publishing Company, 1983.
TAYLOR, ROBERT P. (ed.). *The Computer in the School: Tutor, Tool, Tutee.* New York: Teachers College Press, 1980.

REFERENCES

BENNETT, RANDY ELLIOT, "Applications of Microcomputer Technology to Special Education," *Exceptional Children,* Vol. 49, no. 2 (October 1982), 106–113.
BUDOFF, MILTON, and LEAH R. HUTTEN, "Microcomputers in Special Education: Promises and Pitfalls," *Exceptional Children,* Vol. 49, no. 2 (October 1982), 123–128.
GAGNÉ, ROBERT M., "Developments in Learning Psychology: Implications for Instructional Design; and Effects of Computer Technology on Instructional Design and Development," *Educational Technology,* Vol. 22, no. 6 (June 1982), 11–15.
GAWRONSKI, J. D., and CHARLENE E. WEST, "Computer Literacy," *ASCD Curriculum Update* (October 1982) 1–5.
GOLES, GORDON G., "Games as Teaching Tools: Effective Uses of the Child in All of Us," *Educational Computer Magazine* (November-December 1982), 12–14.
HENNEY, MARIBETH, and VICKI BOYSEN, "The Effect of Computer Simulation Training on Ability to Administer an Informal Reading Inventory," *Journal of Educational Research,* Vol. 72, no. 5 (May-June 1979), 265-270.
LABERGE, DAVID, and S. JAY SAMUELS, "Toward a Theory of Automatic Information Processing in Reading," *Cognitive Psychology,* Vol. 6, no. 2 (April 1974), 293-323.
LATHROP, ANN, and BOBBY GOODSON, *Courseware in the Classroom,* Menlo Park, Calif.: Addison-Wesley Publishing Company, 1983.
SALTINSKI, RONALD, "Microcomputers in Social Studies: An Innovative Technology for Instruction," *Educational Technology,* Vol. 21, no. 1 (January 1981), 29-32.
ZEISER, EDWARD L., and STEVIE HOFFMAN, "Computers: Tools for Thinking," *Childhood Education,* Vol. 59, no. 4 (March–April 1983), 251-254.

FOUR

SOFTWARE FOR READING

Upon completing this chapter, you will be able to

— 1. Describe how teachers of reading can use microcomputer software.

— 2. Discuss how software can be used to teach readiness skills, decoding, comprehension, and study skills.

— 3. Explain some of the cautions that need to be exercised when selecting and using software to teach reading.

— 4. Identify commercial software that can be used to teach reading.

INTRODUCTION

The Role of Technology

Today's teachers of reading have many more software programs available to supplement their teaching of reading than did the teacher of five years ago. Microcomputers, coupled with high-quality software, can augment a teacher's instructional efforts by providing activities to reinforce previously taught skills. Furthermore, tests can be administered and scored by computer, which, in turn, allows educators to monitor student performance. Microcomputers also serve as extrinsic rewards for students who complete conventional assignments such as worksheets or workbooks. In short, microcomputers can play an important part in a teacher's efforts to help students become better readers.

Educators and Microcomputers

According to a recent Carnegie Report ("Two New Studies," 1983), "all students should learn about computers; learn with computers; and, as an ultimate goal, learn from computers" (p. 18). The report goes on to point out that computers should play a role in the revitalization of the American schools. Interestingly, the benefits derived from using computers are consonant with what we know about quality reading teachers. In a review of the literature, for example, Lass (1981) identified a number of characteristics that typify good teachers of reading. These include the

1. Ability to organize and manage instruction
2. Ability to attend to individual needs
3. Ability to pace instruction correctly
4. Skill at maintaining student attention
5. Monitoring of student achievement
6. Provision of one-to-one instruction when needed
7. Use of supplementary material

High-quality computer software can complement teachers in their efforts to attain many of these goals.

A major hurdle that educators need to overcome, however, is their reluctance to use this new technology. Rose (1982) believes that many teachers and administrators don't embrace computer-assisted instruction because they are inherently resistant to change. Since some may lack an understanding of the technology, they may perceive microcomputers as threats to their jobs. Others may not want to be bothered with what they think is just another educational fad.

A first step in helping educators accept microcomputers would be to have software developers produce material that has both high technological and pedagogical quality. Once these two criteria are met, teachers should be more willing to use microcomputers in the classroom. This chapter explores a variety of reading software and discusses possible uses in school settings. While some of the software is of high quality, other programs possess serious limitations. The intent here is to highlight both types of programs, thereby making the reader a more aware consumer.

READINESS SKILLS

Finding and using software to reinforce reading readiness skills can be a challenging experience for a teacher just moving into the computer age. This is so for a number of reasons. First, the area of readiness instruction is perhaps the initial encounter many students will have with computers. Hence, special consideration must be given to the age and maturity level of the users. Next, it is difficult to discern where "readiness" ends and "reading" begins. This makes the title "readiness software" somewhat arbitrary. The net result is that some programs that are entitled "readiness" are more advanced than many teachers would expect. The opposite is also true. Some "reading" software has more of a "readiness" flavor. Program titles, therefore, can be misleading. Finally, teachers must decide on an operational definition of "readiness" and then determine whether the software fits their definition and expectations. Each of these concerns will be discussed in this chapter.

Computers and Nonreaders

Television commercials aired by computer manufacturers sometimes lead parents to believe that a preschooler without a microcomputer will be at a disadvantage upon entering school. This attitude of "It's never too early" can also permeate the school environment. Before long, kindergarten and first-grade teachers begin to wonder, "How early is early enough?" The answer to this question depends to a large degree on the software that is to be used.

An analysis of reading readiness software leaves one wanting. There are a number of reasons for this. One is that many students do not have sufficient letter discrimination ability to permit the use of software without extensive teacher supervision. This severely limits the number of programs from which a selection can be made. Second, young children have only limited keyboarding skills. Programs that are selected should have easy-to-use commands that require only minimal typing. Third, some reading readiness programs use such low-resolution graphics for letter discrimination exercises that the letters only vaguely represent their typeset counterparts. This leads to some teachers questioning whether there can be transfer between what is learned on the computer and what is required of students when using print material. Finally, some programs require the reading of on-screen directions. One program, for example, asks students, "Can you match this letter?" and then proceeds to flash a letter on the monitor's screen. If children can read the directions, they certainly don't need letter matching activities! These reasons necessitate the careful screening of readiness software. Buyers should be aware that the word "readiness" in a program's title doesn't imply appropriateness for young learners.

Readiness and Reading

A persistent question facing early childhood educators is, "Where does readiness stop and reading begin?" This question, of course, is not unique to computer software only. It also pertains to other educational materials. Durkin (1978) suggests that reading readiness and reading are on a continuum and that it is impossible to separate where one ends and the other begins. If that is the case, kindergarten and first-grade teachers should consult each other before software is purchased. In this way, each will have similar expectations of the child and appropriate software can be ordered for each of the respective levels.

A Theory of Readiness

Selecting readiness software implicitly is tied to a teacher's theory of reading. This is because the teacher's perception of what is appropriate and inappropriate often reflects his or her beliefs about readiness training. A teacher who believes that color recognition is related to reading, for instance, might select microcomputer software that requires students to match geometric shapes of similar color. Activities such as these are found in *Matchmaker* (Counterpoint Software). This program requires students to match objects by size, shape, and color. Letter—matching activities are not included in the program.

A teacher who believes that readiness is more "readinglike" may insist on programs that address discrimination training such as letter detail, letter order, and letter orientation skills. These, along with sound matching and sound blending skills, have been labeled "high-priority" readiness skills by Otto, Rude, and Spiegel (1979).

One product that addresses some of these high-priority skills is *Getting Ready to Read and Add (MECC—Elementary,* Volume 7). This diskette includes nine programs, four of which are specifically related to these reading readiness skills. *Caterpillar*, for example, requires students to supply the missing uppercase letter from a five-letter sequence. Each correct response results in a segment being added to the caterpillar's body. *Train* is a similar type drill except that lowercase letters are used and cars of a train are added for each correct response. *A is for Apple* is a drill on the initial letters used to spell a word. A high-resolution picture is shown with a choice of four initial consonants. Students identify the letter that represents the appropriate sound. Either upper- or lowercase letters can be selected. *Words* is a "Concentration"-type game with words hidden under a grid. Students attempt to match word pairs hidden under the tiles in the matrix. Teachers may edit the words used in *Words*, thereby providing an opportunity to use either letters or high-frequency sight words. Extensive documentation describing each activity is included with this program.

Another program for children is *Letter Recognition* (Hartley). Easy-to-read letters and numerals are presented on the screen, and the student is required to find the corresponding letter or numeral on the keyboard. Uppercase, lowercase, numerals, or mixed characters can be selected.

Trying to determine the best type of programs for young students is difficult because programs generally cost $30.00 to $40.00, some of them are of questionable quality, many teach only a few basic skills, and the limited reading ability of young children means that special care must be taken to make sure that students can use the programs without extensive supervision. The net result is that in many instances, the skills needed by these students can best be taught without the aid of a microcomputer.

TEACHING DECODING

Decoding skills have traditionally included skills within the following categories: sight vocabulary, phonics, and structural analysis. The role that software can play in each of these areas will be discussed in the following section.

Sight Vocabulary

The term "sight vocabulary" has a number of connotations. To some, it implies the instantaneous recognition of printed words. To others, sight vocabulary means words that appear with high frequency in oral language or print. The Dolch 220 Sight Vocabulary Word List or the Harris-Jacobson Word List are examples of such word lists. A third definition of sight vocabulary includes those words introduced in basal reader programs. For our purposes, however, sight vocabulary is defined as those words presented in software designed to improve a student's reading vocabulary. While this may not be the conventional operational definition found in many reading methodology texts, it serves the purpose of being able to include many vocabulary software packages that might be overlooked if a narrower definition was used. While such an operational definition may not coincide with convention, it is more important at this stage to understand the intended purposes of this software than it is to quibble over an acceptable sight vocabulary definition.

Wedman (1983), after analyzing 253 reading software packages, identified 68 programs (27 percent) that focused on vocabulary development. One reason for this relatively large number may be related to the ease of programming these types of activities.

At the simplest level, some vocabulary software attempts to improve students' vocabularies through the matching of target words and definitions. Here is an example of a technique used in a typical program:

> genesis (Jen uh sis) n.
>   A. unusual event
>   B. a returning to
>   C. origin
>   D. art form

Students are provided immediate visual and aural feedback upon making their selection. At the conclusion of each unit, the computer calculates the student's score. Some programs also provide a listing of missed words accompanied by their appropriate definitions.

Several programs use a screen format similar to the example just provided. Many of the SAT (Scholastic Aptitude Test) preparation programs, for instance, use this technique.

The two-diskette *SAT Word Attack Skills* (Edu-Ware) program uses this drill-and-practice approach to improve students' knowledge of prefixes and root words. At the beginning of each lesson, students choose either the synonyms or antonyms drill format. An example of a synonym problem is

TRANSIENT
a. careless   c. stable
b. responsible   d. cautious
        e. quickly passing

After two incorrect responses, the program provides the correct answer (i.e., "transient" means "quickly passing."). A short tutorial then explains the use of the prefix and root in the target word. Six lessons are supplied on a diskette. Each diskette also contains a timed review program that drills students on the previous six lessons. At the completion of the review, students' scores (based on the number of correct responses selected on the first trial) are displayed on the monitor.

An interesting adaptation of some vocabularly development programs is the approach used by Hartley. Its *Vocabulary—Elementary* program, for instance, uses the cassette-control device (CCD) to permit the cassette recorder to supply the aural stimulus while the printed word appears on the screen. This assures the student of hearing a correct pronunciation of the target word, something some programs overlook.

Hartley also produces a program entitled *Vocabulary—Dolch.* This program drills students on the 220 Dolch Basic Sight Words, again, making use of the CCD. First, the word is presented on the monitor. Next, the student says the word. Then, the cassette tape plays the word. Through a keyboard response, students indicate whether they know the word. A record of each student's responses is stored on the program diskette.

Another package that attempts to teach vocabulary is Davidson & Associates' *Word Attack.* This program presents a target word, a sentence context in which the word is used, and a choice of four possible answers. An arcade-type game provides excitement as students attempt to match words and meanings within a specified time limit. Like the previously mentioned programs, a profile of student responses is stored on the diskette.

Teachers who want to design their own vocabulary word lists can do so with programs such as Hartley's *Create—Vocabulary. Create—Vocabulary* is a template program that permits teachers to add their personalized vocabulary lists to a diskette, thereby allowing the inclusion of basal reader or content area textbook vocabulary.

When previewing vocabulary development software, it is important to consider how individuals learn words. Is it through a simple association between words and definitions or is it a more complex process? If it is the former, the most expedient way of increasing one's vocabulary would seem to be to employ massive quantities of drill-and-practice activities requiring matching of target words and definitions. An increasing amount of evidence, however, leads us to believe that a simple stimulus-response learning paradigm may not adequately explain how words are learned. Today, research suggests that words are retained only if they are learned in meaningful contextual settings that permit a linking of past experiences with the newly introduced words. Software that attempts to teach vocabulary via synonym or antonym matching uses one technique to link the new with the familiar. Using the words in meaningful contextual settings also helps to establish meaningful connections, since many words have more than one meaning. It is important to remember, therefore, that unless embedded in some type of context, new vocabulary words may be quickly forgotten.

Phonic Skills

The phonological, semantic, and syntactic cueing systems comprise the three processes by which students unlock unfamiliar words. Phonics, perhaps more than the other two systems, has always played an important part in reading instruction. Indeed, since Chall's *Learning to Read: The Great Debate* (1967), reading materials have emphasized phonics, often to the detriment of meaning-seeking strategies. Software publishers will no doubt continue to produce phonic-oriented software since there is always a large market for these materials whether the products are computer related or are more conventional paper-and-pencil activities.

Most popular school microcomputers do not possess sophisticated voice synthesis capability. Software developers, therefore, have been faced with the difficult task of designing materials that purport to teach decoding yet they are unable to include a phonological or sound component. Some publishers attempt to overcome this problem by presenting exercises that require students to use consonant or vowel substitutions to derive new words. A typical program, for example, presents a target word on the screen such as BAT. Beneath the target word are three or four consonants such as S, M, Y, and R. Students are asked to select the letters that represent additional "real words." Correct answers would be SAT, MAT, and RAT.

Exercises such as this fall short of being true decoding exercises, though. Decoding, by definition, implies that students focus on target words and then provide the appropriate *sounds* that constitute the words. Having a student identify *letters* that represent other words is not a decoding exercise at all! Rather, it is a spelling (encoding) exercise.

One way to use this software better is to have another child, a volunteer, or the teacher listen to the child read the words as they appear on the screen. Reading the words aloud assures the teacher that decoding is actually occurring.

A related limitation of consonant or vowel substitution exercises is that students may be unable to *read* the words, yet may be able to *recognize* the letters as a word or may even be lucky and simply guess correctly. Teachers, therefore, need to be especially cautious when assigning phonic-related software. Conceivably, students may be able to pass the exercises when placed in front of a computer but may be unable to read the same words aloud during reading class.

Hartley has attempted to overcome the lack of a phoneme generating capability in computers by using its cassette-control device. Its *Vowels* program presents over 1,000 words to students. The program begins by having a word displayed on the computer's screen (e.g., b___gain) followed by an oral stimulus from the cassette tape. In this example, the recorder would play "Type the letters that make the 'ar' sound in 'bargain'." Other lessons cover such skills as "long" and "short" vowels, diphthongs, and the schwa sound. Notice, however, that this is another encoding task and not a decoding assignment.

Structural Analysis Skills

Unlike the area of phonic analysis, numerous programs are available to teach structural analysis skills. Contractions, affixes, plurals, synonyms, antonyms, and homonyms are typical skills that are included under the category of structural analysis. The following paragraphs will identify some of the popular structural analysis programs and examine how they attempt to teach these skills.

Distinguishing homonyms is a skill that appears with recurring frequency in reading software. Four popular programs are *Homonyms* (Hartley Publishing Company), *Homonyms in Context* (Random House), *Homonyms* (Milliken Publishing Company), and *Word Master* (Developmental Learning Materials).

The Hartley *Homonyms* program consists of 20 lessons and includes words such as sun/son, hear/here, see/sea, carat/carrot, capitol/capital, and sheik/chic. A short tutorial precedes each drill-and-practice section of the activity. The program begins

HOMONYMS

Homonyms are words that sound the same, but are spelled differently and have different meanings.
Examples:

        sun   –   son
        blue –   blew
        bare –   bear

The program then moves into the drill:

RAIN is the moisture that falls from the sky. A REIN is used to steer a horse. REIGN refers to the rule of a king or queen.

The program then provides some additional examples before moving on to the following:

The jockey said that the _____ on his horse broke because they had been cut.

   a. rains
   b. reins
   c. reigns

Answer:

The American colonies won their freedom from England during the _____ of King George III.

   a. rain
   b. reign
   c. rein

Answer:

In addition to the lessons, the Hartley program has a record-keeping option that permits up to 50 students' scores to be stored on the diskette.

Random House's *Homonyms in Context* allows the student to select homonyms from two levels. The on-screen directions for using the program are relatively brief.

DIRECTIONS

1. Read each sentence.
2. Look at the words inside the < >.
3. Type the correct word.
4. Press **RETURN** to continue.

Students are given sentences such as

   1. He can <sew * sow> his coat.
   2. The <son * sun> is shining.
   3. It is <two * too> big for me.
   4. He had some <red * read> paint.

After each sentence, students select the appropriate word and type their answer on the keyboard.

The Milliken program, *Homonyms,* uses a different technique to drill students. Users may first select from four program options: (1) Introduction and Directions, (2) Definitions and Examples, (3) Practice Sentences, or (4) Return to Main Menu. The first option presents this screen.

dear   deer

Do you always know which of these words to use? These words are homonyms. You can get them mixed up because they sound the same. But they
   * are spelled differently and
   * have different meanings

The Definitions section of the lessons provides an explanation of the homonym and then uses the word in a sentence context.

ant

1. A small, crawling insect.
   There's an *ant* crawling across my desk.

aunt

1. The sister or sister-in-law of a person's father or mother.
   My *aunt* and uncle live on a farm.

(An interesting footnote is that regional dialects of *ant* and *aunt* may result in their being pronounced differently, and, hence, this pair of words may not be homonyms.)

The Practice Sentences portion of the program uses animated figures to enhance student interest. Sentences are written with two homonyms beneath the deleted word. An animated figure moves between the two homonyms enabling the student to select the appropriate choice simply by hitting the space bar. A correct response results in the homonym being moved across the screen to the blank within the sentence. Four different lists of homonyms are used throughout the program.

Word Master employs graphics to an even greater extent than does the Milliken program. Eight words are arranged in a circular fashion around a target word. Students, using the right and left arrow keys and the space bar, attempt to fire a cannon from the target word to the correct homonym. The arrow keys control the direction of fire. The space bar fires the shot. The objective of the game is to identify and destroy all the homonyms within a specified time limit. The program permits preselecting speed, content, level, run time, paddle control, and sound options.

Some software focuses on the teaching of antonyms and synonyms. Hartley's *Antonyms and Synonyms,* for example, includes twenty-one different lessons ranging from third to eighth-grade reading level. Approximately nineteen items are found at each level. Here is a typical sequence from the Hartley program:

SYNONYMS

Two words can have the same meaning.
BIG means the same as LARGE.
BIG and LARGE are synonyms.

The next screen prepares the reader for the lesson.

This lesson will help you with words that have the same meaning.

Press "Return."

On the third screen,

> Words that mean the same thing are called SYNONYMS. Rock means the same as stone. ROCK and STONE are _____onyms.
>
> Answer:

and

> Type the word that means the same as GIFT.
>
>   girl   jelly
>   present   cave
>
> Answer:

This program produces letters in high-resolution graphics that make the words very legible. A built-in program manager also permits students to analyze their errors upon completing a lesson while an editor permits teachers to add their own word lists to the program.

Programs that attempt to teach prefixes vary considerably in quality from publisher to publisher. The *SAT Word Attack Skills* program from Edu-Ware, for instance, might be considered to be "bare-bones" software. After a brief introduction to the prefix "trans," it moves quickly into drill-and-practice activities. Target words using prefixes are followed by five choices. Two attempts are permitted before the program provides the correct answer. If students are unable to identify the word in the specified number of trials, a more complete definition is given.

Prefixes (*MECC—Elementary*, Volume 5) provides a more substantial introduction to prefixes before launching into the drill segment of the program. Seven lessons covering the prefixes *un, re, dis, pre,* and *in* are provided. The program first provides a definition of a prefix:

> A prefix is found at the beginning of a word. It almost always changes the meaning of that word.

Next, examples are shown:

> *Un* is a prefix.
> *Un* means *not* as in the word
> *Un*happy.

More instruction follows:

> Sometimes un makes a word mean
> the opposite of.
> *Un*pack is *the opposite of* pack.

During this phase of the lesson, animated illustrations are used. To demonstrate the meaning of *unload,* for example, a truck moves across the screen and then dumps a load of dirt. The next segment of the lesson requires students to use the keyboard to "draw" a line under the prefixes in target words. Finally, students must select the appropriate word from a sentence context such as in the following example.

Enter "A" or "B" to complete the sentence.
The lion is hungry because it is _____.
   (A) fed   (B) unfed
    A or B

Upon completing a lesson, students are provided with a score for the number of attempts and the number of correct responses. Worksheets also accompany the program.

   Tennis Anyone—Plurals (Data Command) is a tutorial program that permits individuals to select lessons from one of two difficulty levels. Ample examples are provided to encourage student learning. For instance,

Most words are made plural by adding "s."

Here are some examples.
   Rabbit – Rabbits
   Clown – Clowns

Type the plural endings on the following words:
   Lamb__   Ceiling__

The tutorial continues:

Words that end in s, ss, ch, sh, x, or z are usually made plural by adding "es."
Examples:
   Lunch – Lunches
   Buzz – Buzzes

Type the plural endings on the following words:
   Ostrich__   Class__

Words ending in vowel + "y" and consonant + "y" are also covered in the tutorial. Once the tutorial is completed, students enter a tennis match with the computer. A tennis court appears on the screen along with rackets and a scoreboard. At one end of the court, the singular form of the word is presented. Students are challenged to type the correct plural in the opposite court. For each correct response, the player's racket returns the serve of the computer and the child scores a point (using the tennis scoring system, of course). The game continues until there is a winner.

   Another example of a structural analysis program is *Contractions* (Educational Activities, Inc.). This software covers the use of *n't, to be, 'd* and *'ll.* A screen of the two base words along with the contracted form of the word is used as a tutorial. Once the words are read, the computer requires the student to spell the contraction by commanding

> O.K., Bob, you try it.
> I'll keep score.
>   Can + not = ?

Later in the program, students are given exercises that require them to identify, in a sentence context, the two words to be contracted. Even though the program doesn't use graphics, feedback and an on-screen scoring system provide a high degree of motivation.

A perusal of any software catalog reveals a wide variety of structural analysis programs from which to select. The examples provided in this section should alert the user to the different program formats that are available to consumers.

TEACHING COMPREHENSION

The teaching of reading, be it decoding, comprehension, or study skills, results in observable, definable behaviors. These behaviors are reflections of the teacher's beliefs about the reading process. On the one hand, for example, some teachers stress the teaching of decoding skills. Students of these teachers may become "bottom-up" processors of textual information. Metaphorically speaking, a "bottom-up" reader is believed to comprehend only after every word is correctly decoded. Some children bring so much information to the reading act that they may predict what is on the page before having read all the words. These readers are called "top-down" processors. Here, the metaphor implies that the brain is actively searching for meaning and printed words are used simply to confirm or reject hypotheses that students hold about text information. Ideally, teachers require students to use both strategies when reading, switching between the two as needs arise. Students who use this strategy are following an "interactive model" of reading.

Teacher-held beliefs about the reading process are nowhere more evident than in the teaching of comprehension. How these beliefs affect the selection of comprehension software will be explored in the next section of this chapter.

Skills or Schema?

Witness the following scenario. Two elementary school teachers were sitting in the teachers' lounge discussing the comprehension problems of their students. Mr. Jones, the fifth-grade teacher, remarked that he had used every material at his disposal to improve the comprehension of his low-reading group. Materials to teach main idea, sequence, following directions, as well as a host of other worksheets and exercises had been employed.

Ms. Roberts, the fourth-grade teacher, had followed a different strategy. Her low-reading group had difficulty comprehending materials, not because they didn't understand the main ideas of paragraphs, not because they needed help listing sequences of events, and not because they couldn't follow directions. This group's problems were caused primarily because they lacked the background experiences that permit them to bring relevant personal experiences to bear when reading many of the stories.

Mr. Jones' and Ms. Roberts' perceptions of their students' problems typify the state of comprehension instruction in our nation's schools. Mr. Jones believes reading comprehension is a series of distinct skills that can be taught to students in an attempt to improve their comprehension of printed material. Ms. Roberts, on the other hand, has a much different perception of what her students need. They need firsthand and vicarious experiences to enable them to link what they read with what they know about a topic.

Mr. Jones, and other teachers like him, hold a skill-centered belief about comprehension. This position is espoused by prominent learning theorists such as Robert Gagné (1982), who states,

> I say you have to start from the bottom up. Starting from the bottom up means you have to start with skills.
> I think they have to be firmly established before one can free the human mind for the kind of thinking that has to be done, even in reading a page of text. (p.14)

In his search for reading comprehension software, Mr. Jones will probably select materials that focus on specific comprehension activities.

Ms. Roberts attacks this problem from another front. She believes that the world knowledge (i.e., background information) of each student has a heavy bearing on an individual's comprehension. Her understanding of reading comprehension has been labeled *schema theory* by cognitive psychologists and reading educators. According to Durkin (1981), schema theory states that a comprehension question may have a number of correct answers depending upon the text as well as the reader's background knowledge (schemata).

The attitudes and beliefs that teachers hold about comprehension, then, will determine the materials they use. As you have just seen, Mr. Jones and Ms. Roberts approach the teaching of comprehension from widely different perspectives.

Reading as a Communication Skill

Reading, most would agree, is a communicative act. The primary reason for learning to read is not to answer workbook or worksheet exercises but to gain a deeper understanding of the world in which we live. For whatever reasons, however, we, as educators, sometimes lose sight of this purpose. When this occurs, comprehension becomes a standardized test score or a completed worksheet rather than a process by which we enrich our understanding. Mason (1982) feels that a possible reason for this may be that these types of activities serve as a symbol of effort and accomplishment, since they represent tangible, measurable commodities.

Much of the computer software designed to teach comprehension doesn't teach at all—it assesses students' abilities to answer workbook-type questions. When this occurs, computers function as electronic workbooks. The preponderance of these activities is largely because these fixed or prescribed responses are relatively easy to measure. Comprehension, however, if viewed as a communicative act, does not lend itself to predetermined responses. According to Rubin (1983), reading, as well as the other language arts, is a more dynamic and creative undertaking. This is nowhere more true than in the area of reading comprehension. Teachers might be better off permitting students to read independently for fifteen or twenty minutes rather than requiring them to complete some of the software comprehension exercises. This is not to say that the computer has no place in the teaching of reading comprehension. It does. What needs to be understood, though, is that many materials that purport to improve reading comprehension may have little if any relationship to what we know about the comprehension process.

Comprehension: Assessing or Teaching?

Durkin (1978), in an analysis of classroom reading practices, discovered that comprehension *instruction* accounted for only a small portion of the reading period. While her study examined conventional instructional practices, it is reasonable to expect that a study of comprehension software use would reveal similar results. This is so because few software materials have been designed to utilize known comprehension teaching strategies.

A survey of methods that have been suggested as means of improving reading comprehension includes the following:

1. Use children's dictation for developing reading material. These dictated stories permit use of familiar semantics and syntax, thus aiding comprehension.
2. Have children read material that is familiar and within the realm of their world knowledge.
3. Encourage students to use "prediction strategies" such as those taught in the directed reading-thinking activities where children are successively asked to predict what events will occur throughout the reading of a selection.
4. Require readers to rely on context by providing exercises that use the cloze or maze procedures (i.e., *n*th word deletion exercises, in which teachers may choose to provide two or three synonyms for each deleted word).
5. Ask students to paraphrase sentences or paragraphs once they have been read.
6. Use divergent questioning techniques that require students to read beyond the literal level of the material.
7. Use previewing techniques, such as having students jot down personal experiences they may have had that relate to the material to be read. Students share these experiences before reading the material.
8. Implement the request procedure, whereby students work in pairs reading a sentence or paragraph. Students take turns reading and asking their partner a question about the material.

9. Provide students with a series of questions to be answered while they are reading.
10. Use adjunct questioning guides to keep student attention focused throughout the reading assignment.

An examination of software intended to improve students' reading comprehension, however, seldom includes any of these techniques. There are some notable exceptions.

Milliken's *Cloze Plus,* for instance, does require students to use sentence syntax to determine appropriate answers. *Cloze Plus* is designed for students in grades 3 to 8. The program consists of six diskettes and the accompanying documentation. Each diskette includes a Manager program that allows teachers to make individual assignments, review individual and class performance, and receive printed records of student performance. Eleven different types of clues are used throughout the program (e.g., synonyms, antonyms, time-order sequence, pronoun referents). Here are two examples of exercises from this program:

Today, honey is one of our few natural foods. Nothing needs to be _____.
Everything is already in it. Honey keeps for months or years. Nothing needs to be done to it.

    a. added   d. said
    b. cooked   e. frozen
    c. read

TYPE THE LETTER OF THE BEST CHOICE
OR PRESS SPACE FOR CLUES.

A second example is

The starfish is not really a fish at all. In many countries it is called the "sea star."
This is a more correct _____ for this animal than starfish.

2. Type a word that fits in the blank.

PRESS RETURN WHEN FINISHED.

In the second example, two to four different words are acceptable, and the student is given credit if any one of the words is selected. Assistance is provided to overcome any spelling difficulties.

Programs that use the cloze technique offer students several advantages. Among them are that (1) they require students to integrate meaning across sentences, (2) they provide opportunities to understand extended passages, (3) they require the use of a variety of contextual analysis strategies, (4) students must use predictive strategies, and (5) users develop test-taking skills.

Another software program from Milliken that should help to develop comprehension ability is *Sentence Combining.* This two-diskette package requires students to combine sentences using words such as *and, but, before,* and *after*. Using a modeling approach, these lessons introduce the skill to be taught and then provide a demonstration of how the skill is to be used. Students are provided at least one opportunity to interact with the keyboard to build a new sentence. Practice is provided using graded exercises that follow the demonstrated format. An example of adding describing words to a sentence follows:

> I have a < > kitten.
> My kitten is black.
> I have a <u>black</u> kitten.

In this example, students find the describing word in the second sentence. They then decide whether the word needs an -ly ending. Finally, they indicate where the word should be inserted in the first sentence.

Using this program develops students' sentence sense, sentence fluency, and selected usage and transcription skills. With the renewed interest in the reading-writing relationship, teachers of reading may be interested in exploring this program further.

Another Milliken program, *Comprehension Power,* employs a more "traditional" skills approach. *Comprehension Power* is a 48-diskette program that covers twenty-five major comprehension skills. Among the skills are literal understanding of details and sequences, evaluation of author's purpose, understanding persuasion, interpreting main idea, predicting outcomes, drawing conclusions, classifying, recognizing cause and effect, interpreting characters, and identifying mood and tone. Additional skills are also covered.

Once the program has been loaded into the microcomputer, students select the story on which they will be working. Here is an example of a lesson entitled "Computers Can't Wait" (approximately fifth- or sixth-grade level) from Level F.

COMPUTERS CAN'T WAIT

Press letter you would like to see

> A. Key Word Sentence
> B. Preview
> C. Segment 1
> D. Segment 2
> E. Segment 3
> F. Segment 4
> G. Segment 5
> H. Segment 6
> I. Segment 7
> J. Segment 8

Selecting option A, Key Word Sentence, results in the key words being displayed in a sentence context. Here are three examples:

Years ago, people could not *communicate* by telephone.

I *deposit* $20 of my pay in my savings account each pay period.

The Boy Scout *encoded* the words of the message in the dots and dashes of the Morse Code.

Selecting the Preview option presents advanced organizers that prepare the reader for the lesson. Here is one example from a story entitled "Computers Can't Wait." Sentences appear on the screen one at a time.

Alicia Jaramillo grumbled and rubbed her eyes.

Alicia groaned, rolled over, and turned on the light.

But these thoughts made it no easier for her to get up at 4 in the morning.

As Alicia sat up, she thought, "Almost six years since I was moved up from programmer to programmer/systems analyst."

"I've done well for someone with no college education."

"I've been on this project for the bank for a long time," Alicia's brain reminded her.

"Tom complained that his check-processing system relied too much on people and not enough on machinery."

"Tom showed me how his department processed checks every day."

"I met with Tom every day to discuss this project, sometimes for an hour or more."

The Preview continues for another five sentences. Students are then quizzed on their recollection:

TYPE THE LETTER OF THE BEST ANSWER

1.   Your preview told you that this selection is about Alicia Jaramillo and
     a. the training program she is running at the bank.
     b. the kinds of things she does as a systems analyst.
     c. how she operates the bank's computer.
     d. the reasons she likes her job in a bank.

The appropriate response evokes a "Correct Answer, Student." The program continues:

Press Y if the statement is correct.

Press N if the statement is incorrect.

2. Based on what you learned from your preview,
    a. Alicia has to get up at 4:00 A.M.
    b. Alicia works as a programmer/systems analyst.

Once the Preview section of the story has been completed, students are ready to move into the segments. At this point, users are able to select a pacing option that presents words on the screen from between 50 and 650 words per minute. A manual override is also available for those who opt not to use the pacing feature. From this point on, the computer presents a line-by-line screening of the story. Comprehension questions are presented at the conclusion of each section. An example of one of the questions is

TYPE THE LETTER OF THE BEST ANSWER

1.   According to Alicia Jaramillo, systems analysts
      a. work a regular 9 to 5 day.
      b. have to be on call at all times.
      c. work only at night.
      d. start to work at 4:08 A.M.

The *Comprehension Power* program is a comprehensive program that focuses on over two dozen skills. Educators looking for a complete system to augment their conventional classroom instruction may find *Comprehension Power* made to order.

A special category of comprehension programs that has proven successful with youngsters is the adventure-type activity. These programs have also been called interactive stories, participatory novels, or graphic-text games. Unlike conventional comprehension software, these programs do not include predetermined skills lists or traditional comprehension exercises. Instead, they rely on developing comprehension through student involvement.

Two of the easiest-to-use interactive stories are *Troll's Tale* and *Dragon's Keep* (Sierra On-Line). In the former, readers wander through an enchanted land filled with labyrinths and treasures. At each turn, students must make decisions as they attempt to find the sixteen treasures for the Dwarf King. The program requires only a minimum of keyboarding skills, so even primary-age children can play. The text is written at a third-grade level. By playing the game, students learn basic map reading skills as well as developing inferential and predictive comprehension strategies. Three frames from the game are shown in Figures 4.1, 4.2, and 4.3.

Dragon's Keep is a similar type of game where students free friendly animals trapped in an old house by a mischievous dragon.

Older students with more developed reading skills may enjoy programs such as *Enchanter, The Witness,* and *Suspended* (Infocom). These are sophisticated interactive novels that require perseverance as well as astute reading ability. Unlike *Troll's Tale* and *Dragon's Keep,* these games require some typing skill since players continually interact with the computer by asking questions or typing commands such as "walk south," "lock door," "look under," and "drink water." *Enchanter* is a dungeons-and-dragon type of game, *The Witness* is a mystery, and *Suspended* is a cryogenic nightmare. Don't expect junior or senior high school students to finish these activities in an hour or two, though. Some individuals play them up to the twelve-hour time limit and still don't solve the mysteries. Fortunately, the game may be suspended at any point and saved to be continued at a later time. While these types of programs aren't for everyone, those who enjoy puzzle solving and have good reading skills usually find them enjoyable and challenging.

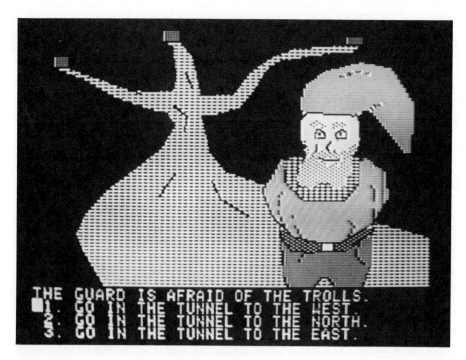

FIGURE 4.1   Frame from *Troll's Tale* (Sierra On-Line Inc.)

FIGURE 4.2   Frame from *Troll's Tale* (Sierra On-Line Inc.)

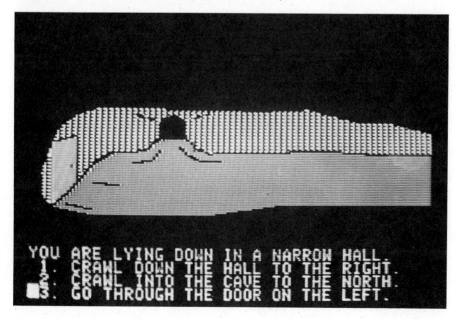

FIGURE 4.3   Frame from *Troll's Tale* (Sierra On-Line Inc.)

An interesting approach to reading comprehension with young children is Spinnaker Software's *Story Machine*. This program is based on a forty-word dictionary that includes words such as *boy, girl, dog, cat, tree, runs, hops,* and *sings.* Typing simple sentences such as "The boy sings" produces a boy on the screen with musical notes emanating from his mouth. "The dog runs to the boy" results in the appearance of a dog that then bounces to the boy's side (Figure 4.4).

While *Story Machine's* vocabulary is limited, the program does make excellent use of computer technology and demonstrates an important concept to young readers—namely, language has a communicative function.

Story Maker (Bolt, Beranek, and Newman, Inc.) attempts to improve comprehension in another fashion. It lets students design stories by selecting prewritten story segments and then adds the segments in a treelike fashion to an existing story stem. These branches permit a story to take a number of different forms, each with a different ending. Each path forms a complete story. The beginning of one story opens:

Lace opened the front door and . . .

Students then choose one of three existing alternatives:

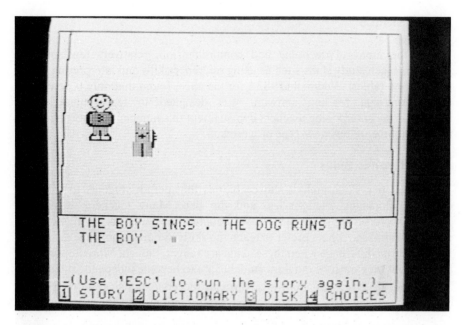

THE BOY SINGS . THE DOG RUNS TO
THE BOY . ▪

(Use 'ESC' to run the story again.)
1 STORY 2 DICTIONARY 3 DISK 4 CHOICES

FIGURE 4.4   Screen Display from *Story Machine* (STORY MACHINE (TM) Spinnaker Software
Corp., One Kendall Square, Cambridge, MA 02139.)

saw the joker
slipped into what looked like a big bowl of spaghetti
stepped on a mouse

The story continues with additional choices until the last branch of the tree is reached. Stories may be printed on a printer for all students to share. *Story Maker* also has several other programs, one of which permits students to compose their own stories.

As teachers might expect, a fine line exists between programs that provide legitimate comprehension strategies and those that resemble paper-and-pencil assessments. Unfortunately, many comprehension programs lack a defensible theoretical foundation. Instead, they are simply electronic transcriptions of workbook activities. Shannon (1983), in a study of the use of conventional reading materials in American elementary schools, posited that one reason why teachers relied extensively on commercial materials to teach reading was based on their belief that the materials actually would improve students' comprehension. Almost certainly, comprehension software will be viewed in the same light. Unfortunately, unless the software is rooted in sound theory, these materials may do little more than provide exercises that test students' test-taking abilities rather than foster the improved understanding of text material.

Teachers should be skeptical when selecting materials that purport to *teach* reading comprehension. Most software simply assesses an individual's ability to answer test questions.

STUDY SKILLS

Unlike the areas of decoding and comprehension, relatively few software programs teach study skills such as using reference skills and interpreting maps, graphs, and tables. Wedman (1983), for instance, found that only 6 percent of the commercial reading software was designed to teach these skills. Nevertheless, enterprising teachers can augment this number by resorting to the use of a number of business-type programs.

Reference Skills

Reference skills include those abilities that permit students to use card catalogs, almanacs, dictionaries, and the like. Many teachers attempt to integrate the teaching of these skills with content area subjects such as science and social studies. Others prefer to teach the skills as part of language arts units. It makes little difference when these skills are taught, though. More important is the fact that they must be taught if students are to become independent learners. This is because, as students move through the educational system, they increasingly rely on reference skills to gain information in all their studies.

Commercial Materials.   Searching for computer software to teach study skills can be frustrating since there are so few materials from which to select. One program designed to teach the principle of alphabetization is Milliken's *Study Skills: Alphabetization Sequences*. This two-diskette program leads students through ninety-four problem levels, ranging from such simple tasks as discerning likenesses and differences in similar lowercase letters to listing words and variations in alphabetical order by fifth letter. Problems within the sequence include activities such as

What letter is missing?

P __ R S
S T U __
W __ Y Z

and

Put these words in a-b-c order.

talk, nap, jug, book

Teachers are able to specify mastery and failure levels as well as determine the minimum number of problems a student will encounter. To supplement the computer activities, accompanying duplicating masters provide teachers with a profile chart of student performance and a User Schedule that can be used to assign individuals to specific lessons.

Data Bases.   Some teachers feel that data bases can be more exciting teaching tools than commercial reference skill materials. Data bases are designed to assist in the retrieval of information. One of the easiest to use is *PFS: File* (Software Publishing Corporation). *PFS: File* is best understood by thinking of it as a series of electronic notecards. The user designs the template on which all information will later be recorded. Once the template is produced, information is entered and stored on a data diskette. *PFS: File* has innumerable uses. One teacher (Hunter, 1983) used this program to list information from almanacs, encyclopedias, and textbooks. A "States" data base, for example, was created to record information about each of the fifty states. The state's name, capital, state flower, year entered the union, land area in square miles, acreage of state forests and parks, mean altitude in feet, highest point, and lowest point were included in each record (Figures 4.5 and 4.6). Once the information was added to the templates, students could use the computer to seek information such as

1. What state has the highest peak?
2. The violet is the state flower of what state(s)?
3. What is the capital of Nebraska?
4. How many states entered the union prior to 1848?
5. Name all the states that have a mean altitude of 2,000 feet or higher.

Another excellent use of data bases is to develop a file of student-recommended tradebooks. Each file might include the author's name, the name of the book, the call number, a category designation, a review by a prior reader, and the reader's name. Students interested in finding a peer-recommended book simply need to search through the data base to find something to their liking.

Baker (1983) used *PFS: File* to catalog software that was available in her schools. This inventory application allows individuals to search quickly for software by name, general use, price, description, and whatever other categories are used to catalog the materials. Students or teacher could inventory software available throughout the school. The author has used *PFS: File* to create a similar inventory of software at an institution of higher education. At the touch of a button, the data base can search for all word processing programs available throughout the institution. The program can also sort by specified parameters. A request to identify all word processing programs whose price is less than $100.00, for example, can be handled in a matter of seconds.

Another excellent use of data bases is to establish a classroom information base about students. Students can record their names, addresses, telephone numbers, birthdates, hobbies, favorite recording artists, and other interesting facts on the computer. Once the date base is complete, individuals can print a list of names and birthdates, identify the most popular rock artist, and distribute a listing of telephone numbers.

If enough computers are available, some junior and senior high school students may want to use the data base to take notes for upcoming papers. By using a format similar to that in Figure 4.7, individuals can print notes to correspond to outlines they draw up. Obviously, though, individuals must have adequate typing skills to benefit from such a system.

Creative teachers can no doubt think of numerous other applications for data bases. Saltinski (1981) describes how social studies teachers can make the microcomputer the focus of much study since social phenomena lend themselves to the collection and manipulation of sociological data. Data from economics, politics, geography, and ecology can all provide fruitful references that can be used to understand the world around us. Data base use is limited only by the imagination of the user.

Maps, Graphs, and Tables

If students are to be literate consumers of books, newspapers, magazines, and reports, they must be able to interpret maps, graphs, and tables. Maps appear in a variety of forms (e.g., inset, topographical, climatic, and political) and projections (e.g., polar, mercator, and conical). Graphic information is also presented in many different ways such as with picture graphs, line graphs, bar graphs, and circle graphs. Tables, likewise, appear in numerous formats ranging from simple two-column lists to complex airline and train schedules. The following paragraphs identify some of the programs that are available to teach these skills.

Commercial Materials.   Several publishers have developed programs that present facts about the United States through drill-and-practice activities. Typically, these programs drill students on the capitals or information concerning each state. Some programs provide additional information such as identifying the location of major cities and providing demographic data. Some software even calculates the distances between selected cities.

The problem with some of these programs is that they fail to provide experiences whereby the learned information can be transferred to other situations. While it is important to know the capital of New York, it is even more important to possess the knowledge of how to locate Albany or any other state capital. Unfortunately, the bulk of these programs are more intent on having youngsters memorize what some individuals consider to be meaningless facts than they are on teaching specific skills that can be transferred across many disciplines. For this reason, teachers should be cautious when selecting programs that purport to improve students' map reading skills.

Hurkle (MECC Elementary—Mathematics, Volume 1), on the other hand, does an excellent job of teaching coordinates on number-letter grids, a skill that is needed to read maps. Hurkle is a fuzzy-looking character that hides on a screen grid. The objective is to find Hurkle in the fewest possible tries. Four different types of number lines and grids are used: horizontal, vertical, horizontal and vertical using positive integers, and horizontal and vertical using positive and negative integers. Typing the coordinates results in feedback

```
STATE:     ABBREV:
CAPITAL:
FLOWER:
YEAR ENTERED UNION:
1980 LAND AREA (SQ.MILES):
STATE FORESTS, PARKS (IN ACRES):
MEAN ALTITUDE (IN FEET):
HIGHEST PT. NAME:
ALTITUDE:
LOWEST POINT NAME:
ALTITUDE:
```

FIGURE 4.5   *PFS: File* "States" Data Base
(PFS® is a registered trademark
of Software Publishing Corp.)

```
STATE: CALIFORNIA   ABBREV: CA
CAPITAL: SACRAMENTO
FLOWER: GOLDEN POPPY
YEAR ENTERED UNION: 1850
1980 LAND AREA (SQ.MILES): 158693
STATE FORESTS, PARKS (IN ACRES):
MEAN ALTITUDE (IN FEET):
HIGHEST PT. NAME: MT. WHITNEY
ALTITUDE: 14495
LOWEST POINT NAME: DEATH VALLEY
ALTITUDE: 282 FEET BELOW SEA LEVEL
```

FIGURE 4.6   *PFS: File* "States" Data Base (PFS® is a registered trademark of Software
Publishing Corp.)

specifying where Hurkle is hiding relative to the student's guess. Responses are given using intermediate and cardinal directions such as "Go northeast."

Spreadsheet Programs   Students with good reading ability may be able to explore simple spreadsheet programs as a way of increasing their understanding of the use of tables. One of the earliest programs was *VisiCalc* (Software Publishing Corporation). For the most part, spreadsheets allow individuals to design numeric tables ranging from simple two-column formats to multicolumn examples. By changing data within the table, the program "automatically" recalculates answers to problems. Teachers, however, should be aware that spreadsheet programs require the use of mathematical formulas that may make them difficult to use with some students.

Associated with some spreadsheet and data base programs are companion programs that permit the graphing of tabular information. *PFS: Graph* (Software Publishing Corporation) and *VisiPlot/VisiTrend* (Personal Software, Inc.) are two such programs. Line, bar, and circle graphs can be produced by using data supplied by the data base or spreadsheet. Spreadsheets, data bases, and graphing programs permit students to assume the role of beginning scientists as they become familiar with terms such as mean, range of scores, and percentages.

SUMMARY

The 1980s have been a time of mushrooming computer use in our nation's schools. These machines are both powerful and flexible and they can help teachers of reading provide focused instruction for students of all capabilities.

```
AUTHOR(S):
TITLE:
SOURCE:
LOCATION:
PUBLISHER:
DATE:
PAGES:
OTHER:
CODE NUMBER:


AUTHOR(S): VERNON, LIBBY
TITLE: PARENTS CONSIDER COMPUTERS THE CH
ALLENGE OF THE '80S
SOURCE: CHILDHOOD EDUCATION
LOCATION:
PUBLISHER:
DATE: MARCH/APRIL, 1983
PAGES: 167, 270
OTHER: VOLUME 59, NUMBER 4
CODE NUMBER: 129
```

FIGURE 4.7   *PFS: File* A Data Base for Use in a Research Paper (PFS® is a registered trademark of Software Publishing Corp.)

Before computers find widespread use, however, educators will need to accept them and the accompanying software.

At early reading levels, students using microcomputers may be handicapped because of inappropriate reading readiness software and lack of sufficient keyboarding skills. To foster the best use of readiness software, it is imperative that educators are able to articulate the relationship between the readiness instruction and the reading program. Once this has been done, it is easier to select appropriate readiness software.

Decoding is one area in which there appears to be an abundance of reading software. Because of its nature, though, it is difficult to design programs that truly require decoding, not encoding skills. Furthermore, some learning theorists question the learning paradigm used to teach selected decoding skills.

Recent advances in comprehension research have led many teachers of reading to question the skills approach to improving a students comprehension. Schema theory and the importance of world knowledge have been demonstrated to play a major part in determining whether comprehension occurs. Reading teachers are faced with the difficult task of trying to match comprehension software with their beliefs about the comprehension process.

There are few software packages available to teach the study skills. This chapter has identified how reading teachers may adapt programs that were originally intended to serve other purposes.

As more and more reading software becomes available, the quality and sophistication of these materials should improve. Furthermore, as the power of microcomputers increases, the programs that drive these machines should also change. For the present time, however, reading teachers will need to be cautious in their selection of software designed to teach reading skills.

RELATED READINGS

DUFFY, GERALD G., LAURA R. ROEHLER, and JANA MASON. *Comprehension Instruction: Perspectives and Suggestions.* New York & London: Longman, Inc., 1984.
GEOFFRION, LEO, and OLGA P. GEOFFRION. *Computers and Reading Instruction.* Reading, Mass.: Addison-Wesley Publishing Company, 1983.
JOHNSTON, PETER H. *Reading Comprehension Assessment: A Cognitive Basis.* Newark, Dela.: International Reading Association, 1983.
MASON, GEORGE E., JAY S. BLANCHARD, and DANNY B. DANIEL. *Computer Applications in Reading,* 2nd ed. Newark, Dela.: International Reading Association, 1983.
RUDE, ROBERT T., and WILLIAM OEHLKERS. *Helping Students with Reading Problems.* Englewood Cliffs, N.J.: Prentice-Hall, Inc., 1984.

REFERENCES

BAKER, PATTI R., "A Software Filing System for Elementary Schools," *Educational Computer Magazine,* Vol. 3, no. 5 (September 1983), 46–47, 50, 91.
CHALL, JEANNE S., *Learning to Read: The Great Debate,* New York: McGraw-Hill Book Company, 1967.
DURKIN, DOLORES, *Teaching Them to Read,* 3rd ed., Boston: Allyn & Bacon, Inc., 1978.
    What Classroom Observation Reveals About Reading Comprehension Instruction, Technical Report No. 106, Champaign: Center for the Study of Reading, University of Illinois, October 1978.
    "What Is the Value of the New Interest in Reading Comprehension?" *Language Arts,* Vol. 58, no. 1 (January 1981), 23–43.
GAGNÉ, ROBERT M., "Developments in Learning Psychology: Implications for Instructional Design and Effects of Computer Technology on Instructional Design and Development," *Educational Technology,* Vol. 22, no. 6 (June 1982), 11–15.
HUNTER, BEVERLY, "Powerful Tools for Your Social Studies Classroom," *Classroom Computer Learning,* Vol. 4, no. 3 (October 1983), 50, 55–57.
LASS, BONNIE, "What Research Says About the Quality Reading Teacher," *Educational Technology,* Vol. 21, no. 6 (June 1981), 28–31.
MASON, JANA, *A Description of Reading Instruction: The Tail Is Wagging the Dog,* Reading Education Report No. 35, Urbana: University of Illinois at Urbana—Center for the Study of Reading (August 1982) 1–30.
OTTO, WAYNE, ROBERT T. RUDE, and DIXIE LEE SPIEGEL, *How to Teach Reading,* Reading, Mass: Addison-Wesley Publishing Company, 1979.
ROSE, SYLVIA NOID, "Barriers to the Use of Educational Technologies and Recommendations to Promote and Increase Their Use," *Educational Technology,* Vol. 22, no. 12 (December 1982), 12–15.
RUBIN, ANDEE, "The Computer Confronts Language Arts: Cans and Shoulds for Education," *Teaching Writing Through Technology,* Chelmsford, Mass.: Northeast Regional Exchange (1983) 15–40.
SALTINSKI, RONALD, "Microcomputers in Social Studies: An Innovative Technology for Instruction," *Educational Technology,* Vol. 21, no. 1 (January 1981), 29–32.
SHANNON, PATRICK, "The Use of Commercial Reading Materials in American Elementary Schools," *Reading Research Quarterly,* Vol. 19, no. 1 (Fall 1983), 68–85.
    "Two New Studies See Major Role For Computers In Education," *Electronic Learning,* Vol. 3, no. 3 (November–December 1983), 18, 20.
WEDMAN, JUDY, *Media and Methods* (February 1983) 25, 27.

FIVE

WORD PROCESSING AND RELATED SOFTWARE

Upon completing this chapter, you will be able to

— 1. Discuss the relationship between language and writing.

— 2. Explain what is meant by the term "word processing."

— 3. Describe a variety of applications for word processing programs.

— 4. List the advantages and limitations of word processing programs.

— 5. Discuss the operation of electronic spelling checkers and thesauruses.

Picture the following scenario. Tamara Bernstein, a sixth-grade student, has just begun the school year. This year will probably mark the most dramatic change in Tamara's schooling since she was enrolled in a preschool program eight years ago. This change will be largely attributable to the technological changes that our society has undergone in the past decade.

One of the first things Tamara will learn this year is how to type. There is no typing class in her school, however. Nor does she take private typing lessons. Instead, Tamara has read a five-page pamphlet that describes a typing tutorial program available for her classroom's microcomputer. Twice a week, she carefully places her fingers on the home row of keys just as the pamphlet pictures. The program requires her to type a short selection of words. From this selection, her typing ability is automatically diagnosed and she is provided with appropriate skill-level lessons. At the end of twelve weeks, Tamara is typing twenty words per minute with 85 percent accuracy.

One of the major goals of Mr. Erickson, Tamara's teacher, is to improve the writing ability of his class. Mr. Erickson has methodically planned three major units of study. Each carefully parallels the path through which fluent writers progress when composing. During the Prewriting Unit, he shows his class how to gather information and design an outline from which the writing will emanate. Next comes the actual act of writing. Finally, there is the Rewriting Unit. This is where the writer revises, edits, and applies the final polish to the work.

Tamara and the other students in her class have a distinct advantage over students who graduated from Pinehurst School a few years earlier. The school is now equipped with a collection of microcomputers that are used, in part, for student writing. Mr. Erickson has found that his students develop longer works, are more creative, have fewer spelling errors, and make better use of language. A closer examination of how Tamara utilizes the microcomputer reveals why there is an improvement in writing at Pinehurst School.

To begin, Mr. Erickson requires all students to submit an outline of their proposed writing assignments. Students prepare the outline on the word processor, thereby enabling them to edit the original outline once it has undergone the eagle-eye editing of Mr. Erickson. The final outline must also accompany the written report.

As Tamara was collecting data for her outline, she noticed a lack of information on one aspect of the topic. To fill that void, she consulted the appropriate books in the school library as well as those in the city library. Still, more information was needed. As a last resort, Tamara instructed the school computer to address electronically a large data base information service located in the adjoining town. Only a few keystrokes were needed to link the school computer electronically with the massive mainframe computer at the information service. Quickly the monitor displayed a variety of up-to-the-minute reports on Tamara's topic. For each pertinent reference, Tamara simply struck another key to make a printed copy of the report. In less than fifteen minutes she had five additional articles to augment her report. Now she was ready to finish her outline and submit it to Mr. Erickson.

Once the outline had been returned to Tamara, she was ready to begin the first draft. As she sat at the keyboard, there was little apprehension about making typographical mistakes. Instead, she was intently focusing on the content of her work. Finally, the double-spaced rough draft had been completed. As she reread her work on the screen, she noticed an overused adjective. This looked like a job for a thesaurus! Rather than paging through a paper thesaurus, however, Tamara simply placed the blinking cursor over the first letter of the recurring word. She excitedly punched the keyboard twice. The screen flashed and suddenly was filled with a list of synonyms. Tamara moved the cursor to the desired replacement and pushed another key. Once again the screen flickered and the original document appeared before Tamara, this time with the new-found synonym neatly in place.

Now it was time for a quick check for misspellings. Tamara slid a diskette into the disk drive. The screen read "Spelling Checker." She hit the Return key on the keyboard. As the computer leaped into action, typographical errors were identified one by one, accompanied by possible alternative spellings. Tamara made the necessary corrections on the screen, which in turn were automatically inserted into her original document.

The spelling check completed, it was now time to submit the paper to Mr. Erickson. Tamara flipped the switch on the printer and instructed the computer to print a "hard copy" of her work. After several minutes, she removed her completed report. As she submitted the paper to Mr. Erickson, he smiled and said . . .

Does this scenario read like a voyage through the school of the future? It could be, but it could also be the school next door since this technology already exists. It is only a matter of time, therefore, before it works its way into more of our nation's schools. As teachers become increasingly familiar with the technological capabilities of today's electronic world and as more computers appear in our educational institutions, students will be encouraged to use these time-saving tools. While all these electronic marvels are not currently being used in schools, this chapter explores how microcomputers can be used today to improve students' reading and writing skills.

WORD PROCESSING

Perhaps more than any other microcomputer application, word processing has the potential to change the way in which we communicate and learn from one another. Watt and Parham (1983) state "the word processor offers the prospect of substantially narrowing the gap between the immediate but fluid world of speech, and the past but fixed world of print" (p. 74). Collins, Bruce, and Rubin (1983) believe that word processing provides an environment where children write for the same reason adults write—to communicate with each other. Anderson (1983) contends that it will revolutionize students' outlooks concerning the sphere of reading and writing by showing them how rewarding writing can be. Sherman and Hall (1983) and Squire (1983) also articulate the advantages of using word processors in school settings. Even Seymour Papert, the developer of the Logo programming language, is a strong proponent of word processing (Schwartz, 1982). Praise rings so high for word processing applications that many individuals have begun to consider the word processor the pencil of the future. In the following pages, we will explore the reading-writing relationship and how word processors can be used in school settings.

Writing

Many children are writers before they enter school. Preschoolers, for example, try to emulate the writing of older brothers and sisters who are already in school. For these youngsters, crayons, chalk, pencils, pens, or felt-tipped markers are the tools with which they try to communicate.

Other youngsters first encounter print upon entering kindergarten or first grade. In some classes, teachers use the language-experience approach to illustrate the interrelationships among speech, print, and reading. The formation of letters, words, and syntactic sense are stressed.

Later in the elementary grades and into junior high and high schools, grammar drills abound. The purpose of these exercises is purportedly to improve students' writing abilities. Schwartz (1983), Watt and Parham (1983), and Smith (1981) point out the futility of these exercises as means of developing writing ability, however. They contend that only through writing does writing improve. Other experts, such as Don Graves of the University of New Hampshire, contend that the problem with writing instruction in our schools is that there is no writing!

Later, during the college years, writing continues to play an important part in the curriculum, since most professors require written assignments. Unfortunately, in many cases, these papers are last-minute synopses of loosely related facts assembled virtually hours before the assignments are due.

After college, writing is practiced by only a few. Individuals who work in the communicative arts continue to polish their writing ability, but for the majority of individuals, writing becomes a bothersome chore to be undertaken only when corresponding to friends and relatives.

The Importance of Writing.   Simply put, to be literate implies having the ability to read and write. The importance of writing goes far beyond this, however. Writing is one means of becoming a better reader. This is so because of the interrelationship that exists between writing and reading. As Wittrock (1983) states,

> When we write with clarity we generate meaning by relating our knowledge and experience to the text. Writing also involves building relations among the words and sentences, the sentences in paragraphs, and the paragraphs in texts. In these important ways reading comprehension and effective writing relate closely to each other. (p. 601)

Others (Hanley-James, 1982; Lickteig, 1981) also point out the close relationship that exists between writing and reading.

Another reason that educators need to be concerned with writing is that nationwide test data reveal that students are far poorer writers than they are readers. The 1981 National Assessment of Educational Progress (NAEP), for example, an assessment of over 100,000 nine-, thirteen-, and seventeen-year-olds, found that while students were able to comprehend a wide range of passages, they appeared to have difficulty examining, elaborating, or explaining their ideas in writing (Langer, 1982). The study also found that the older students were no better at defending their written ideas than were the nine- and thirteen-year-olds.

In another analysis of NAEP data, Squire (1983) reported that while 85 percent of all thirteen-year-olds were able to respond correctly to a multiple-choice type of comprehension check, only 15 percent could write an acceptable sentence summarizing a paragraph read. According to him, one possible reason for this is that less than 10 percent of junior and senior high school English teachers provide opportunities for students to compose their own thoughts in writing.

These findings are not new. An earlier NAEP report, for example, revealed that students did not have problems with the mechanics of writing but were unable to deal successfully with connected discourse (Deford, 1981). These data illustrate the need for teachers to reexamine language arts instruction at all levels. What is needed is not isolated drill on the mechanics of reading and writing but, instead, practice using these skills in lifelike settings, for it is only in these situations that transfer of newly learned skills will occur.

Speech and Writing.   Speaking, reading, and writing are interrelated skills that, to a large degree, determine the success a student experiences at school. These three skills are influenced, in part, by our past experiences. Numerous authors remind us of the importance of experiential background because experiences are the foundation of speech (Lickteig, 1981; Moffett, 1983; Wall and Taylor, 1982).

Schema theory holds that comprehension of written material is possible largely because individuals bring past experiences (schemata) to the printed page. As individuals encounter connected text, they consciously and subconsciously reconstruct meaning (Sanacore, 1983).

Before thoughts can be expressed in print, the writer must have a mental image of what is to be said. This inner speech requires the continual refocusing and editing of thoughts before they can be transferred to print. Unlike spoken communication, however, written communication is not as fluid or as alterable. This is because spoken communication presents numerous opportunities for feedback and adjustment of the message; written communication lacks these opportunities.

The Stages of Writing.   Experts agree that writing is a multistage process. While some individuals contend that writing skills exist along a continuum, others believe that writing is best envisioned as a series of distinct stages. In reality, however, there is little difference between these viewpoints. Since a "stage" model permits a clearer examination of the writing process, a summary of how writers mature will be presented.

In a "stage view," three distinct steps are suggested: prewriting, writing, and rewriting. Each is important, for together they contribute to a product that is greater than the sum of its parts.

The prewriting stage is the brainstorming period when the writer begins to first think about the topic. Some individuals take notes during this period. Others try to rough out early drafts. Still others use generating ideas such as making rough outlines or penciling ideas on pieces of paper. Some writers spend the majority of their total writing time concentrating on this prewriting stage. It is during this period that inner speech and the creative talents of an individual must rise to the occasion.

The second stage is that of actually putting the pen (or pencil, typewriter, or computer) to the paper. This is the composing or writing stage. A written record of the ideas and thoughts of the earlier prewriting stage now appears.

The final stage is that of rewriting. For most writers, there must be a substantial period of time between the writing and rewriting stage. This is necessary because during the rewriting process the original work must be carefully reviewed, proofread, reworked, and rewritten. In one sense, the writer must be able to divorce himself or herself from the earlier drafts and bring objectivity and perspective to the editing task.

In an excellent explanation of these processes, Flowers (1981) describes the different personalities a writer must possess before fluent writing can occur. The personalities are that of madman, judge, architect, and carpenter. Her madman role describes the thought processes necessary during the prewriting stage. The madman must be full of ideas but not overly concerned with writing style. The main objective of the madman is simply to produce material. The responsibility of the judge, the second personality, is to recognize sentence fragments and other mechanical flaws. The judge, however, is unable to create ideas or text. The architect's role parallels that of the writing stage. The architect selects large chunks of material and arranges them in logical order. Flowers calls this paragraph-level thinking. The architect doesn't worry about sentence structure or related matters. The fourth role is that of a carpenter who nails all the ideas together and sees that everything fits in a logical fashion.

Using the model described by Flowers can lead students to recognize that writing is not a one-shot operation but is instead a dynamic, fluid representation of our thoughts. As time passes, these thoughts change. Almost all authors would agree that shortly after putting their thoughts to paper, their ideas have been modified. Given enough time, the works of these authors would continually change, constantly reflecting the new experiences and ideas that have transpired between the time of creation and the present.

A final perspective on writing stages is to look not at the writing process itself but instead to explore the stages through which writers pass. Graves (1982) has presented a detailed analysis of these stages. He contends that the stages are relatively age independent.

According to Graves, the primary concern of most beginning writers is spelling. This is understandable since spelling instruction plays such an important part in a school's curriculum.

Stage 2 appears when students begin to focus on aesthetics and form.

Students at this stage become concerned with neatness and orderliness.

In the third stage, students become concerned with punctuation and capitalization. Perhaps this is, in part, caused by the constant admonition to "Begin all sentences with a capital letter and end with a period!"

It is not until the fourth stage that the content of the writing begins to take precedence. Heretofore, writers have been more concerned with the mechanics of writing, but now, for the first time, the topics and content take on new meaning.

The final stage is that of revision. It is not until students are able to achieve the fourth stage that they will move into this final and more mature stage of writing. It is during this time that problems of organization and style begin to surface and multiple drafts of a document may be labored over until a final polished product is achieved.

The Teacher's Role.   Before exploring the teacher's role in encouraging students to write, it is important to examine existing writing practices so that we may proceed in a logical fashion toward improving instruction. Here is what some writing authorities have to say about writing in our schools.

1. "No one writes enough to learn more than a small part of what writers have to know" (Smith, 1983, p. 560).
2. There is rarely any discussion of writing (Wall and Taylor, 1982).
3. The teacher feedback that students receive is frequently focused on low-level details such as grammar and spelling (Wall and Taylor, 1982).
4. Students view revising as punishment (Schwartz, 1982).

If these statements truly represent the current situation that exists in our schools, much could be done to improve writing. A common adage in reading instruction is that the teacher is more important in determining student progress than are the instructional materials. This is also true in writing instruction, for without a knowledgeable and understanding teacher, there is apt to be little improvement in students' writing.

One important facet of a successful writing program is a supportive teacher and an environment that is conducive to constructive criticism (Lickteig, 1981; Esbensen and Esbensen, 1983; Holt and Vacca, 1981). In addition to the writing climate, teachers need to view writing as a process where one continually experiments with language and polishes drafts. Teachers who establish this milieu nurture writers who continually improve their writing ability. Teachers who stress mechanics, on the other hand, tend to impart an imbalanced view of the writing process.

To practice writing, students need multiple opportunities to put thoughts to paper. Meaningful writing assignments require an interested audience ready to read the aspiring author's work. Later in this chapter, specific writing suggestions will be offered. At this point, however, both teachers and students must perceive writing as having meaning and not as a ritualistic act that is undertaken simply because it is required by a curriculum guide or textbook. Smith (1983) suggests that the first step in establishing a meaningful writing environment is for teachers simply to be able to discern the difference between meaningful and nonmeaningful writing. The second step is to discuss these differences with students.

It would be a relatively easy task to change the state of writing instruction if all one needed was to provide opportunities for writing. Unfortunately, changes in writing instruction will come about only when educators become writers. Unless we serve as models for our students, and unless we understand the processes that transpire as ideas evolve from a creative thought to the final product—the printed word—there is apt to be little change in how we teach writing.

Classroom Uses

A basic principle students need continually to have reinforced is that writing is a communicative act. When students see a purpose for writing, they become more enthusiastic about writing and before long perceive themselves as writers. This chapter will examine the hurdles that students face as they strive to become fluent microcomputer users and then provide ideas that will encourage students to use the computer for communicative purposes.

Keyboarding Skills.   The lack of typing ability or keyboarding skills has been called an "educational time bomb" (Dacus and Dacus, 1983). The implication is that unless students become proficient typists, their use of microcomputers will be severely restricted.

Typing instruction is usually considered the domain of high school business teachers. With the skyrocketing number of microcomputers available in homes and schools, however, educators are feeling increased pressure to provide keyboarding skills to young children. Kaake (1983), after a review of the literature, contended that typewriting increases children's reading, spelling, grammar, punctuation, and creative writing abilities. According to her, elementary school children have no difficulty learning touch typing skills. Some students, in fact, are able to type at a speed of 40 words per minute. The exact age at which this training should begin has not been determined, however. While educators discuss the implications of early keyboarding skills, many computer users are learning these skills through drill-and-practice tutorial programs that are available for microcomputers. At least a half dozen or more of these programs are presently available.

Three of the most popular typing tutorial programs are *MasterType* (Scarborough Systems), *Typing Tutor III* (Microsoft Corporation), and *Type Attack* (Sirious Software). *Typing Tutor III* is a revised version of two earlier programs. The new version includes a student record-keeping function, a test creation function, and an arcade-type drill-and-practice game. The program requires students to reproduce a set of characters that appear on the screen.

Both speed and accuracy are calculated. The program is very easy to use. Once students learn the finger placement for the home row of keys, they rapidly improve their typing ability.

MasterType and *Type Attack* are arcade-type tutorials where students attempt to reproduce target words within a specified time limit in a gamelike setting. Both programs are highly motivating and are appropriate for use with elementary school children.

Unlike the typing teacher, these tutorials cannot provide supervised practice. With the exception of short instructional booklets, all three programs rely on students practicing correct finger movements as they attempt to locate specific keys. Some individuals, attempting to type faster, disregard the importance of finger placement and rely instead on the "hunt-and-peck" method. The advantages of this technique, of course, are that it permits a clear view of the keyboard and may initially be somewhat faster than the preferred touch-typing style. The persevering student will soon overcome the initial limitations of touch typing, however, and quickly surpass the individual who continues to hunt and peck.

The long-range impact of microcomputers and typing programs on young children has not yet been determined, and it is difficult, therefore, to make specific recommendations regarding their use. Some reading teachers, in an attempt to impart good typing habits, hover over the students, chiding them to place their fingers on the home row of keys. Other teachers have actually instituted typing "minilessons" in their classrooms. Still others have devised their own techniques, such as coloring keys, assisting correct hand usage by tapping students on the appropriate shoulder when searching for a key, and placing placards and wall charts in the room illustrating proper finger placement. Until more data are available to guide rational decision making, however, the best advice is to use common sense and not pressure young students to perform beyond their physical capabilities. Encouragement, rather than pressure, should direct students toward proper keyboard usage.

Student Stories.   Many years ago, this author envisioned a magical typewriter that would permit reading teachers to take dictation from students and simultaneously display it on the typewriter as well as on an overhead screen. This was long before the word "microcomputer" became part of everyone's vocabulary. Fortunately, today's reading teachers have such a machine—the powerful microcomputer coupled with a word processing program.

When working with primary-age students, the word processor can visually depict the process of print being generated from left to right across the screen. Furthermore, to the beginning reader, it presents a vivid illustration of how speech can be transcribed into text. While the typewriter, the chalkboard, and the wall chart can illustrate the same process, the microcomputer permits text to be easily corrected on screen, thereby illustrating, at an early stage, the necessity for occasional editing. Moreover, when connected to a printer, the microcomputer can reproduce an unlimited number of copies of students' stories. This capability permits students to receive their creations within seconds of dictation.

Dictated stories may range from simple "one liners" to more lengthy undertakings. Here are several examples of language-experience stories dictated to a reading teacher who then transcribed the efforts using a word processor. First, look at the following short "treasures."

"Ted and Bill ride a bike."
"Fred and Jill look at the duck."

With other individuals, lengthier renditions may be forthcoming:

MY GUINEA PIG

When I get my guinea pig, I will put it in the cage and make sure Pincushion, our cat, doesn't get it or eat it. If it's white, I'll name it Snowball or if it's white and brown, I'll name it Penelope.

I want a guinea pig because they are so cute and if you put them on your lap they don't move away. You can hold them and they won't bite. You have to put newspaper under their cage so they won't go to the bathroom on the floor. I am going to feed it carrots and lettuce. You shouldn't squeeze it because it will maybe break its bones or something.

A derivation of the experience story is the individually authored story. Once students demonstrate reasonable keyboard facility, they can create their own masterpieces. Eventually, of course, the word processor can be used whenever written assignments need to be produced.

Some teachers have found that collaborative writing assignments foster improved writing (Rubin, 1983). These activities require that one individual dictates while the other types. Joint ventures such as these demonstrate to children the value of working together. Not only does pairing of students reduce the demand for additional computers, but it also illustrates that writing is a dynamic process in which collaboration, revision, and proofreading are all important ingredients.

An interesting word processing technique used with older students in an effort to improve their writing is to use what Marcus and Blau (1983) identify as "invisible text." Invisible text is created when the brightness and contrast controls of a video monitor are dimmed until print on the screen becomes invisible. According to the authors, writing using the invisible text forces students to attend to their emerging thoughts and to disregard typographical errors. Once the creative aspect of their composition is concluded, students readjust the monitor's controls to view their text. Invisible writing may be a technique that some teachers could try with older students who are fluent typists. Some students may still need to reread what they have composed and may, therefore, find invisible writing difficult.

Newspapers. Student-generated newspapers are an excellent example of how word processors can contribute to meaningful communication among students. Students can elect an editorial board, feature editors, and staff editors. Typically, such a newspaper includes an editorial page, sports section, foods, cartoons, entertainment guides, and personal messages. All students can be encouraged to submit articles for inclusion in such a venture. When manuscripts are created on the word processor, students can be asked to edit their work to conform to a predetermined standard.

As sophisticated microcomputers and printers become more user friendly, different type styles and fonts may be used in the newspaper setup. Some microcomputers now permit the integration of high-resolution graphics with text. Student newspapers can truly become artistic ventures limited only by students' imaginations and the computer hardware available.

Recipes. Recipes can be a meaningful way for students to share information as well as to illustrate the importance of following directions. Once the recipe has been entered into the computer, it can be saved on a diskette. After all recipes have been typed, the teacher can merge the collection into a printed version to be shared by all members of the class. A variation of this activity is to collect recipes of one category such as cookies, desserts, and so on.

Letters and Messages. If the primary purpose of writing is communication, letters and other messages must surely be the epitome of the printed word. Letters can take a variety of forms. They might be written to pen pals, to producers of commercial products, or to other classmates. Frequently, letter writing is integrated with the language arts program, and children are shown examples of the many different types of letters that can be written. Protest letters, letters to the editor, invitations, and congratulatory letters are but a few of the many types that adults confront on a daily basis.

Lists. List making is recommended by a number of individuals (Goodman and Goodman, 1983; Schwartz, 1982). Lists may take a variety of forms. There are Christmas lists, birthday lists, telephone number lists, student lists, and movie lists. Lists are so popular, in fact, there are even tradebooks that consist of nothing but lists. Students may create their own "Book of Lists." Such books are great for trivia buffs. Even reluctant readers can usually find a list that appeals to them. Word processing programs are great for "lists", since it is easy to add, delete, or insert additional items to an existing list.

Diaries and Journals. Teachers may want students to maintain a diary or journal for a period of weeks or months. Again, the ease with which files can be retrieved and edited makes word processing an excellent way to encourage writing. By requiring students to have their own disks, each entry can be a separate file. Diaries or journals may be read by the teacher upon invitation.

The Quill Program. A commercial program that has attempted to increase students' writing is *Quill* (D. C. Heath). This program actually consists of five distinct programs: a children's text editor, a publication system, a message system, an information exchange, and an activity kit (Collins, Bruce, and Rubin, 1983). Students using the program join a "club" early in the school year. A variety of different clubs may be formed (e.g., computers, books, sports, automobiles, jokes, dinosaurs, cooking, skiing, hiking). The word processing capabilities of the *Quill* program permit students to design a student newspaper that has a variety of formats and page layouts. Students submit articles to be reproduced in the newspaper.

A message system within the *Quill* program permits students to experience a variety of types of writing. An electronic bulletin board permits users to add messages that may be read by other students. Other portions of the program encourage descriptive, persuasive, and story writing.

Sentence Combining. One activity that has been demonstrated to improve student's writing is sentence combining. Teachers who have access to word processors can design their own sentence combining activities. Using this process, students examine two or more sentences and combine them into one compound sentence. The following two sentences, for example, could be combined to make a third.

> The boy used the word processor.
> The boy combined two sentences.
> The boy used the word processor to combine two sentences.

According to Bradley (1982), sentence combining allows students to manipulate text without emphasizing the rules of grammar, since it utilizes students' own unconscious knowledge of language.

Teachers who plan to use sentence combining activities on the computer should first select a word processor that is simple to use. Students must then be taught simple commands (such as insert and delete) so they will be able to manipulate the text.

Additional Uses. Creative teachers will find many additional uses of word processors. Some teachers create lessons that include typographical or grammatical errors and then encourage the students to be "detectives" in an effort to find and correct the mistakes. Other teachers have students use word processors to create joke books, song lyrics, plays, and the like. As you probably have surmised by now, the computer truly is a tool that permits a host of interesting applications. Unlike many of the computer-assisted instruction applications where the student is a recipient of preprogrammed information, word processing applications involve the student as an active participant in the learning process. As such, the computer becomes a powerful tool that not only provides high motivation but, when used appropriately, results in improved learning.

Advantages of Word Processing

Word processing is rapidly becoming one of the most influential applications of microcomputers in our nation's schools. Anyone who has experienced word processing sings its praises. Some contend that word processing will be especially beneficial for those who lack the confidence and skill to play with language (Schwartz, 1982). Others contend that children can become computer literate by learning how to write and edit using word processors (Hennings, 1981). Still others believe that word processing demonstrates to students the power of writing (Flowers, 1981). But perhaps the greatest advantage perceived by students is the freedom from having to recopy edited text (Watt and Parham, 1983).

Ease of Correction.   A major impediment experienced by student writers is the fear of making mistakes. While young children writing with pencils simply have to erase writing errors, once they begin to write with pens, they soon realize the importance of proper transcription. To err usually means having to recopy. Once students learn to type, a fear of commiting typographical errors arises. Even using erasable typing paper, correcting tape, or "white out" still requires having to interrupt the thought process to make a correction. Word processors, however, reduce or even eliminate the fear of improper transcription. Typographical errors are easily corrected by backspacing and overtyping or by using one of the many editing functions.

Even the simplest word processor permits the user to effortlessly erase letters, words, sentences, or entire paragraphs with the stroke of a key. Watt (1983) contends that if computers did no more than serve as correctable typewriters, they would make the act of writing easier for most students. This newly discovered freedom permits students to devote a greater portion of their energies to more important aspects of writing such as revising content, style, and mechanics.

Ease of Revision.   While ease of correction is an important facet of word processing, an even more powerful feature is the ease with which revisions can be made. Anderson (1983) calls revision "the backbone of coherent writing" (p. 33). Experts in the field of writing continually stress the importance of the revision process. Graves (1982), for instance, writing about the revision process says,

> The last article I had written, called "A New Look at Writing Research," took me four months of writing before I arrived at the one simple thing the whole article was about, research in context (p. 175).

Smith (1981) contends that the idea that writing is a linear, left-to-right process is a myth. Instead, he calls writing a plastic art where words and lines can be moved around on a page just as pages can be reshuffled to form different sequences.

Whereas some teachers believe that writing should proceed only when a nonalterable outline has been developed, a more contemporary view is that writing is a fluid process whereby the order of text may be revised during the actual writing process. This chapter, for example, began as an outline draft that was set aside to "ferment" for eight weeks. Once writing actually began on the chapter, it was necessary to revise the outline, changing substance as well as order. As various drafts of the chapter evolved, so did the outline. Roughly a month transpired between each draft. New experiences, thoughts, and beliefs continually affected the author's perceptions and, hence, the content of the writing.

Formatting Ease.   Once documents are stored in the memory of a computer, they can be manipulated in a variety of ways. Text, for example, can be changed from single spacing to double spacing. Margins can be reset to produce printed material that can take any number of forms. Many word processors permit the user to align the print in at least three fashions: left justified (make all left-hand margins line up), right justified, or full justified. Most programs also permit the user to add automatic page numbering with headers or footers.

Since these features can be performed after the text is stored in memory, the physical appearance of a document can take many forms. If you are unhappy with a single-spaced creation, you simply instruct the computer to change the print option to reflect a double-spacing option. Once the printer is activated, a double-spaced version of the paper is produced. Margins might also be revised after examining a draft of the document. In short, innumerable printing options are available to the user.

While all of this may sound too good to be true, there is one caveat. Whereas some word processors present information on the monitor exactly as it will appear when printed (i.e., "screen-oriented" text), other word processors lack this feature, and, hence, the user is unable to envision how the final draft of a document will appear until it is actually printed. A screen-oriented word processor, therefore, is considered superior to others without this feature, since it permits on-screen editing of virtually all aspects of the text. Programs without this capability become cumbersome to use whenever lists or columns of figures are included in the written document. Screen-oriented word processors, on the other hand, permit the user to align lists and columns on the screen; the other programs don't.

Time and Effort.   Another advantage to teaching reading and writing with a word processor is that the turnaround time between revisions of documents is reduced when compared with longhand or typewritten preparation. Revision is usually a matter of inserting, deleting, or changing the order of words or sentences rather than undertaking massive rewritings. Thus, the actual time and effort needed to revise documents is diminished (Bennett, 1982).

Quantity and Quality of Writing.   An interesting outcome of using a word processor is that students tend to increase the quantity of their writing (Rubin,

1983). This is important when one considers that so little writing is done in schools in the first place. Some students find that the blinking cursor serves as a prod to keep them generating material. Schantz (1983) contends that the computer itself serves as a motivating force to increase productivity. Collins (1983) believes that a reduced fear of making mistakes and the fact that texts appear better when produced on a word processor may contribute to longer papers.

Increased production, of course, is not the ultimate goal of teachers of writing. Improvement in the quality of writing is even more important. In all likelihood, because editing becomes such a painless task (relatively speaking), students using word processors will be more apt to revise and, hence, improve the quality of their writing. Whereas revising was once perceived by students as punishment, with word processing, today revision is seen as one step in the writing process.

While research into the effects of word processing is still preliminary, teachers who have used it with students offer high praise for its educational potential. It may well be that within the next few years, virtually all students will use word processors to prepare written assignments. At that time, we will be more able to judge the long-term effects of word processing on the communicative skills of our young people.

Limitations of Word Processing

While word processing is an excellent application of computer technology, it is not without its limitations. Some of these are directly related to the hardware and software, while others are related to the application of the technology into the existing school curriculum.

Multiple Key Use.   Microcomputer hardware is continually being refined at such a dizzying rate that new developments appear on the market on a daily basis. For the most part, however, microcomputers are produced with the stan-

FIGURE 5.1   Special Function Keys for *Word Juggler* Word Processing System (Used with permission of Quark Incorporated.)

dard qwerty keyboard supplemented by a few additional function keys. Word processing software relies heavily upon most keys serving dual functions. The word processor on which this manuscript was typed, for example, generates the letter "d" by simply striking the keyboard. When a control key is held down simultaneously, however, the character at the blinking cursor is deleted (many word processors make use of mnemonics such as "d" for delete and "g" for glue. To create a capitalized "d," the Escape key must first be struck followed by the "d." Thus, one key serves three distinct functions in this software package.

A variety of schemes have been developed to overcome the hurdle of learning the multiple functions of individual keys. Some programs come with pressure-sensitive gummed labels that are affixed to the keys until their functions become second nature. One word processing program, *Word Juggler* (Quark, Inc.), aids the user by supplying nineteen new keys that replace the original keys on the keyboard. Editing commands such as Delete Paragraph, Tabs, and Help are embossed on the front of each key, thereby aiding the new user (Figure 5.1). Another technique that some publishers employ is to supply a laminated template of the keyboard with color-coded keys depicting the multiple functions of specific keys. Regardless of the aids provided, it usually takes the first-time user a minimum of ten hours to become comfortable with an operating system (Anderson, 1983). Since most students have only limited access to school computers, it is imperative that an easy-to-learn system is selected.

Upper- and Lowercase Letters. A second limitation inherent when using some word processing programs is that a few microcomputers do not have the ability to produce upper- and lowercase letters on the screen. Instead, uppercase letters are represented by an inverse character (i.e., black character on a white background instead of a white character on a black background). This may be confusing for beginning readers who need practice discerning both upper- and lowercase letters. As computers become increasingly sophisticated, however, virtually all machines will have the capability of producing both styles of letters. Parenthetically, it is interesting to note that Apple Computer's Macintosh microcomputer has the capability to produce not only upper- and lowercase letters, but it can also generate a variety of different type styles as well as font sizes (Figure 5.2).

Editing Functions. A third limitation is that several word processors and/or computers make the job of editing text extremely cumbersome. This is so for a variety of reasons. First, with some machines, there are no specific cursor control keys to permit cursor movement in the edit mode. This means that cursor movement can occur only by using a Control key in conjunction with other keys (e.g., I, J, K, and M). Some computers, however, have four arrow keys that are used for cursor control. Obviously, this latter arrangement is superior to the former.

Another related shortcoming of some programs is that editing cannot be

FIGURE 5.2   Size and Font Styles from the Apple® Macintosh Microcomputer (Courtesy of Apple® Computer, Inc.)

done in the "composition" mode. Instead, the program must be switched to the "edit" mode, changes made, and then shifted back to the "composition" mode. Such gymnastics make editing cumbersome, especially if numerous editing changes are needed.

Number of Characters Per Line.   Another limitation that has been mentioned throughout this book is the inability of some computers and software to produce at least 65 characters across the screen. This figure marks the minimum number of characters that permit screen-oriented text. Some programs permit only 26 characters per line; others display 40 characters. Programs with these shortcomings are less desirable, especially if your computer and monitor have the ability to produce more text per line with sufficient clarity to permit easy reading.

Users should be aware of two additional concerns that are more curriculum related than hardware or software limitations. They are the seductiveness of computer-generated print and the quality of teaching.

Seductiveness.   Anyone who has seen material printed on a high-quality printer is impressed by the quality and evenness of print. This neatness is what some (Schwartz, 1982) call "smoke screen revision," since quality of the reproduction may cover flaws in reasoning or logic. When this happens, the appearance of the printed material can result in a composition appearing better than it actually is. Merton (1983) describes this print as being "seductively" good. Teachers, therefore, must be able to recognize good writing and not be led to believe assignments are better than they actually are simply because the output is from dot-matrix or letter-quality printers.

Teacher Quality. Finally, word processing programs and microcomputers cannot make a skilled teacher of writing out of someone who knows or understands little about the writing process. Word processing is only a tool or vehicle designed to increase the writer's productivity and ease composition. A good program in the hands of an incompetent teacher is not likely to result in better student writing. While word processing programs and microcomputers will relieve much of the anguish associated with writing, only a knowledgeable teacher can make writing the enjoyable and creative enterprise it should be.

POPULAR WORD PROCESSING PROGRAMS

Scores of excellent word processing programs are available for microcomputers. Furthermore, new programs are being developed monthly and already existing software is being revised at such an alarming rate that it is impossible to keep track of the many options available. Recommending a "best" program is difficult, since selecting a word processing program is a very personal act that has been likened to marriage—different people want and expect different things. To illustrate the variety of programs that are available, three popular systems will be described: *Bank Street Writer*, a system that has seen widespread use in schools; *Magic Window II*, a package that permits the user to use either a 40-, 70-, or 80-column display; and *PFS Write*. Each of these programs is considered to be "user friendly" and possesses most of the features educators need.

Bank Street Writer

This program was developed at the Bank Street College of Education in New York. A primary advantage of *Bank Street Writer* (Scholastic Publishing Company) is that it is a simple program to learn. To assist the first-time user, the back side of the program diskette contains a five-part tutorial that teaches the various commands used within the program. Even individuals who don't read the accompanying documentation can learn to use the program simply by working through the on-screen tutorial.

Another noteworthy feature of *Bank Street Writer* is a screen display that provides a menu of commands available in the program (Figures 5.3 and 5.4). To capitalize a letter, for example, the user simply refers to the top section of the screen to see that Shift-N will shift into the uppercase mode (Figure 5.3). To edit text, the user shifts to the Edit Mode and moves the cursor around the screen by using the I, J, K, and M keys. Another editing mode permits the author to delete or retain text, move blocks of text, find and replace strings of characters, save a composition, delete a composition, rename a file, or print the file on a connected printer. To select any of these options, the operator simply moves a highlighted bar by using the right or left arrow key to make the selection and then presses the Return key to perform the operation (Figure 5.4).

Because *Bank Street Writer* has only 40 characters per line displayed on the screen, the student may select to print his or her document using the 40-column format (called Print Draft) or to utilize the entire 80 columns available on most printers (entitled Print Final on the menu display). The Print Draft option permits students to find typographical and grammatical errors quickly on the screen, since the printed version is an exact replication of the screen version of text. Users are also able to adjust margins to their own specifications as well as to select either a double- or single-space option. Automatic page enumeration with or without headers or footers is also possible.

Bank Street Writer has many noteworthy features. It is easy to use, it doesn't require any hardware modifications when used with the popular Apple computers, it contains an excellent tutorial, and the accompanying documentation is clearly written and easy to comprehend, even for the first-time computer user.

The program also has its limitations. First, editing is cumbersome, since

FIGURE 5.3   Text Mode from *Bank Street Writer* Word Processing Program (Published by permission of Scholastic Publishing Company.)

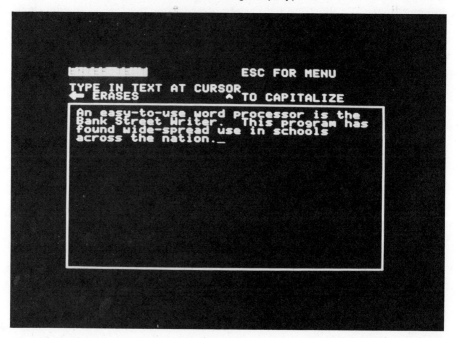

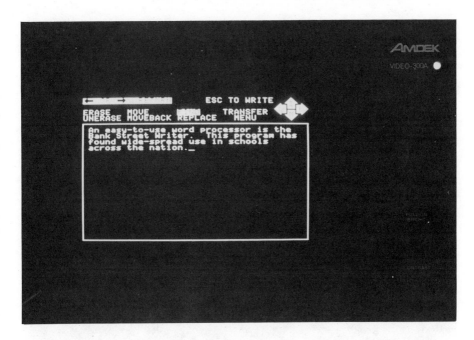

FIGURE 5.4 Edit Mode from *Bank Street Writer* Word Processing Program (Published by permission of Scholastic Publishing Company.)

the user must switch between the composing mode and the editing mode. This makes editing more difficult than it is with some comparable word processors. (A new release of this program has overcome this limitation, however.) Second, only 40 characters per line are displayed. Thus, screen-oriented text is not available. Last, the program lacks some of the more sophisticated commands such as right, left, and center justification, the ability to scroll rapidly through the text, and underlining or boldfacing of type. All these features are found on more powerful programs. Nevertheless, the program is an excellent introduction to the power of word processing.

Magic Window II

Magic Window II (Artsci, Inc.) is an intermediate-level word processor that is a revision of the popular *Magic Window*. The metaphor of a magic window is used to describe the program, since it provides screen-oriented text. The revision permits the user to select from a 40-, 70-, or 80-column screen display. While the choice is dependent upon the components within the microcomputer, each option does present the screen-oriented text. In the 40-column mode, however, only the left or right half of the screen is visible at one time. The result is similar to viewing text through a mailing tube. The screen automatically shifts from the left half to the right half of the page as text is entered. This makes on-screen editing challenging, but this shortcoming is quickly overlooked if the user needs

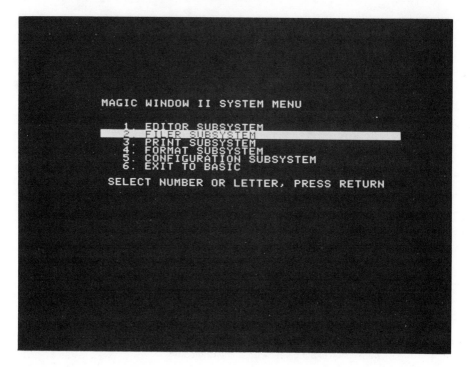

FIGURE 5.5   Main Menu Screen from *Magic Window II* (Magic Window II by Artsci Inc., N. Hollywood, CA.)

to prepare any tabular or columnar information, for then the information from the table lines up perfectly on the screen and the user is assured that it will appear the same way once hard copy is printed. The 40-column display only needs to be selected if the computer is incapable of producing the 70- or 80-column version. Most computers now permit these last two formats to be used.

Magic Window II makes extensive use of the Control key used in conjunction with other alpha characters on the keyboard. To justify text, for example, the user enters Control-J (justify) and then selects from six options such as left, right, or center justify. To open the text to insert a word, phrase, sentence, or paragraph, Control-T (tear) is used. Once the text has been added, Control-G (glue) is entered.

Another feature of *Magic Window II* is the ease with which one can move from one subsystem to another. After a document is created, for instance, the user goes back to the main menu (Figure 5.5). From the six available options, the choices are made by simply selecting the corresponding number or by moving the white cursor bar with the right or left arrow keys. To save a document on disk, the user selects the Filer Subsystem (Figure 5.6). Option 3, Save Formatted File, is selected by pressing the numeral 3 twice. At this point, the user specifies a file name. After the file name is given and the Return key hit, the file is saved onto the data diskette. To retrieve the document at a later time, option 4,

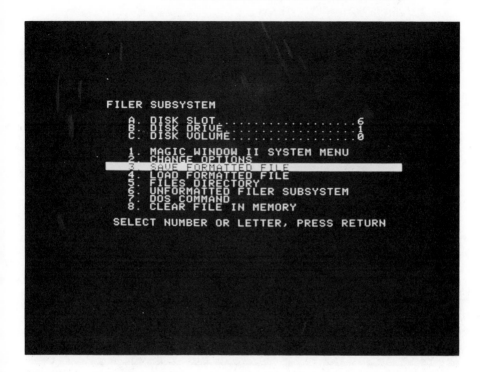

FILER SUBSYSTEM
A. DISK SLOT .6
B. DISK DRIVE .1
C. DISK VOLUME 0
1. MAGIC WINDOW II SYSTEM MENU
2. CHANGE OPTIONS
3. SAVE FORMATTED FILE
4. LOAD FORMATTED FILE
5. FILES DIRECTORY
6. UNFORMATTED FILER SUBSYSTEM
7. DOS COMMAND
8. CLEAR FILE IN MEMORY
SELECT NUMBER OR LETTER, PRESS RETURN

FIGURE 5.6   Filer Subsystem Screen from *Magic Window II* (Magic Window II by Artsci Inc., N. Hollywood, CA.)

Load Formatted File, is selected. The screen then presents a list of current programs residing on the diskette. Entering the number corresponding to the file name automatically loads the selected program.

Magic Window II is so easy to use that many primary-grade students quickly learn the system after watching their teacher use the program for recording dictated language-experience stories. On the other hand, the program has enough features to be used by graduate-level students in the preparation of writing assignments.

PFS: Write

This program is another user-friendly word processing system that is available for several different brands of microcomputers. The program makes extensive use of a menu-driven format and also has a special Help command. Once the program is loaded into the computer, the screen presents a menu of possible functions (Figure 5.7). Type/Edit is the option selected whenever a document is to be created or edited. Define Page permits the user to modify the standard paper size and margin settings. It also allows the use of headings, footers, and page numbers. Print directs the document to be sent to the printer. The Get/Save/Remove option is used whenever one wants to retrieve or store

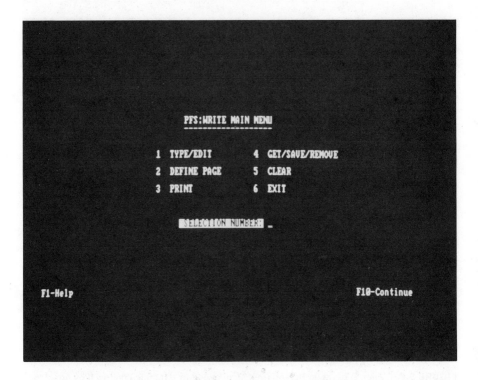

FIGURE 5.7   Main Menu from *PFS: Write* Word Processing Program (PFS® is a registered trademark of Software Publishing Corp.)

information on the disk. A document can also be deleted from the diskette using this command. Clear erases everything in the computer's memory (RAM) and permits a new document to be constructed. When the user is ready to leave *PFS: Write*, the Exit option is selected.

This program has several advantageous features, especially when used with an IBM PC or a PC-compatible microcomputer. First, the cursor is easily moved around the screen with the four arrow keys found on the numeric keyboard. Second, the ten special function keys (F keys) of the PC have been assigned special operations when used with this program. F3, for example, moves the cursor to the previous word in the text. The F4 key moves the cursor to the next word. The F1 key has been designated as the Help key. Pressing F1 brings a screen of prompts into view that explain many of the cursor movements and editing commands of the program. In addition to the already described functions, other operations that can be performed with function keys include deleting words or lines, underlining or boldfacing text, searching and replacing functions, appending documents to each other, then continuing with the program.

PFS: Write is also a screen-oriented word processor. A ruler appears at

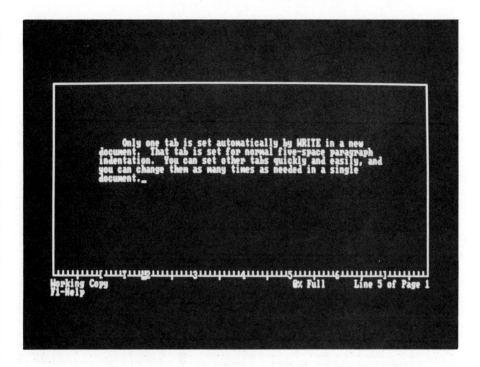

FIGURE 5.8   Editing Screen from *PFS: Write* Word Processing Program (PFS® is a registered trademark of Software Publishing Corp.)

the bottom of the editing screen allowing the user to actually see margin and tab settings (Figure 5.8).

While *PFS: Write* may lack some of the more advanced features that more expensive word processors include, its ease in learning makes it an excellent choice for the first-time word processor user. *PFS Write* provides all the functions necessary for most word processing tasks.

Additional Programs

Selecting the "perfect" word processing program can be confusing. There are so many different computers, word processing programs, price differences, and program features that attempting to find the "best" program can be overwhelming. To help individuals select a program with the features they need, for their machine, and within their price range, the following guide should be helpful (Figure 5.9). Keep in mind, however, the fact that programs are continually undergoing revisions, prices fluctuate depending on market demand and supply, and new programs are being released each day.

EL'S GUIDE TO WORD PROCESSORS

Company Name/Address	Name of Program/Price	Hardware/Minimum Memory	Single Write/Edit Mode	Overwrite/Edit Mode	Insert/Delete Text	Search and Replace	Delete*	Moving Blocks of Text	Transfer to Another File	Transfer to Another Disk	Cursor Movement**	Moving Cursor to B...
A B Computers 252 Bethlehem Place Colmar, PA 18915 (215) 822-7727	Page Mate $40	All Commodore computers (16K-64K)	✓	✓	✓		c, s, p	✓	✓	✓	c	
Apple Computers Inc. 20525 Mariani Ave. Cupertino, CA 95014 (408) 996-1010	Apple Writer II+, IIe, III II+: $150 IIe: $195 III: $225	Apple II and II+ (48K), IIe (64K), III (128K)	✓		✓	✓	c, s, p	✓	✓	✓	c	✓
Artsci, Inc. 5547 Satsuma Ave. North Hollywood, CA 91601 (818) 985-2922	Magic Window II $150	Apple II, IIe, II+ (48-64K)	✓	✓	✓	✓	c, s	✓	✓	✓	c	✓
Atari, Inc. P.O. Box 427 Sunnyvale, CA 94086 (800) 672-1404 (Calif.) (800) 538-8543 (Elsewhere)	Atari Writer $100	Atari family (16K)	✓		✓	✓	c, w, s	✓	✓		c	
Bruce and James Program Pub. 6024 Riverside Drive Columbus, OH 43017 (415) 775-8400 for information (614) 766-0110 to order	Wordvision $80	IBM PC (96K)	✓		✓	✓	c, w, s, p	✓			c, w, s, p	✓
Commodore Business Machines 1200 Wilson Drive West Chester, PA 19380 (215) 436-4200	Easy Script 64 $50	Commodore 64 (64K)	✓	✓	✓	✓	c, w, s, p	✓	✓	✓	c, w, s, p	
Datamost 20660 Nordhoff Place Chatsworth, CA 91311 (213) 709-1202	Write-On $130	Apple II, IIe, II+, IBM PC (48-64K)		✓	✓	✓	c, w, s	✓		✓	c, w	✓
Datasoft, Inc. 19808 Nordhoff Place Chatsworth, CA 91311 (818) 701-5161	Text Wizard $50	Atari 400 or 800 (32-48K)	✓	✓	✓	✓	c, w, s, p	✓	✓	✓	c	✓
Hayden Software 600 Suffolk St. Lowell, MA 01853 (617) 937-0200	Pie Writer Apples: $150 IBM: $200	Apple II, II+, IIe IBM PC (48K)	✓	✓	✓	✓	c, w, s, p	✓	✓	✓	c, w	✓
Human Engineered Software 150 North Hill Brisbane, CA 99005 (800) 624-2442	HES Writer Commodore 64: $45 Vic 20: $40	Commodore 64 (64K) Vic 20 (16K)		✓	✓	✓	c, s	✓	✓		c	✓
IJG 1953 West 11th St. Upland, CA 91786 (714) 946-5805	Electric Pencil $90	TRS-80 Model III, IV, Color Computer (16-48K)	✓	✓	✓	✓	c, w, s, p	✓	✓	✓	c	
	Electric Pencil $300	IBM PC (48-512K)	✓	✓	✓	✓	c, w, s, p	✓	✓	✓	c, w, s, p	✓
Information Unlimited 2401 Marin Ship Way Sausalito, CA 94965 (415) 331-6700	Easy Writer II System $395	IBM PC, TI Professional (128K)	✓	✓	✓	✓	c, w, s, p	✓	✓	✓	c, w, s, p	✓

*Delete by character (c), by word (w), by sentence (s), and/or by paragraph (p).
**Cursor moves by character (c), by word (w), by sentence or line (s), and/or by paragraph (p).
***Print formatting functions are either menu (m), embedded (e), or both (e, m).

FIGURE 5.9 A Guide to Word Processors ("EL's Guide to Word Processors" from *Electronic Learning*, March 1984. Copyright© 1984 by Scholastic Inc. Reprinted by permission of Scholastic Inc.)

114

Use Letters Displayed	Reformatting Paragraphs on Screen	Ability to Make Columns	80/24 Display	Horizontal Shifting	Display Shows Printed Format	Line Spacing	Margin Setting	Right Justification	Page Numbering	Headers and Footers	Underlining	Boldface††	Print Pause	Print Part of a Document	Menus	Tutorial	Index in Manual	Reference Card	Y or N Deletion Verification	Yankback Feature	Mail Merge	Spell Check	Integrated Data Base	Notes
✓	✓		✓		e	e	e	e	h†					✓		✓		✓		✓	In.		Av.	
	✓		✓		e, m	e, m	e, m	e, m	e, m	e				e	✓	✓		✓		✓	✓		Av.	Fairly easy to learn.
	✓	✓	✓		m	m	m	m	h	e	e††			e	✓	✓	✓	✓		✓	✓	Av.	Av. Av.	User can program embedded print commands; has to make room for inserts.
✓		✓	✓		e, m	e, m	e, m	m	m	e	e††	m	m			✓	✓			✓	In.		Av.	Easy to learn; good documentation; cartridge-based.
	✓	✓	✓		e, m	e, m	e, m	m	m	e	e††		e, m	✓	✓	✓			✓					
✓		✓			e	e	e	e	e	e	e††	e	e		✓	✓	✓		✓		In.	Av.	Av.	Avail. on disk and cartridge.
	✓	✓	✓		e	m	m	m	m	e	e	e	m		✓	✓					In.		Av.	Particularly facilitates letter writing; includes form letters.
					e, m	e, m	e, m	e, m	e	e††			e		✓	✓							Av.	*Letter Wizard* avail. Feb.; relies on commands, not menus.
	✓				e, m	e, m	e, m	e	e	e, m	e, m††	e, m	e, m	✓	✓	✓	✓		✓	✓	In.	Av.	Av.	Flip-screen feature.
					e, m	e, m	e, m	e, m	e, m			m	e, m			✓	✓	✓						Cartridge-based; new manual coming out.
✓					m	m	m	m	h	m		m	m			✓	✓					Av.	Av.	Six windows; Spanish/French keyboard.
✓	✓		✓		e, m	e, m	e, m	e, m	h	e, m	e, m††	e, m	e, m		✓	✓	✓	✓		✓	In.	Av.	Av.	
✓	✓		✓		m	m	m	m	m	e	e††	e	e	✓	✓	✓				✓	In.	In.	Av.	

...ers only (h).
...talics, subscripts, and superscripts.
...ams are either included in program (In.) or available from company or third-party vendor (Av.).

MARCH 1984 ● 61

FIGURE 5.9 (continued)

ELECTRONIC DICTIONARIES

With the increased use of word processing, it is perhaps only natural that electronic dictionaries (i.e., spelling checkers) have been developed. The following paragraphs describe these programs and list some of their advantages and limitations.

Frequently, electronic dictionaries are marketed by the same companies that produce word processing programs. Artsci, the company that publishes *Magic Window II*, for example, also has a companion electronic dictionary entitled *Magic Words*.

Electronic dictionaries are programs that permit users to check the spelling of all the words in a document against a dictionary of known words that is stored in the computer's random access memory. Just as with printed dictionaries, the number of words contained in each electronic program varies considerably. The printed version of *The Random House Dictionary of the English Language* contains over 260,000 words and Webster's *New Collegiate Dictionary* contains over 150,000 words, but electronic dictionaries are considerably smaller. According to Kimmel (1982), though, an electronic dictionary should contain a minimum of 10,000 words, for the greater the number of

FIGURE 5.10   Screen Menu from *The Sensible Speller* (Reprinted by permission of Sensible Software, Inc. Sensible Speller and Sensible Software are trademarks of Sensible Software.)

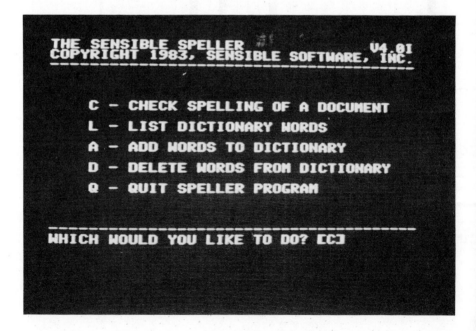

words in the dictionary, the fewer words the program will fail to recognize.

To use a typical electronic dictionary, the program is first loaded into the computer's memory. Once it is loaded, the word processing data diskette is inserted into the disk drive and the document to be checked is specified. Words from the document are then checked against known words stored in the RAM of the microcomputer. Document words that are not in the computer's memory (i.e., in the electronic dictionary) are identified either on the monitor screen or printed in a list format on a connected printer. Most electronic dictionaries highlight unrecognized words on the screen and ask the user whether the spelling is correct or incorrect. If an incorrect spelling is specified, the user can select an option to change the word in the existing file or simply mark it to be changed at a later time (Figure 5.10). Some programs even offer alternative spellings of unrecognized words (Hertz, 1983). The more words in the dictionary, of course, the less interaction needed between the user and the computer (all other things being equal).

Advantages of Electronic Dictionaries

An obvious benefit of having access to an electronic spelling checker is that compositions can be proofread quickly and accurately. In most cases, documents can be checked automatically while the user goes about some other chore.

Another advantage of using spelling checkers with children is that it frees students to concentrate on the content of a composition rather than worry needlessly about spelling. Once the composition is complete, the spelling checker can do a quick scan to reveal any typographical mistakes.

Disadvantages of Electronic Dictionaries

While spelling checkers initially appear to be a salvation for poor spellers, these programs are not without their faults. Their biggest disadvantage is that they only tell the user what words they think should be checked. Usually, the user must still resort to a dictionary to obtain the proper spelling.

A second limitation is that programs with limited dictionaries overidentify many words that are spelled correctly but are not in the dictionary and, hence, are considered misspellings. Content-specific words, therefore, such as "spinnaker," "microcomputer," and "klister" may be spelled correctly in the document but may be identified as possible misspellings. The larger the dictionary, therefore, the fewer incorrectly identified words.

Another limitation is that some dictionaries require a second disk drive. To purchase an electronic dictionary for $200.00 only to discover that a second disk drive must be added to your microcomputer can be an expensive, hard-learned lesson.

Some educators feel that electronic spelling checkers foster sloppy spelling habits and, hence, have no place in education (Bell, 1983). While inappropriate applications could result in such an outcome, with proper guidance, these shortcomings can be avoided.

A more real danger in using spelling checkers is failing to understand that these dictionaries are unable to discern the differences between homonyms. Hence, while selected words may be spelled correctly, their use may be inappropriate in a given setting. Sentences such as "The bare chased the man" and "We will meat the boys after school" fit the constraints of spelling appropriateness, but they fail the test of semantic acceptability. So, while spelling checkers do search for inappropriate spellings, they do not negate the necessity of a careful proofreading of compositions.

Spelling Insights

It is too soon to evaluate the effectiveness of using spelling checkers in schools. Perhaps the major spin-off of their use will be to demonstrate to students the importance of correct spelling and to instill a sense of pride in spelling. Some individuals contend that the common practice of having children commit to memory long lists of "spelling words" is a much different task from spelling words in written assignments (Rule, 1982; Hodges, 1982; and Morris, 1981). Spelling, they believe, is a multifaceted skill that proceeds in stages and develops as students are exposed to reading and writing activities (more about this in the following chapter). Spelling checkers, when viewed from this perspective, can be seen as alerting users to potential misspellings in their work. Through this awareness, students can develop a greater understanding and appreciation of spelling and its importance in written work.

Examples of Electronic Dictionaries

To acquaint the reader with some of the popular electronic dictionaries available, four programs will be presented. They are *Magic Words* (Artsci, Inc.), *The Sensible Speller* (Sensible Software, Inc.), *Lexicheck* (Quark, Inc.), and *The Benchmark Spelling Checker* (MetaSoft Publishing Company). These four include many features that are found in other electronic dictionaries.

Magic Words.   *Magic Words* is a 14,000-word spelling checker that can be used with its companion program, *Magic Window II*, or with a number of word processors that use the Apple II disk operating system. The dictionary checks documents at the rate of approximately 1,600 words per minute. In addition to checking a document, it also permits the user to build a new document that incorporates any spelling corrections that have been instituted. Furthermore, *Magic Words* allows the user to develop "customized" dictionaries from his or her existing files, thereby expanding the original number of words in the basic dictionary. Another feature is its ability to print a list of unrecognized words. This list includes the page number, line number, the misspelled word, and the context in which the error occurs (Figure 5.11). This automatic print feature permits the user to go about other tasks while the document is being

```
MAGIC WORDS ERROR LIST FOR FILE: WELLS


   WORD              PAGE   LINE              CONTEXT

Wells                 1      7      H.G. Wells or by his fu
Herbert               1      7      name Herbert George Wells
George                1      7      rbert George Wells was bo
Wells                 1      7      George Wells was born   Sa
occured               1      9      This occured   at the Atla
Bromley               1     11      e in Bromley near North K
Kent                  1     11      r North Kent which is now
London                1     13      eater London. (2)   He was
Sarah                 1     13      son of Sarah and Joseph
Joseph                1     13      h and Joseph   Wells. (3)
Wells                 1     15      oseph   Wells. (3)   They w
's                    1     15      n their 40's at the time
shopkeepers           1     17      shopkeepers. (4)   Mrs. W
Mrs                   1     17      rs. (4)   Mrs. Wells taugh
Wells                 1     17         Mrs. Wells taught Herbe
Herbert               1     17      ught Herbert the alphabet
village               1     21      mall village school then
Bromley               1     21      then Bromley Academy whic
refered               1     21      h he refered to as   "a be
beastly               1     23         "a beastly little priva
draper                1     25      for a draper at   Windsor.
Windsor               1     27      at  Windsor. (7)   He mad
chemist's             1     31      a chemist's assistant an
Midhurst              1     33      the Midhurst School in 18
draper's              1     35      g a draper's apprentice.
unhappy               1     37      most unhappy hopeless per
suicide               1     39      ting suicide he dropped t
```

```
occured              10     27      ion occured.
Wells                10     27      ured.   Wells warns people
warns                10     27      Wells warns people of th
story                10     31      in the story.   Wells want
Wells                10     31      tory.   Wells wants people
invasion             10     33      an invasion could happen
Wells                10     39            Wells was trying t
story                10     41      e the   story which are "a
salutary             10     41      "a salutary warning agai
warning              10     41      tary warning against the
complacency          10     41      complacency of  optimism
optimistic           10     43      o optimistic  about this
invasion             10     45      of invasion that occurs
sympathy             10     47      man sympathy  is negative
destructive          10     49      -destructive, (31) which
Martians             10     51      the Martians progress in
sympathy             10     51      man sympathy and  that it
destructive          10     53      destructive to  mankind.
Wells                10     55      e that Wells was trying t



warning              11      7      tely warning humans to co


      2699 WORDS CHECKED.
```

FIGURE 5.11   Sample Error List from *Magic Words* Spelling Checker (Magic Words by Artsci Inc., N. Hollywood, CA.)

scanned for the misspellings. The program is menu driven and, hence, is easy to use. While the program contains a number of subsystems, its heart is the Checker Subsystem. Once a document begins to be scanned, a screen such as that in Figure 5.12 appears on the monitor. The unrecognized word, the page on which it occurs, the line number in which it occurs, and the contextual setting of the word are presented. The bottom of the screen presents the options available to the user. If it is correct, the user enters "Y" for yes or strikes the Return key; if it is not, "N" is struck. "I" represents "ignore" and the program continues. "C" represents "change" and the correct spelling is then entered on the keyboard.

Overall, *Magic Words* is an inexpensive program that has most of the functions available on other electronic dictionaries.

The Sensible Speller.   This program consists of over 80,000 words derived from the Concise Edition of the *Random House Dictionary*. If two disk drives are available, the program can have roughly 10,000 additional words added to the dictionary.

Sensible Speller identifies each unrecognized word in a three-line contextual setting. Once the word is "flagged," the following options are available:

1. Add the word to a dictionary (assuming that it was correctly spelled).
2. Ignore the word.
3. Look up the correct spelling.
4. Suggest the correct spelling.
5. Mark the misspelled word so it can be located later with the word processor.
6. Correct the misspelled word.

The program can search through a ten-page document in approximately one

FIGURE 5.12   Screen Display from *Magic Words* Spelling Checker (Magic Words by Artsci Inc., N. Hollywood, CA.)

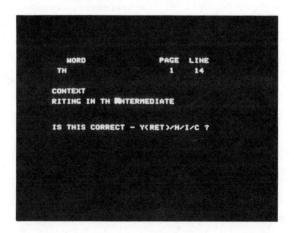

minute (providing there are no errors). Encountering misspellings increases this time to two or three minutes.

Sensible Speller works with many different Apple-compatible word processors such as *Apple Writer, Bank Street Writer, Letter Perfect, Magic Window*, and a host of others. Like *Magic Words*, this program is menu driven. An interesting difference, however, is the program's ability to suggest alternate spellings if an unrecognized word is encountered. This permits the user to survey other words spelled similarly to see if one of the words on the list might be the correct spelling of the unknown word.

Lexicheck IIe.   Unlike the previously described programs, this spelling checker is specifically designed for an Apple IIe with 128K of RAM. It will not work with a 64K machine nor will it work with any word processor except its companion program, *Word Juggler IIe*. The program consists of a 50,000-word dictionary, but additional dictionaries can be created as the user checks the spelling of other documents. Like all the other spelling checkers, *Lexicheck IIe* does not check for capitalization, punctuation, or correct grammatical usage.

One beneficial feature of this program is an on-disk tutorial that walks the first-time user through the checking process. Once the user is ready to proofread documents, they are scanned at a rate of about 7,000 words per minute.

The Benchmark Spelling Checker.   This program is designed to run on an IBM PC or a PC-compatible microcomputer that is using *The Benchmark Word Processing Program*. A 27,000-word dictionary is used to verify the spellings of words contained in the word processing documents. Unusual or low-frequency words can be added to the dictionary, thereby customizing it for specific user applications.

The program is menu driven, although once the spelling checking commences, words and text do not appear on the screen. After the checking has been terminated, the screen displays information that informs the user as to the number of words checked, the number of misspelled words, and the number of "flagged" words. "Flagged" words, in this case, refers to the frequency of misspelled words in the document. Six words, for example, could continually reappear any number of times.

The user can, at any point, check the words in any dictionary and add words to an already existing dictionary. Thus, it is simple to build a customized checking program. Unrecognized words in a document are marked with left and right brackets, thereby making it easy to spot potential misspellings. The user has the option of deciding what action to take whenever a marked word is encountered.

Concluding Remarks.   Having access to a spelling checker that automatically scans documents is indeed enticing. Not only can these programs quickly alert the author to potential misspellings, but they can also enhance an appreciation for correctness when composing. The programs are not without their limitations, however. When one considers that all of the electronic dictionaries have memory restrictions and that words not contained within the dictionaries are identified as potential misspellings, it becomes apparent that documents containing specialized vocabulary are apt to create "bottlenecks" in the checking process. When this occurs, the checker may take more time than the author is willing to spend. Coupled with the fact that spelling checkers are unable to discern the appropriate use of capital letters, don't discriminate between homonyms, and are not able to check grammatical appropriateness of words (e.g., when singular and plural forms of words should be used), it is not surprising that some individuals are skeptical of their use. Nevertheless, for the teacher who wants to instill an awareness of spelling, these electronic dictionaries might be worthwhile investments.

ELECTRONIC THESAURUSES

Electronic thesauruses are more recent developments than spelling checkers. These thesauruses usually require microcomputer systems with two disk drives, since one drive is needed to access the word processing document that has been created while the other diskette contains the thesaurus. This, in addition to their recentness, is why they have not found widespread use in schools. Another reason is that there simply aren't that many electronic thesauruses from which to select.

The operation of a computer-based thesaurus is straightforward. First, the word processed document is loaded into the microcomputer's memory and is brought up on the monitor. Next, the thesaurus is inserted into the second disk drive. The cursor is then moved to the selected word for which a synonym is sought. A keyboard command then activates the thesaurus. The screen usually divides itself with the available synonyms shown on the bottom of the screen. Moving the cursor to the selected synonym and entering a keyboard command "plucks" the word from the thesaurus and enters it into the document under review. All this occurs in a time frame faster than it takes to describe.

Advantages of Electronic Thesauruses

An obvious benefit from such an electronic aid is the speed at which synonyms can be found and inserted into text. More time is spent deciding on the appropriate synonym than is needed to perform the mechanical manipulations necessary to complete the operation. Another advantage is that it doesn't require a separate book cluttering the writer's workspace. Since it is an integral part of the total electronic system, it is easy to recall and use. There is no more fumbling through papers and notes trying to find a misplaced thesaurus since it is available at the touch of a finger. A final benefit is that writers begin to play with the various shadings and meanings of words. The thesaurus (whether paper or electronic) allows them to color their writing to better reflect the intent or mood of a passage.

Limitations of Electronic Thesauruses

Electronic thesauruses are not inexpensive. At this writing, they are available only as part of integrated and expensive word processing packages. Expect to pay between $200 and $400 for an integrated word processing/thesaurus software package. Thus, price alone puts them beyond the reach of many school budgets.

A second limitation is that, unlike their paper- or hardback brethren, electronic thesauruses have memory restrictions, which means that the number of synonyms available per word is usually fewer than that found in a hard-copy version. Whereas an electronic version may have only four or five synonyms per entry, a hard-copy version may have twice that number.

A last caution regarding the use of thesauruses relates to all versions, be they electronic or hard copy. This is what Tamor and Walmsley (1983) describe as an overreliance on the thesaurus. While there is widespread agreement regarding the importance of the thesaurus, they argue that students may be inclined to use it too frequently, and as a result, their writing may reflect an overuse of "million dollar" words. Good writers, they contend, already have broad and active vocabularies and rely on the thesaurus only to jog their memories to allow them to choose between words they already know. Beginning writers should focus on the careful expression of written ideas. The thesaurus can be used thereafter by the author to refine the semantics of a composition thereby producing a polished final copy.

An Example of an Electronic Thesaurus

Peachtext 5000 (Peachtree Software, Inc.) is one example of an integrated information processing package. The company describes the complete system as a "comprehensive personal productivity system for word processing and related information handling tasks." The thesaurus is but one piece in a five-part program. The other components contain a word processor, a spelling proofreader, a list manager and report generator, and an electronic spreadsheet.

When used with an IBM PC or compatible machine, the thesaurus resides in the first disk drive while the word processing document occupies the second drive. To activate the thesaurus a function key is depressed (F10). The thesaurus listing then occupies the lower part of the screen, separated from the document itself by a horizontal broken line. By depressing the right or left arrow keys, a pair of brackets moves horizontally across the list of synonyms. To replace the target word (i.e., the word on which the cursor is located), the synonym in the thesaurus is selected and the Return key is struck. The target word disappears to be replaced by the chosen synonym. The thesaurus is very simple to use—much more so than any word processing program.

SUMMARY

To be considered truly literate, not only must students be able to comprehend written material but so too must they be able to express themselves. Accessibility to word processing programs should provide students with numerous opportunities to draft and edit written documents. The key to written literacy, however, is the teacher. It is important that educators understand not only the importance of writing but that they also are insightful into the process by which students evolve into articulate individuals. Word processors in the hands of individuals who know little about the writing process are apt to have only a minimal impact on the educational process.

This chapter has attempted to describe some applications that have been demonstrated to be meaningful to students as they begin to learn the operation of word processors. Throughout the chapter, the point has been made that the real purpose for writing is to communicate. Writing is not simply the mechanics of grammar or punctuation but is instead a richer, deeper process that develops throughout an individual's life.

This chapter has also illustrated several "user-friendly" word processing programs that are used in schools throughout the country. Many of the features important to users were described and explained. While it is impossible to touch on every word processing software package available, the characteristics found in most popular programs were presented.

In addition to discussing word processing, this chapter also acquainted the reader with electronic dictionaries and thesauruses. The operation, advantages, and limitations of each type of program were also discussed. Finally, examples of currently available programs were presented.

Word processing is a powerful application of computer technology. This decade should mark an exciting time for students since computers and word processing will become more and more a part of their world. Availability of these tools, it is hoped, will play a part in strengthening our written literacy.

RELATED READINGS

KORENBLIT, JOAN, and JUDY PRIVEN. *Language Arts Through Writing.* Chicago: Children's Press, 1984.

Language Arts, Vol. 60, no. 5 (May 1983). Entire issue.

NEWKIRK, THOMAS, and NANCIE ATWELL (eds.). *Understanding Writing: Ways of Observing, Learning and Teaching.* Chelmsford, Mass.: Northeast Regional Exchange, 1982.

MOSENTHAL, PETER, LYNNE TAMOR, and SEAN A. WALMSLEY. *Research on Writing: Principles and Methods.* New York: Longman, Inc., 1983.

SMITH, FRANK. *"Myths of Writing," Language Arts,* Vol. 58, no. 7 (October 1981), 792–798.

_____ *Writing to Learn: A Resource Notebook.* Chelmsford, Mass.: Northeast Regional Exchange, 1982.

REFERENCES

ANDERSON, JOHN J., "Bank Street Writer," *Creative Computing*, Vol. 9, no. 6 (June 1983), 33–34, 37, 39.

BELL, TRUDY, "Computer Literacy: The Fourth R," *Personal Computing*, Vol. 7, no. 5 (May 1983), 63–69.

BENNETT, RANDY ELLIOT, "Applications of Microcomputer Technology to Special Education," *Exceptional Children*, Vol. 49, no. 2 (October 1982), 106–113.

BRADLEY, VIRGINIA N., "Improving Students' Writing with Microcomputers," *Language Arts*, Vol. 59, no. 7 (October 1982), 732–743.

COLLINS, ALLAN, BERTRAM C. BRUCE, and ANDEE RUBIN, "Microcomputer-Based Writing Activities for the Upper Elementary Grades," in *Teaching Writing Through Technology*, Chelmsford, Mass.: Northeast Regional Exchange, 1983.

DACUS, JUDY, and DAVID M. DACUS, "Time Bomb in Educational Computing," *Educational Computer*, Vol. 3, no. 6 (October 1983), 50–51.

DEFORD, DIANE E., "Literacy: Reading, Writing, and Other Essentials," *Language Arts*, Vol. 58, no. 6 (September 1981), 652–658.

ESBENSEN, BARBARA, and THORWALD ESBENSEN, "Word Weaving: Computer-Assisted Creative Writing," *Educational Computer Magazine*, Vol. 3, no. 5 (September 1983), 36–38, 58–59.

FLOWERS, BETTY S., "Madman, Architect, Carpenter, Judge: Roles and the Writing Process," *Language Arts*, Vol. 58, no. 7 (October 1981), 834–836.

GOODMAN, KENNETH, and YETTA GOODMAN, "Reading and Writing Relationships: Pragmatic Functions," *Language Arts*, Vol. 60, no. 5 (May 1983), 590–599.

GRAVES, DONALD H., "How Do Writers Develop?" *Language Arts*, Vol. 59, no. 2 (February 1982), 173–179.

HANLEY-JAMES, SHIRLEY M., "When Are Children Ready to Write?" *Language Arts*, Vol. 59, no. 5 (May 1982), 458–463.

HENNINGS, DOROTHY GRANT, "A Writing Approach to Reading Comprehension," *Language Arts, Vol. 59, no. 1 (January 1982), 8–17.*

HERTZ, ROBERT M., "Problems of Computer-Assisted Instruction in Composition," *The Computing Teacher*, Vol. 11, no. 2 (September 1983), 62–64.

HODGES, RICHARD E., "On the Development of Spelling Ability," *Language Arts*, Vol. 59, no. 3 (March 1982), 284–290.

HOLT, SUZANNE, L., and JOANNE L. VACCA, "Reading with a Sense of Writer: Writing with a Sense of Reader," *Language Arts*, Vol. 58, no. 8 (November–December 1981), 937–941.

KAAKE, DIANNE M., "Teaching Elementary Age Children Touch Typing as an Aid to Language Arts Instruction," *The Reading Teacher*, Vol. 36, no. 7 (March 1983), 640–644.

KIMMEL, STEPHEN, "Hte Proofreader Porgrams," *Creative Computing*, Vol. 8, no. 3 (March 1982), 14, 16, 18–19.

LANGER, JUDITH A., "Reading, Thinking, Writing…and Teaching," *Language Arts,* Vol. 59, no. 4 (April 1982), 336–341.

LICKTEIG, SISTER M. JOAN, "Research-Based Recommendations for Teachers of Writing," *Language Arts*, Vol. 58, no. 1 (January 1981), 44–50.

MARCUS, STEPHEN, and SHERIDAN BLAU, "Not Seeing Is Relieving: Invisible Writing with Computers," *Educational Technology*, Vol. 23, no. 4 (April 1983), 12–15.

MERTON, ANDREW, "Computers in the Classroom," *Technology in the Classroom*, Vol. 3, no. 9 (September 1983), 39–42, 44, 46.

MOFFETT, JAMES, "Reading and Writing as Mediation," *Language Arts*, Vol. 60, no. 3 (March 1983), 315–322, 332.

MORRIS, DARRELL, "Concept of Word: A Developmental Phenomenon in the Beginning Reading and Writing Process," *Language Arts*, Vol. 58, no. 6 (September 1981), 659–668.

RUBIN, ANDEE, "The Computer Confronts Language Arts: Cans and Shoulds for Education," in *Teaching Writing Through Technology*, Chelmsford, Mass.: Northeast Regional Exchange, 1983.

RULE, REBECCA, "The Spelling Process: A Look at Strategies," *Language Arts*, Vol. 59, no. 4 (April 1982), 379–384.

SANACORE, JOSEPH, "Improving Reading Through Prior Knowledge and Writing," *Journal of Reading*, Vol. 26, no. 8 (May 1983), 714–720.

SCHANTZ, LETTY M., "The Computer as Tutor, Tool and Tutee in Composition," *The Computing Teacher*, Vol. 11, no. 3 (October 1983), 60–62.

SCHWARTZ, LAWRENCE, "Teaching Writing in the Age of the Word Processor and Personal Computers," *Educational Technology*, Vol. 23, no. 6 (June 1983), 33–35.

SCHWARTZ, MIMI, "Computers and the Teaching of Writing," *Educational Technology*, Vol. 22, no. 11 (November 1982), 27–29.

SHERMAN, SALLIE J., and KEITH A. HALL, "Preparing the Classroom for Computer-Based Education (CBE)," *Childhood Education*, Vol. 59, no. 4 (March–April 1983), 222–226.

SMITH, FRANK, "Myths of Writing," *Language Arts*, Vol. 58, no. 7 (October 1981), 792–798. "Reading Like a Writer," *Language Arts,* Vol. 60, no. 5 (May 1983), 558–567.

SQUIRE, JAMES R., "Composing and Comprehending: Two Sides of the Same Basic Process," *Language Arts*, Vol. 60, no. 5 (May 1983), 581–589.

TAMOR, LYNEE, and SEAN WALMSLEY, "Using a Thesaurus in the Elementary School: Some Cautions," *Language Arts*, Vol. 60, no. 5 (May 1983), 554–557.

WALL, SHAVAUN M., and NANCY E. TAYLOR, "Using Interactive Computer Programs in Teaching Higher Order Conceptual Skills: An Approach to Instruction in Writing," *Educational Technology*, Vol. 22, no. 2 (February 1982), 13–17.

WATT, DANIEL, "Word Processors and Writing," in *Teaching Writing Through Technology*, Chelmsford, Mass.: Northeast Regional Exchange (1983) 109–111.

WATT, MOLLY, and CHARLES PARHAM, "Child Appropriate Word Processing in the Language Arts Curriculum," in *Teaching Writing Through Technology*, Chelmsford, Mass.: Northeast Regional Exchange, 1983.

WITTROCK, M.C., "Writing and the Teaching of Reading," *Language Arts,* Vol. 60, no. 5 (May 1983), 600–606.

SIX

SPECIALIZED CLASSROOM APPLICATIONS

Upon completing this chapter, you will be able to

— 1. Describe the advantages and limitations of using microcomputer software to determine readability levels.

— 2. Explain the underlying theory behind speed-reading training software.

— 3. Identify the operation of selected programs that permit teachers to design their own instructional material.

— 4. Discuss how spelling ability is acquired and whether commercially available software enhances students' spelling achievement.

— 5. Articulate how administrative software can be used by teachers of reading.

In addition to the many programs already described in this text, there are still others that cannot be classified in any of the previously mentioned categories. Readability analysis and speed-reading software, for example, are two types of programs that should be of special interest to reading teachers yet do not fit into any aforementioned category. Authoring systems and spelling programs might also be used by reading teachers. Reading teachers and supervisors may have a need occasionally to use administrative software for particular applications such as when working with Chapter 1 reading programs. This chapter describes this potpourri of educational software.

READABILITY ANALYSIS PROGRAMS

Readability of instructional materials has long been of interest to educators. This is especially true of teachers of disabled readers, those who have to contend with the day-to-day dilemma of finding material that is of sufficient interest to these readers and yet is easy to read. Commonly, appropriate material for these students is determined by employing a readability formula to compute the reading level. For the most part, these formulas have the user examine such factors as sentence length, number of syllables, or number of frequently used words in a 100-word sample. The formula then yields a score that represents a grade-level approximation of the material.

School Use

Readability software is sometimes used by both the reading teacher trying to find materials that are suitable for individuals with reading problems and librarians establishing special collections of books for poor readers.

FIGURE 6.1   Screen Menu from a Microcomputer Readability Program *(MECC School Utilities,* Volume 2.)

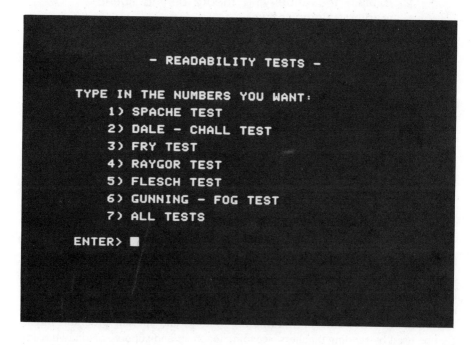

Occasionally, content area teachers might also rely on readability formulas to assist them in selecting textbooks for students. In each of these cases, the teacher attempts to achieve a match between the students' reading level and the material to be read.

Advantages of Readability Software

Anyone who has computed readability levels by hand can attest to its tediousness. Words, sentences, and syllables must be counted to determine the level of the material. Some formulas require that each word be checked against a list of common or uncommon words. Furthermore, most authors of readability formulas suggest that three or more samples be drawn from the material before an accurate representation of readability can be determined.

Readability software greatly eases the chore of determining reading level of materials. Most of these programs simply require the user to type sentence samples (roughly 100 words) on the keyboard, omitting all punctuation except periods. A screen menu (Figure 6.1) permits the user to select the analysis of his or her choice. The computer scans the entered data, and within roughly thirty to sixty seconds the computed analysis appears on the screen.

Computer analysis of text material is quick when compared with hand calculation. To speed the process even more, some teachers even use two computers to expedite the analysis. While one machine is calculating the keyboarded data from a passage, the teacher is busily entering another sample passage on the second computer. Depending upon one's typing ability, using a computer to determine readability can shorten the time needed to conduct an analysis considerably. Using two computers speeds things up even more!

Limitations of Readability Software

There are a number of limitations inherent in readability formulas. First, the formulas are only reflections of difficulty rather than the cause of it. Second, readability formulas only measure a limited portion of what actually constitutes readability. Even their developers recognize that factors such as figurative use of language, technical terms, sentence structure, the coherence of topics, and the connectives used between clauses and sentences all have a bearing on the readability of material. Readability formulas fail to account for these factors. Finally, readability formulas are only indirect measures of reading difficulty. They should not, therefore, be construed as offering guidelines for the rewriting of material. Davison (1984) argues that readability formulas "are such crude models of reading difficulty that they cannot be used to find out anything not already known" (p. 130). Durkin (1981) also questions the value of readability formulas when she states, "The importance schema theory assigns to world knowledge . . . makes it natural to wonder about formulas that fail to consider what a reader knows about the content of a passage" (p. 32).

With these limitations in mind, readers are cautioned to examine readability software with a critical eye. The following programs are offered simply as illustrative examples of existing readability software. As with the other programs mentioned throughout these chapters, readers should not construe these descriptions to be recommendations to purchase particular programs.

Popular Readability Analysis Programs

One program designed to measure readability is the *Readability Analysis Program* (Random House). The popularity of this program is based on the fact that it is able to compute six separate analyses simultaneously. The formulas and a short description of each follow.

1. The Flesch Index—designed to analyze material from fifth-grade through college graduate level. Uses a syllable per sentence average to determine grade level.

2. The Fog Index—designed to analyze grade 6 through graduate-level reading material. It is based on the number of words of three syllables or more as an indicator of difficulty.

3. The Dale-Chall Index—designed to measure fourth-grade through college materials. It is based on two types of counts: average sentence length and percentage of unfamiliar words (i.e., those words that do not appear on the Dale List of 3,000 Commonly Used Words).

4. The SMOG Index—an estimate of grade level that a person must attain to comprehend the text that is being analyzed. This analysis assumes that ten consecutive sentences will be used in the computation.

5. The Wheeler-Smith Index—a primary-grade analysis that is based on the number of polysyllabic words (i.e., three or more syllables).

6. The Spache Index—based on the number of words and sentences and affected by words not on Stone's revision of the Dale-Chall 769 Easy Word List.

To use the *Readability Analysis Program,* the user first selects samples of approximately one hundred words. It is suggested that nine such samples be selected when computing a book's readability. Each sample is entered on the keyboard. Once the words have been typed, a screen menu offering the following options is displayed.

A. Do Another Analysis
B. Primary Analysis (grades 1–3)
C. Regular Analysis (grades 4–adult)
D. Complete Statistics
E. Display Words > 2 Syllables
F. Display Non-Dale Words
G. Display Alpha List
H. Change a Word
I. Change a Stat
J. Add a Word
K. Exit

When option B, the Primary Analysis, is selected, a list of all words on the Dale-Chall Easy Word List, the number of words not on this list, the Spache readability level, and the Wheeler-Smith readability level are generated.

Option C, the Regular Analysis, computes the Dale-Chall Index, the Fog Index, the Flesch Grade Level, the SMOG Index, and an average grade level for the combined Dale-Chall, Fog, and Flesch indices.

A request for complete statistics, option D, produces the number of sentences, number of characters, average number of characters per word, number of words with more than two syllables, the total number of syllables, the number of words, the average number of words per sentence, the average number of syllables per word per sentence, and the readability indices provided under the option C category.

The *Readability Analysis Program* also provides additional features that are beyond the scope of this text. Each of the options is explained in detail in the technical documentation accompanying the program. Programs such as the *Readability Analysis Program* can ease considerably the task of computing readability as determined by existing formulas. Prudence should be exercised, however, when interpreting what these data actually mean.

Another popular readability program is the *Reading Level Analysis* (Bertamax, Inc.). This program also requires at least a hundred-word sample. After the passage(s) have been entered on the keyboard, the program is capable

```
DISPLAY WORDS > 2 SYLLABLES                      COMPLETE STATISTICS
---------------------------                      -------------------

NUMBER OF SYLLABLES       BIG WORD
-------------------       --------       # OF SENTENCES            7
         3                ANOTHER        # OF WORDS                108
         3                POPULAR        # CHARACTERS              559
         5                READABILITY    # WORDS/SENTENCE          15.4
         4                ANALYSIS       # CHAR/WORD               5.1
         3                BERTAMAX       # SYLLABLES/WORD          1.7
         3                CAPABLE        # WORDS > 2 SYLLABLES     20
         3                WHEELER/SMITH
         3                DALE-CHALL
         3                CALCULATED
         3                SIXTY-PAGE     FRY COORDINATES
         3                FORMULA        # SYLLABLES/100 WORDS     170.37037
         3                SHORTCOMINGS   # SENTENCES/100 WORDS     6.48148148
         5                READABILITY
         3                FORMULAS
         4                ADDITIONAL
         3                TECHNICAL      1. ESTIMATED DALE         3.9202
         4                INFORMATION    2. FOG INDEX              13.578836
         4                ANALYSIS       3. FLESCH GRADE LEVEL     13.9451445
         3                PARAGRAPH      4. SMOG INDEX             10.4535599
         3                ANALYZED       AVERAGE (OF 1, 2, AND 3)  10.4
```

FIGURE 6.2   A Microcomputer Readability Analysis (Reading Level Analysis Program, Published by BertaMax Inc., Seattle, WA.)

of computing the Wheeler-Smith Index and Spache Index for grades 1 to 3. For grades 4 and above, the Flesch, Fog, Dale-Chall, and SMOG indices can be calculated. The program includes a sixty-page booklet that explains each formula, cautions the user about shortcomings of using readability formulas, and supplies additional technical information. An actual analysis of this paragraph as it was analyzed by this program is found in Figure 6.2.

SPEED-READING PROGRAMS

Over twenty years ago, I was involved in a large-scale remedial reading program that served a variety of communities. The teachers who worked in this project each were provided with a controlled reader designed to help students overcome their reading difficulties. These machines permitted the user to adjust the rate at which words would be displayed on a screen set up in the room. A shutterlike device would move across the screen revealing words at the predetermined rate. Today, technology has advanced to the point where the projector, screen, and filmstrips are no longer needed. Instead, today's reading teachers have microcomputers and software to provide the same instructional techniques. Some would suggest that these microcomputer pacing programs are nothing more than old wine in new bottles.

The underlying theory of these programs is to improve the user's comprehension by training the eyes to move rapidly across the page. The belief is that efficient eye fixations will lead to more rapid reading and, hence, improved comprehension. The speed-reading programs allow the user to adjust the rate at which words will appear on the screen. As reading rate and comprehension increase, the user can continue to increase the speed at which words appear. Through continuous practice, individuals supposedly become more mature readers.

Advantages of Speed-reading Programs

When compared with the cost of enrolling in a commercial speed-reading course, microcomputer speed-reading programs are a considerable bargain. Most cost less than $75.00 and some even sell for under $50.00. This is substantially cheaper than enrolling in a "course" with an enrollment fee of more than $200.00.

A second advantage of speed-reading software is that it is "user convenient." Unlike a course that meets once per week, the speed-reading software can be used whenever desired. This may be especially advantageous for high school students and adults who often cannot afford to sacrifice an evening to attend a class.

Another advantage of these programs is that they are easy to use. Most of the programs are menu driven; the user simply needs to specify the type of lesson he or she wants to do (e.g., eye movement lesson, columnar reading drill, paragraph reading, or timed test). In most cases the packages contain comprehensive manuals that describe, in step-by-step detail, each program's operation and objectives.

Another positive feature of speed-reading programs is that they contain stories that have widespread appeal for students of many grade levels. Some programs even permit teachers to add stories of their choosing to the diskette, for example, basal reader or content area passages.

A final feature of these programs is that they do an excellent job of student record keeping. Students receive an ongoing profile of their performance regarding reading rate (words per minute) and comprehension accuracy.

Limitations of Speed-reading Programs

With so many commendable features, you might wonder if there are any limitations in speed-reading programs. Indeed, there are several.

First, some programs only present information in uppercase letters. This may present only a minor distraction to the accomplished reader, but to the struggling remedial student, it may be confusing and troublesome. In this author's view, reading material should be presented in as natural a form as possible. The allographs used in print, therefore, should closely resemble those the student will be expected to read. This is especially true with young readers.

Second, some programs provide short phrases that exist in no contextual setting and, hence, are relatively meaningless. Reading should be done in meaningful settings. Simply flashing words, letters, or phrases on the screen may send inappropriate messages to students as to what constitutes the ultimate goal of reading.

Finally and most important is that eye movement training has not been documented to be any more effective than traditional instructional techniques, such as reading printed matter, for improving reading ability. Moreover, the use of eye-training techniques is so outdated that practically no reading methods textbooks or journals advocate its use. In most college and university reading clinics, diagnosing reading eye movements is no longer undertaken. According to Moore (1983), "instruments and practices devoted to training eye movements are the dinosaurs of the reading profession" (p. 16).

While good readers do demonstrate better eye movements than poorer readers, the less efficient movements are only symptoms of poor reading and not its cause. Whereas at one time educators wee quick to recommend eye movement training in an attempt to increase poor readers' reading ability, it was discovered that such reasoning was fallacious and that the teaching efforts were misdirected. Today, it is hoped, we will not pursue that avenue of illogical reasoning.

AUTHORING SYSTEMS AND LANGUAGES

Authoring systems and languages, while having their own unique characteristics, possess a common characteristic; they can be used by educators to design instructional material for students. That common element is why they have been grouped together in this chapter. There are many authoring systems and authoring languages that are available to ease the development of instructional programs. Each of these categories could be a chapter unto itself. But, for the sake of brevity, only an introduction to these programs will be presented. Individuals interested in learning more about these programs might consult any one of a number of textbooks available.

Before exploring the specifics of authoring systems and languages, it is important to understand their origins. By doing so, we gain a better perspective and, hence, appreciation for what their designers have attempted to do.

Authoring software is the result of a need by individuals to produce instructional material without having to learn the intricacies of learning a complex computer language. In a sense, they are a type of shorthand communication that permits the teacher to communicate with the computer. Authoring systems and languages permit the user to design computer-assisted instructional material, usually of a drill-and-practice or tutorial variety, with only a minimum of training.

Many educators feel there is a lack of quality educational software. It is perhaps only natural, then, that teachers feel that they can develop better instructional materials. Authoring systems and languages are intended to ease this task.

Authoring systems are programs that resemble skeletal outlines or templates in the sense that the user simply fills in the template to produce the computer-assisted instructional materials. Generally, these programs require the user to provide information for text material, test questions, anticipated responses, unanticipated responses, feedback responses, and hints. Some systems even permit the user to select from a number of test formats such as multiple choice, short answer, or true and false. Typically, the system includes a record-keeping capability that permits the teacher to examine the scores of individuals who have used the program. Some programs also provide item statistics that are gathered as students are administered the tests.

Authoring systems lack most of the operation or command statements that are available in authoring languages and other programming languages. For this reason, their formats tend to be inflexible. This linear programming style does not permit branching to allow a student to follow a special learning sequence (Cohen, 1983). All students, in other words, pass through the same set of materials; only the learning pace varies.

Authoring languages, while easier to use than standard programming languages such as BASIC, are not nearly as simple as authoring systems. The most popular authoring language is PILOT. PILOT is an acronym for *Programmed Inquiry, Learning or Teaching*. It was devised in the late 1960s to create material for use with college-aged students (Lathrop and Goodson, 1983).

PILOT has become a popular language in some quarters since it was specifically designed for educational applications and is much easier to use than most programming languages. While there are several dialects of PILOT, most of them include less than a dozen frequently used commands such as Type (T), Accept (A), Match (M) and Jump (J). Even the nonprogrammer can begin to visualize how a program might be designed by examining the following short excerpt.

T: Who was the first president of the U.S.?
A: George Washington
A: Washington

In this three-line example, the teacher has specified the question (T, or Text) as well as two acceptable answers (A, or Accept): George Washington or Washington. Notice that in PILOT, the commands are abbreviated, thereby increasing the speed at which a program can be typed on the keyboard.

The relative ease with which instructional materials can be produced with PILOT makes it an excellent language to use for drill-and-practice or tutorial programs. PILOT has more flexibility than an authoring system, but it is more complex to learn.

Advantages

Authoring systems and languages have a number of positive attributes. One of the most important is the fact that they are so easy to learn. This ease of learning increases the chances that teachers will use the programs or languages to create their own instructional material. In this writer's experience, many teachers believed that they could write their own instructional materials using a common language such as BASIC. The lack of time to learn the BASIC language, however, soon dampened any hope that these individuals held about material generation. The simplicity of authoring systems and languages may change that, though. In the matter of a few hours, educators can begin to create their own materials using cloze procedures, multiple-choice activities, and fill-in-the-blank drills (Holmes, 1982).

A second advantage of these programs is that some of the simpler ones are relatively inexpensive. For under $75.00, for instance, teachers can purchase a program that permits them to design simple drill-and-practice materials. (It is important to understand that some authoring systems, however, are much more expensive and may run as much as $300.00 or $400.00!)

Limitations

These programs are not without their limitations. In fact, some authorities believe the limitations are so great that their use is questionable (Roblyer, 1983; Steinberg, 1983; Merrill, 1982). Here are some of the common criticisms levied against these programs.

Perhaps the most frequently heard problem surrounding these programs is the amount of time needed to develop materials. It is not uncommon to spend as

TECHNOLOGY IN THE CLASSROOM

SOME MINI-AUTHORING SYSTEMS

Editor's Note: This table provides information on mini-authoring systems.
Check with the producer/distributor for memory and other hardware requirements.

PRODUCER/ DISTRIBUTOR	PROGRAM NAME	DESCRIPTION	COMPUTERS	COST	NUMBER OF QUESTIONS	STUDENT MANAGEMENT?	SENTENCE PARSER?
APPLE COMPUTER, INC. 10260 Bandley Dr. Cupertino, CA 94017 (408) 996-1010	Shell Games	Multiple choice, true/false, and matching quizzes	Apple II	$30	Unlimited (typically 20-40 per quiz)	No	No
AUTOMATED SIMULATIONS 1988 Leghorn St. Mountain View, CA 94043 (415) 964-8021	Jabbertalky	Four game options including sentences and word scrambling	TRS-80; Apple II; IBM PC	$29.95	Varies with game	No	No
COMPUTATIONS PO Box 502 Troy, MI 48099 (313) 689-5059	Study Quiz File	Question and answer with complete sentence or matching with correct answer number	Apple II; Atari 400, 800	$24.95	30 per file	No	No
	Multiple Choice File	Multiple choice test	Same	$24.95	30 per file	No	No
COMPUTER ADVANCED IDEAS 1442-A Walnut St., #341 Berkeley, CA 94709 (415) 526-9100	The Game Show	Game based on "Password" with words and definitions	Apple II	$39.95	30-40 per subject	No	Yes
	Tic-Tac Show	Tic Tac Toe board with questions and answers	Apple II	$39.95	18 per subject	No	Yes
EDUCATIONAL COURSEWARE 3 Nappa Lane Westport, Conn. 06880 (203) 227-1438	Testing Series (5 disks)	Tests include multiple choice, true/false, completion, matching and spelling	Apple II	$160 or $35 each	Up to 100 per test; 60 tests per disk	No	No
HARTLEY Dimondale, MI 48821 (616) 942-8987	Create Series	Six programs with variety of lesson and game formats	Apple II	$26.95	Unlimited	Yes	Varies with each one
THE LEARNING CO. 4370 Alpine Rd. Portola Valley, CA 94025 (415) 851-3160	Magic Spells	Scrambled word spelling game	Apple II; TRS-80	$45 (Apple); $40 (TRS-80 cassette); $55 (TRS-80 disk)	Unlimited	No	No

FIGURE 6.3   Some Mini-Authoring Systems ("Mini-Authoring Systems" from Electronic Learning, March 1984. Copyright© 1984 by Scholastic Inc. Reprinted by permission of Scholastic Inc.)

much as two hundred hours to produce one hour of instructional material. Even with some of the simpler programs, the author has found that teachers developing material for their own classrooms need fifty to seventy-five hours to develop an hour's worth of material. Whether teachers are willing to spend this amount of time is a question that remains to be answered.

A second limitation of authoring systems is that while the programs are easy to learn, teachers soon become disenchanted with the simple, linear programming paradigm that is used as a template. Unlike some commercial programs that include branching capabilities, authoring systems do not permit

MECC 2520 Broadway Dr. St. Paul, MN 55113 (612) 638-0613	Teacher Utilities Package Vol. 1	Crossword and hidden word puzzles, tests, and posters	Apple II	$37	About 100	Yes	Yes
MONUMENT COMPUTER SERVICE Village Data Ctr. Box 603 Joshua Tree, CA 92252 (619) 365-6668	The Professor	Lesson and test questions	Apple II	$49.95	50 per lesson; 400 per disk	Yes	Yes
MSSS D INC. 3412 Binkley Dallas, TX 75205 (214) 522-8051	Create A Lesson	Lesson and test questions	Apple II (Commodore & IBM by April 15, 1983)	$125	Unlimited	Yes	Yes

JOSEPH PETERSON 35 Tobey Brook Pittsford, NY 14534 (716) 385-2997	Wordsearch	Puzzle in which players find word in string of letters	TRS-80	$15	Up to 30 lines	No	No
RADIO SHACK EDUCATIONAL DIVISION 1400 One Tandy Center Fort Worth, TX 76102 (817) 390-3832	Quick Quiz	Multiple choice quiz	TRS-80	$39.95	Up to 40	Limited	No
RANDOM HOUSE SCHOOL DIVISION Dept. 9039 400 Hahn Rd. Westminster, MD 21157 (800) 638-6460	Quiz Master	Lesson and multiple choice quiz	TRS-80; Apple II	$49.50 (disk versions); $39 (TRS-80 cassette)	Disk—40; Cassette—20	Yes	No
SCHOLASTIC WIZWARE 902 Sylvan Ave. Englewood Cliffs, NJ 07632 (201) 567-7900	Square Pairs	Matching boxes of information	Apple; Atari; TI; VIC-20	$39.95 (Apple and Atari); $29.95 (TI and VIC-20)	Unlimited	No	No
TEACHING TOOLS PO Box 50065 Palo Alto, CA 94303 (415) 493-3477	Spelling Package	Spelling test	PET; Apple II	$99.95 (includes tape recorder interface)	Up to 50 items	No	No
TYC 40 Stuyvesant Manor Geneseo, NY 14450 (716) 473-2858	Individual Study Center	Matching and completion tests and games	Apple II; TRS-80	$54.95 (Apple); $59.95 (TRS-80 disk); $69.95 (TRS-80 cassette)	50 per set	No	No
XPS INC. 323 York Rd. Carlyle, PA 17013 (717) 243-4373	Drill Instructor	Question and answer test	Apple II	$39.95	400 per disk	No	Yes

* A sentence parser gives the teacher the option of allowing for more than one correct answer. For example, it will accept "L" as well as "left" as correct and will allow for misspelling.

FIGURE 6.3 (continued)

users (to any great degree, at least) to pursue alternate paths to learn similar information. In most of these systems, everyone is exposed to the same material. Only the rate at which students pass through the content is varied.

Another limitation of these programs is that many are very unsophisticated. Unlike simulations that are highly engrossing, authoring systems and languages are primarily designed to drill or tutor students. Individuals often find the programs to be tedious and boring. In many cases, the programs are nothing more than electronic workbooks or dittos.

A final criticism is not directed at the programs as much as it is at the individuals who produce the content. Scandura (1981) has argued that in order to develop quality programs, the user must be knowledgeable about subject matter as well as the rudiments of instructional design, a combination that few people possess. For this reason, many of the computer-assisted instruction programs that have been developed by educators are of an uneven quality and have limited appeal to students.

Examples of Authoring Systems

One of the easiest types of program on which to create personalized software is what Bockman (1983) calls "miniauthoring systems." These systems allow the user to use an existing program template but to add information specific to a teacher's needs. Two popular miniauthoring systems are *The Game Show* and *Tic Tac Show* (Computer Advanced Ideas). Both are drill-and-practice games that permit the user to play with the existing information contained in the program editor, or additional data diskettes can be made by the teacher to impart information about virtually any topic.

The Game Show program pits two contestants against each other. The contestants are teamed with two players who appear in the program: Joe and May. The objective of the game is to accrue as many points as possible by trying to guess a mystery word in the least number of tries. Clues are given before each try, and the quicker the answer is provided, the more points a team gathers.

Programs like *The Game Show* can be excellent sources of motivation for reluctant or disabled readers. Popular topics sure to interest students would be sports figures or teams. Some individuals might enjoy trying to name popular recording artists. In today's society, it is important not to stereotype interests by gender, so be aware that students' interests might be quite different from those a generation ago. It's necessary, therefore, not to have preconceived ideas about sexual preferences.

Teachers wanting to design their own activities for use with *The Game Show* would first think of topics and clues. Suppose, for example, a teacher wanted to design a game entitled "Hockey Teams." Some of the clues developed for the game might be

1. They play in the Adams Division.
2. Their nickname is a bear.
3. It is one of the game's oldest franchises.
4. It is an East Coast team.
5. Bobby Orr is a former player.
6. Gerry Chevers is a former goalie.
7. Rick Middleton is a star.
8. They own their arena.
9. Former great was Phil Esposito.
10. Red Sox play in this city.
    (Answer: The Boston Bruins)

Students can also design games using any number of topics. The resourceful teacher might even have a schoolwide contest between reading groups that come to him or her for reading assistance. These easy-to-use programs permit even the novice computer user to design personalized instructional software. A list of some other popular miniauthoring systems is given in Figure 6.3.

A more comprehensive authoring system is *Courseware Development System I,* or *CDS* (Bell and Howell). This program permits the teacher to develop curricular materials in which students are presented information, asked questions, and provided feedback. The system automatically keeps track of student performance as they move through the program.

CDS is organized into two modes. The first, the authoring mode, allows the teacher to prepare the instructional material. The second, the presentation mode, presents the teacher-developed materials to the child. The building blocks of the *CDS* are called sections. Each section consists of seven parts. A brief description of each part follows:

1. Text Pages—This is where information is presented to the student.
2. Question—Once the student has read the text pages, he or she is questioned about the material.
3. Correct Answer Group or Responses—Anticipated answers expected from the child are specified.
4. Wrong Answer Groups and Responses—These are responses that are unacceptable but are within the realm of possible responses. The teacher may offer remedial feedback to correct misconceptions held by the student.
5. Unanticipated Answer Responses—Since it is impossible to anticipate every conceivable response to a question, this subsection allows the teacher to supply feedback when an unexpected answer is given.
6. Failure Message—This is the response provided to the student when an unacceptable answer is given.
7. Hints—Hints are clues that can be provided if desired. Since the *CDS* program permits the teacher to specify the number of trials per question, it is frequently desirable to provide hints to assist students.

Here is an excerpt from a lesson entitled "What Am I?" composed by a reading teacher.

Text Page 2

WELCOME TO "WHAT AM I?"
THE COMPUTER WILL GIVE YOU CLUES.
CAN YOU GUESS WHAT I AM?

Text page 2

I HAVE RED SKIN.

Question: 1

WHAT AM I?

Correct Answer Group: 1

APPLE
APPEL
APPL   (Here the teacher has allowed for six possible spellings.)
APEL
APL
APLE

Response:

THAT'S RIGHT, I AM AN APPLE.

Unexpected Answer Response:

ASK FOR A HINT.

Failure Message:

DON'T WORRY. LET'S TRY THE NEXT ONE.

Hint: 1

I GROW ON A TREE.

Hint: 2

YOU CAN MAKE PIES FROM ME.

The teacher continues to program sections using this template. When finished, he or she saves the entire lesson onto a blank diskette.

Another authoring system that differs substantially from the *CDS* program is *The Learning System* (Micro Lab Learning Center). This system also allows the user to create tutorial programs but has the added feature of being able to create fill-in, matching, or multiple-choice tests. Once the tests are created and have been administered to students, test item statistics are generated, thereby providing an analysis of pupil performance. This summary can then be used to determine if a weakness exists in the instructional program or in the test items.

Another feature of *The Learning System* is that material can be administered on the computer or be reproduced on a connected printer. This option can come in handy especially if only a limited number of computers are available for student use.

This program also includes a management system that stores students' test performances. This feature permits the teacher to call up names of students and examine their individual test scores. When connected to a printer, the program will print the student's name followed by the tests taken, the percentage scores, and the average percentage score.

Two limitations of this system are that two disk drives are desirable (but not necessary) and that the three diskettes require the frequent changing of disks between the drives. These limitations notwithstanding, the system is easy to use and offers a number of features not found in other authoring systems.

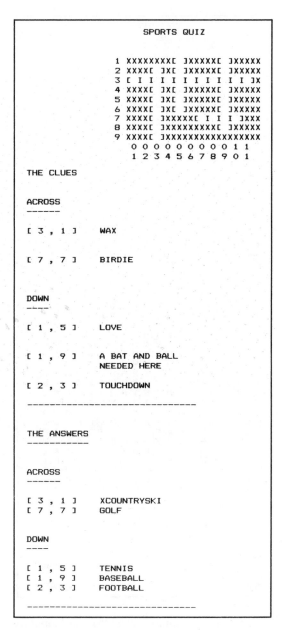

```
                              SPORTS QUIZ


                    1 XXXXXXXXC JXXXXXC JXXXXX
                    2 XXXXC JXC JXXXXXC JXXXXX
                    3 C I I I I I I I I I I JX
                    4 XXXXC JXC JXXXXXC JXXXXX
                    5 XXXXC JXC JXXXXXC JXXXXX
                    6 XXXXC JXC JXXXXXC JXXXXX
                    7 XXXXC JXXXXXC I I I JXXX
                    8 XXXXC JXXXXXXXXXC JXXXXX
                    9 XXXXC JXXXXXXXXXXXXXXXXX
                      0 0 0 0 0 0 0 0 0 1 1
                      1 2 3 4 5 6 7 8 9 0 1

        THE CLUES


        ACROSS
        ------

        C 3 , 1 J    WAX


        C 7 , 7 J    BIRDIE



        DOWN
        ----

        C 1 , 5 J    LOVE


        C 1 , 9 J    A BAT AND BALL
                     NEEDED HERE

        C 2 , 3 J    TOUCHDOWN

        ------------------------------------

        THE ANSWERS
        -----------

        ACROSS
        ------

        C 3 , 1 J    XCOUNTRYSKI
        C 7 , 7 J    GOLF


        DOWN
        ----

        C 1 , 5 J    TENNIS
        C 1 , 9 J    BASEBALL
        C 2 , 3 J    FOOTBALL

        ------------------------------------
```

FIGURE 6.4
A Microcomputer-Generated
Crossword Puzzle

TEACHER UTILITY PROGRAMS

Teacher utilities is a catchall title that encompasses programs that can be used to fulfill special requirements such as making crossword puzzles and tests. The utilities do not require learning a new language since most of them are menu

```
                    COMPUTERS

. . . . . . . . D I S K    D R I V E E .
. . . . . . . . . . R . . . . . L . .
. . . . . . . . . O . . . . . P . . .
. . . . . . . . T . . . . E P . . . .
. . . . . . . . I . . . R A . . . . .
. . . . . . N . . . . A . . . . . . .
. . . . . O . . . . W . . . . . . . .
. . . . M . . . . T . . . . . . . . .
. . . . . . . F . . . . . . . . . . .
. . . . . . O . . . . . . . . . . . .
. . . . . . S E . . . . . . . . . . .
. . . . . . R . . . . . . . . . . . .
. . . . . A K Y . . . . . . . . . . .
. . . . . W . R E . . . . . . . . . .
. . . . D . O . . Y . . . . . . . . .
. . . R . M . . . . B . . . . . . . .
. . A . E E . . . . . O . . . . . . .
. H . M T . . . . . . . A . . . . . .
. . . Y . . . . . . . . R . . . . . .
. . B . . . . . . . . . . D . . . . .

IF YOU WISH, YOU MAY INSERT A DITTO
MASTER AT THIS TIME.  PRESS THE RETURN
KEY WHEN YOU WANT THE PUZZLE TO PRINT.


                    COMPUTERS

S Z U H S T C W D I S K   D R I V E E T
B G V X T G N L E D A R P T Q N C L F E
F R N P T L F T J K O J G D Q Y P M M T
R E U E Q J V C N T U M X R E P X Q X I
O X F U F L H J I Z Q M G R A Y V G S N
F R U K H V C N X F X N A Q K A L I A P
G O F M F S O E B W R W K Z R T X U L J
G E M Q U M Y P O I T P B K S N P W J U
I B G M M F V V D F X C Y U Y K O G K G
D U M G X E M M O J S I H U T B E F O E
A J S L X K Q S E U T O P Y F T L J H H
T M C F U Y H R R I C N B E I F H A P A
C S T Z G X A K Y R P I P U L F P P Q Z
Z S A K T W K R E G I G F U I T H W I H
T A Q I D M O S Y Y P Q C E R K B S R W
T U U R O M L D R C B U I H E Z I I A Y
V M A D E E U Q P V C O T D F Q Z R G I
K H Q M T Q B M D Y I U A S O Z T W W S
J Y Q Y Z H W M Q B O Y V R B A W C C Y
T N B K T I T E J T Y F V U D F Y Y Z D


THERE ARE 8 WORDS HERE - CAN
YOU FIND THEM?

HERE ARE THE WORDS TO LOOK FOR:

APPLE                      BYTE
DISK DRIVE                      HARDWARE
KEYBOARD                   MEMORY
MONITOR                    SOFTWARE
```

FIGURE 6.5
A Word Search Puzzle
Generated by a Microcomputer

driven and only require straightforward input from the user.

Some utility programs, such as *MECC—Elementary—Language Arts,* Volume 2, permit the user to create crossword puzzles by simply typing the clues and the target word. The computer automatically formats the grid accompanied by the words supplied by the developer (Figure 6.4). A second example of a teacher utility program is Hartley's *Wordsearch.* This program permits a teacher to enter a series of words to be used in a word search puzzle.

Program options permit the user to specify whether overlapping words should be used as well as the directions the words may run (e.g., frontward, backward, diagonally, left to right, or top to bottom) (Figure 6.5). A third example of a utility program is *Banner* (Sam Wilson & Associates). As the name implies, *Banner* is a program that creates banners using letters of various specified sizes. Using specified codes, a variety of character fonts may be produced.

MICROCOMPUTER SPELLING PROGRAMS

Spelling is typically taught in the elementary school by providing students with lists of words to be committed to memory. Each week, students' mastery of these words is checked with a criterion-referenced test. Students who do well on the test supposedly demonstrate spelling competence. This type of instruction lends itself well to programming materials on the microcomputer.

Most spelling software programs use the stimulus-response (S-R) model in an attempt to improve spelling ability. Some programs provide an aural stimulus and then require students to reproduce the correct spelling on the keyboard. Other programs incorporate gamelike formats to encourage student participation. Virtually all programs rely on lists of words on which students drill themselves. It is important to understand the advantages and limitations of using this model when teaching spelling using the computer.

Advantages

Using a microcomputer to teach spelling permits the teacher to assign lessons, according to need, throughout the school year. Better spellers quickly master easier lessons and can move on to more advanced skills. Poorer spellers work at a slower pace. Some programs permit the teacher to predetermine lesson assignments. Through a password system, only identified students are able to access specific lessons.

A second advantage in using computer-assisted spelling is that a variety of practice formats can be selected. By using the same word list but altering the program format, students receive repeated instruction on the same words but in a variety of settings. This may result in transfer of learning outside the spelling practice sessions.

A third advantage is that students can work on spelling lists as time permits. The computer can patiently drill them, over and over, whenever scheduling permits. No longer must the entire class march together through the same lessons at the same time.

Limitations

According to some experts, learning to spell lists of words and learning to spell may be two different processes (Rule, 1982). While some individuals believe that learning to spell is based on memory and simply requires repeated drill until words are committed to memory, a closer examination of our orthography reveals that this is not necessarily the case. This is because spelling is largely a predictable act based on the regularity of our language. In fact, spelling instruction should not focus exclusively on the graphic components of our language (which is what many spelling programs do) but rather should emphasize the phonological aspects. The regularity of our orthographic system was demonstrated when Hanna and his associates examined 17,000 words. They discovered that the spelling of 15,000 words could be accounted for by consistent phonological and morphological rules (Hodges, 1982). This led them to believe that language is predictable and specific generalizations can be taught to improve students' spelling. Since spelling is a predictable representation of speech, it is probably best not taught as rote memorization.

A second limitation of spelling software is that most programs fail to

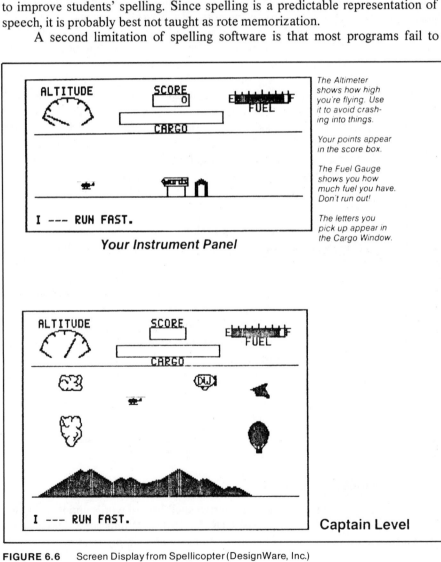

FIGURE 6.6   Screen Display from Spellicopter (DesignWare, Inc.)

account for the spelling stages through which students pass. These are not linear stages but instead are recognizable points where children become increasingly aware of the function of language and print and develop a deeper understanding of how the many factors of language interact with one another. According to Morris (1981), there are four spelling stages through which learners pass, from primitive prephonetic spelling to more mature correct spelling. These nonrigid stages represent a continuum of learning.

Another limitation of most spelling software is that the programs tend to isolate spelling as a separate topic rather than integrate it as part of a broader language arts approach toward learning. The outcome of such instruction frequently results in students who perform beautifully on the weekly spelling tests only to misspell these same words hours later on other written assignments. When spelling is placed in a broader context, such as in the preparation of a

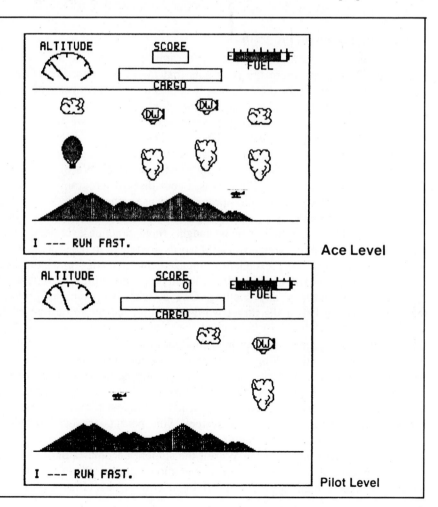

Ace Level

Pilot Level

composition, correct spelling may not be the major goal to be accomplished. But most teachers would agree that before a final draft of the paper is submitted, students should have enough pride in their work to scan it for misspellings. This is what we must emphasize in spelling—pride. Good spellers are those who eventually spell the word correctly. Morris (1981), in support of such a position, states, "it is in the context of a supportive, natural language environment that children may have the best opportunity to develop conceptual knowledge about words" (p. 667). It is only through this type of rich language environment that the true importance of spelling and writing is learned. This is because learning to be a good speller is learned not only in school but wherever print is encountered.

To summarize, spelling is not a low-order skill that can be simply drilled until words are learned. The fact that there are so many different words to be learned prohibits a simple stimulus-response model from being applied. Instead, learning to spell is a complex cognitive task that continues throughout life.

Popular Spelling Programs

The quality of computer spelling programs varies considerably. At one end of the continuum, there are programs that might be better identified as "copying" programs, since the user simply copies words from a list supplied on the screen—a mindless task at best. On the other hand, some programs do a respectable job in helping students to become better spellers. Five programs will be briefly described in this section. They are *The Spelling System* (Milliken Publishing Company); *Spellicopter, Spellakazam,* and *Spellagraph* (all from DesignWare); and *DragonWare: Spelling Bee Games* (Edu-Ware).

The Spelling System (Milliken) is a four-diskette program that covers grades 3 to 10. The program is appropriate to use with remedial-, developmental-, or enrichment-level students. Each lesson contains three parts: a brief introduction to the skill to be taught, three practice exercises, and a mastery test. In all, approximately 1,400 words are taught in the system. High-resolution graphics, an excellent management system, and thorough documentation are the earmarks of the Milliken program. Some of the exercises, however, require little if any spelling. One activity, for example, provides the student with a list of the target words accompanied by an outline of the configuration of the word to be spelled. Students must copy the word from the top half of the screen to the outlined configuration. Whether activities of this type lead to improved spelling is questionable. A management system is also part of the program. Students can be assigned specific lessons through a password system. Once the practice activities have been completed, the child takes the mastery test provided on the diskette. Student files are stored and accessed through this management system. This permits teachers to call up class or individual records in a matter of seconds.

Using *Spellicopter* (Design Ware), the student becomes a pilot and tries to fly a mission of transferring letters over mountainous terrain and around hazardous objects such as storms and flying enemy objects (Figure 6.6). This program is a drill-and-practice, arcade-type game. Four hundred words, divided into forty word lists, are used in *Spellicopter*. The correct spelling of a letter is selected by flying the helicopter over each letter, finding the appropriate one, and pressing the space bar. Once the order of letters has been determined, the pilot flies back to his or her home field and presses the Return key. A scoreboard accumulates points as well as bonus points for safe flying. The pilot also must safely return with the correctly spelled word before running out of fuel.

The arcade-type format of this program makes it an appropriate choice for a remedial setting. Another positive feature of this program is that students must determine the missing word from a sentence context (e.g., The _____ ran to the store). Once students become proficient pilots, they can increase the skill level of the game by selecting to be a "Captain" or an "Ace."

Another arcade-type spelling game is *Spellakazam* (DesignWare). This program requires the student to move a pac-man–type creature around the screen picking up letters in correct order. The creature must outrace a fast-moving magician. Keyboard control allows movement in all four directions. Like *Spellicopter*, this program requires the user to determine the missing word from a sentence context and then to spell the omitted word correctly. Three skill levels can be selected. Between twenty and thirty words are available on each spelling list. The program is simple to use and is entirely menu driven. Students may select to study five, ten, or thirteen words from a list. Thus, the amount of time needed to play the game can vary somewhat.

The contextual application of spelling words is an excellent feature of this program. Students must not only *read* and comprehend, but they must also *spell* the word correctly. Feedback is supplied through statements such as "You spelled the words correctly on the first try four out of five times. Words that you need to practive are . . .". One unanswered question regarding this program and others like it is, "Is the amount of time and energy needed to play the game in line with the purported payoff in improved spelling ability?" Since a considerable amount of time and effort is needed to manipulate the pac-man character on the screen, some teachers may feel that this time may be better devoted to writing or other more conventional spelling activities. Unfortunately, there is no clear-cut answer to this question.

Spellagraph (DesignWare) is reminiscent of the television game *"Concentration."* Students are required to spell a word missing from a sentence context. Each time the correct spelling is supplied, a square from a matrix reveals part of a rebus message. The message "Home is where the heart is" is shown in Figure 6.7. Figure 6.8 illustrates a partially revealed rebus message.

An advantageous feature of this program, and others like it, is the capability of making personalized data diskettes, thereby enabling a teacher to design his or her own spelling lists. The cloze technique is also an excellent way of forcing students to attend to meaning within sentences. When combined with the gamelike format of programs such as *Spellagraph*, both reading and spelling should improve.

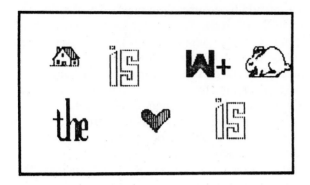

The rebus says
"Home is where the heart is."

FIGURE 6.7   Rebus Message from Spellagraph (DesignWare, Inc.)

FIGURE 6.8   Partially Revealed Rebus Message from Spellagraph (DesignWare, Inc.)

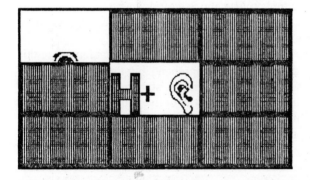

DragonWare: Spelling Bee Games (Edu-Ware) actually contains four different games: *Squadron, Skyhook, Puzzle,* and *Convoy.* In order to play the first two, however, game paddles must be connected to the computer. (This points out the importance of determining the hardware needed to run a program before actually investing in any computer software. Unless game paddles are connected to the computer, half of the programs on this diskette are unusable.) Program selection is very simple, since it entails simply selecting the game from the supplied menu (Figure 6.9). Twenty-two study units are available on the diskette. They include the following skills:

1.   Simple two-and three-letter words
2.   More simple three-letter words
3.   Four-letter, one-syllable words
4.   Double vowel/consonants

FIGURE 6.9 Spelling Bee Games Menu (Courtesy of Peachtree Software, Inc.)

5. Hard c's/silent e's
6. More hard c's/silent e's
7. One syllable with diphthongs
8. More with diphthongs or consonants
9. Simple multisyllable words
10. Difficult multisyllable words
11. Directions and numbers
12. Shapes
13. Animals
14–22. Assorted words

These units are typical of the spelling categories found in many of the commercially available programs.

Squadron pits two players against each other. Using the game paddles, each player attempts to fly to the word illustrated in high-resolution graphics. Points are scored for each correct response. This is *not* a spelling game; rather, it is a drill of reading isolated vocabulary words from a list.

Skyhook is similar to *Spellicopter* in that a helicopter moves across the screen controlled in this case by game paddles. The student attempts to pick up scrambled letters in the correct order. It is impossible, however, to pick the letters up in the incorrect order. Up to four players may play the game, each attempting to accrue the most points and become the winner.

Puzzles is a "Concentration"–type game where the target word appears in the lower right-hand corner of the screen. A six-celled matrix hides the picture of the target word. The objective of the player is to find the picture represented by the supplied word. Obviously, no spelling ability is required in this activity. Instead, this is another case of students having to read words in isolation.

The last game on the diskette, *Convoy,* does assess spelling ability. A picture appears in the upper-left portion of the screen. The right side of the screen is used as a slate on which students construct the correct spelling of the word. As each correct letter is typed on the screen, a truck inches across the bottom of the screen. The first truck to reach the right-hand edge of the screen scores a point. Up to four players may play the game at one time.

There are many different types of activities that are used to teach students spelling. Some of these activities require decoding rather than encoding. Other programs require virtually no spelling or reading ability. They simply require students to choose letters from a supplied array. Still other programs fail to use spelling words in contextual settings. For these reasons, teachers are urged to use special caution when selecting programs to enhance their spelling programs. Theoretical issues aside, the fact that some programs use such questionable procedures to teach spelling should make the buyer of spelling software especially wary.

ADMINISTRATIVE SOFTWARE

Reading teachers, supervisors, or administrators are sometimes responsible for maintaining student reading records. The format of the records varies considerably, however, from district to district. In small districts without reading supervisors, the reading teacher may be responsible for simply keeping student rosters and test scores. In larger systems where someone oversees the total system's reading program, though, there may be the need for more extensive record keeping such as reports, test summaries, school reading score profiles, and district reading averages. The size of the district, to a degree, plays a part in determining what type of record keeping is needed.

For the most part, administrative software is based on the principles of data base management. Typically, these programs manipulate data according to user-defined specifications. Before the manipulations can be performed, though, information such as the student's name, address, telephone number, parents' names, grade, school, and test scores must be entered into the computer. Once these data have been entered, they can be sorted or retrieved in an infinite number of ways. Typical applications for these programs might be to list names of students who need to be evaluated by a school reading specialist, to generate student count reports, or to print mailing labels (Bennett, 1982). Budgetary and special services information is also easy to call up once it is entered into the data base.

A few school districts have experimented with using computers to store, retrieve, and produce Individualized Educational Plans for students (Williams,

Smith, and Esch, 1981). Some of these programs also include the option of selecting a computerized listing of educational materials that have been matched to learning objectives. This permits a teacher to assign activities that can be used to correct a reading disability.

It is only recently that sufficiently powerful microcomputers have been able to perform many of the administrative functions required in school settings. (Some individuals may argue that low-cost microcomputers with adequate memory are still unavailable.) Today, most of the technical problems found in earlier microcomputers have been surmounted. This, plus the fact that there has been a rapid decrease in computing costs—no longer is expensive time sharing necessary—means that many of the obstacles that have delayed computer use by school administrators have been overcome (Jones and Dukes, 1983). This is not to say there are still not limitations. It does imply, however, that computers are now available to a much larger percentage of administrators than ever before.

Advantages of Administrative Software

A major advantage of administrative software is that it permits the user to have untold amounts of information at his or her fingertips. Schedules, rosters, budget information, plus a host of other applications are available in simple-to-use programs. Never before has such convenience been available. Some software even permits the user to customize the programs to fit explicit school system needs. Never before have so many programs provided the user with access to information that heretofore was difficult or impossible to access.

Another advantage of administrative software is that it reduces the amount of repetitive paperwork. Before computers, paper-and-pencil or typewritten editions of rosters, inventories, and the like needed to be completely redone whenever a change was made. These software packages, however, allow the easy addition and deletion of information without the necessity of retyping entire rosters. Producing an up-to-date report is as easy as activating a printer and pressing a button on the computer's keyboard.

Limitations of Administrative Software

One of the major limitations a reading supervisor or administrator will find with administrative software is cost. A simple data base program, with no predefined templates, may cost more than $200.00. It is not unusual to find some data bases running upwards of $500.00. Unless there is an explicit need for this type of program, reading personnel may find it difficult to justify such expenditures.

A second limitation may arise when the size of some school districts' information bases becomes so large that the data to be stored exceeds the memory capabiities of the machine. Adding a hard disk drive to the computer system may be the solution to this problem. A hard disk drive operating system may add $1,000 to $2,000 to the price of the system, however. This added hardware, in turn, may not be able to run the software, since adding an additional component to the operating system of some computers affects their ability to run the software.

A final limitation may be the complexity of the software itself. Unlike most classroom applications software, many administrative packages are complex and less user-friendly than software designed for students. Furthermore, the program may be so specific in intent that few others in the district may understand its operation. This can be a problem if the system fails to operate and the vendor is unavailable to render quick assistance. Or the user may discover that the software may not be able to produce the type of reports needed. It behooves users, therefore, to be thoroughly trained with its operation before beginning to add information to the data base. It is conceivable that untold amounts of data could be entered before it is discovered that the program may be unable to produce the needed documents. Even worse, an inappropriate keyboard command could result in the loss of important information.

An Example of Administrative Software

One popular software product that a reading teacher, administrator, or supervisor might find valuable is *PFS: School Recordkeeper* (Software Publishing Corporation). This program can be adapted to fit a number of different purposes.

School Recordkeeper consists of four ready-to-use diskettes that work with two other PFS products: *PFS: File* and *PFS: Report.* Together with the *PFS* products, *School Recordkeeper* permits a user to maintain student records; keep tabs on budgetary and requisitioned items; monitor the inventory of a project, school, or room; and schedule special events. Each diskette comes with between five and eight predefined forms that are ready to use. A total of over thirty different forms are included as part of the program. A few of the forms found on the respective diskettes include:

DISKETTE 1—STUDENT RECORD MANAGEMENT

Parent Mailing Labels
Student List
Student/Parent Information
Teacher Class Report
Student Emergency Data
Test Score Warning Report
Special Program Registration
Dominant Language Report

DISKETTE 2—BUDGET AND REQUISITION CONTROL

Year-to-Date Budget Balance for All Departments
Year-to-Date Budget Balance for All Accounts
Outstanding Requisitions Year-to-Date
Items Returned for Credit

DISKETTE 3—SCHOOL PROPERTY MANAGEMENT

School Property Report
Property by Location
Property by Funding Source
Property Values by Category
Property Being Repaired
Maintenance Cost Analysis
Property on Loan

DISKETTE 4—ROOM AND EVENT SCHEDULING

Teacher Locator
Room Fixtures Locator
Public Events Calendar

These are only samples of some of the predefined forms for which information can be retrieved. To begin using the program, the user must first input data that will later be recalled. To use the Student Record Management program, for example, a data form must first be completed (Figure 6.10). Information is required from a number of areas such as name, grade, the counselor's last name, parents' name, and so on. The complete form appears in Figure 6.11. Obviously, reading personnel may not have a need for all this information and, hence, may decide to omit some of these data or modify the form to fit their own purposes.

Once the Student Record Form is completed for all students, mailing labels can be printed (Figure 6.12), Student Lists drawn up (Figure 6.13), Student/Parent Information provided to all teachers (Figure 6.14), Teacher Class Reports generated (Figure 6.15), Dominant Language Reports provided (Figure 6.16), plus a number of other reports produced.

Each of the other three diskettes included in this program operates in a similar fashion. Figure 6.17 is the form that must be completed to obtain information related to budget and requisition control, Figure 6.18 is the form for property management, and Figure 6.19 the form for room and event scheduling.

While many data base management systems permit the user to define forms, the advantage of *PFS: School Recordkeeper* is that the forms are already generated. Furthermore, the program is exceedingly easy to use. Reading personnel who have the need to maintain extensive records, such as Chapter 1 directors or teachers, may find programs of this type enable them to get out from under some of the paperwork that frequently accompanies the job.

SUMMARY

This chapter has explored six different classroom and administrative applications that may be of value to teachers of reading. The value of each type of program depends on two factors: the need for the software and the user's

```
FULL NAME:
STUDENT#:     GRADE:
COUNSELOR:
TEACHER/ROOM:
LOCKER#/LOCK#:
COMBINATION:
PARENT(S):
ADDRESS:
CITY/ST:
ZIP:    HOME TEL:
CONTACT1/TEL:
CONTACT2/TEL:
BUS#:    STOP#:
ENROLLMENT CODE:
BIRTHDATE:
MALE:    FEMALE:   RACE:
HOME LANGUAGE:
DOMINANT LANGUAGE:
MEDICAL TREATMENT APPROVAL (Y/N/?):
TRANSPORTATION APPROVAL (Y/N/?):
DOCTOR/TEL:
HOSPITAL:
MEDICAL CONDITIONS:
VACCINATIONS NEEDED:
CODE1:    CODE2:
CODE3:    CODE4:
CODE5:    CODE6:
TEST1:    TEST2:
TEST3:    TEST4:
TEST5:    TEST6:
PARENTAL INVOLVEMENT:
```

FIGURE 6.10

Student Record Form from *PFS: School Recordkeeper* (PFS® is a registered trademark of Software Publishing Corp.)

```
FULL NAME: WISEMAN ERIC
STUDENT#: 216  GRADE: 7
COUNSELOR: JOHNSON
TEACHER/ROOM: PETERS/111
LOCKER#/LOCK#: 342/123
COMBINATION: 09-06-22
PARENT(S): EZRA WISEMAN
ADDRESS: 2225 ROY ST.
CITY/ST: SUNNYTOWN WI
ZIP: 54701  HOME TEL: 831-7854
CONTACT1/TEL: MOTHER/831-7854
CONTACT2/TEL:
BUS#: 01  STOP#: 01
ENROLLMENT CODE: DISTRICT 2
BIRTHDATE: 73/09/25
MALE: M  FEMALE:   RACE: CAUCASIAN
HOME LANGUAGE: HEBREW/ENGLISH
DOMINANT LANGUAGE: HEBREW/ENGLISH
MEDICAL TREATMENT APPROVAL (Y/N/?): Y
TRANSPORTATION APPROVAL (Y/N/?): Y
DOCTOR/TEL: JONES/864-2176
HOSPITAL: MEMORIAL
MEDICAL CONDITIONS: SOME ALLERGIES
VACCINATIONS NEEDED: NONE
CODE1:    CODE2:
CODE3:    CODE4:
CODE5:    CODE6:
TEST1:    TEST2:
TEST3:    TEST4:
TEST5:    TEST6:
PARENTAL INVOLVEMENT: PARENT VOLUNTEERS
```

FIGURE 6.11

Complete Student Record Form from *PFS: School Recordkeeper* (PFS® is a registered trademark of Software Publishing Corp.)

```
EZRA WISEMAN                    JENNIFER OTTO
2225 ROY ST.                    2431 WAYCROSS LANE
SUNNYTOWN WI   54701            SUNNYTOWN WI   54701



WILLIAM OEHLKERS                ROGER KLUMB
60 ROGERS AVE.                  21 SHAWNO ST.
SUNNYTOWN WI   54701            SUNNYTOWN WI   54701



MANUEL CARDOZA                  HARRY L. BROWN
3435 ELM ST.                    4741 LAFAYETTE DRIVE
SUNNYTOWN WI   54701            SUNNYTOWN WI   54701



JOHN LI                         ARTHUR ANDERSON
1 CRESENT DRIVE                 16 MAPLE BLUFF RD.
SUNNYTOWN WI   54701            SUNNYTOWN, WI   54701



DAVID GUSTAFSON
5 NOLOP HILL RD.
SUNNYTOWN WI   54701
```

FIGURE 6.12 Mailing Labels Printed from *PFS: School Recordkeeper* (PFS® is a registered trademark of Software Publishing Crop.)

FIGURE 6.13 Student List Generated from *PFS: School Recordkeeper* (PFS® is a registered trademark of Software Publishing Corp.)

```
FULL NAME: ANDERSON LAURA  GRADE: 7      FULL NAME: WISEMAN ERIC   GRADE: 7
COUNSELOR: JOHNSON                       COUNSELOR: JOHNSON
TEACHER/ROOM: FRANKS/102                 TEACHER/ROOM: PETERS/111
LOCKER#/LOCK#: 413/215                   LOCKER#/LOCK#: 342/123
COMBINATION: 09-22-21                    COMBINATION: 09-06-22

FULL NAME: BROWN STEPHEN   GRADE: 7      FULL NAME: LI KIM  GRADE: 7
COUNSELOR: JOHNSON                       COUNSELOR: JOHNSON
TEACHER/ROOM: PETERS/111                 TEACHER/ROOM: FRANKS/102
LOCKER#/LOCK#: 234/391                   LOCKER#/LOCK#: 101/211
COMBINATION: 01-24-31                    COMBINATION: 21-23-09

FULL NAME: CARDOZA WILLIAM  GRADE: 7     FULL NAME: OEHLKERS ANN   GRADE: 7
COUNSELOR: JOHNSON                       COUNSELOR: JOHNSON
TEACHER/ROOM: PETERS/111                 TEACHER/ROOM: PETERS/111
LOCKER#/LOCK#: 513/522                   LOCKER#/LOCK#: 323/301
COMBINATION: 02-09-11                    COMBINATION: 30-21-13

FULL NAME: GUSTAFSON RICHARD  GRADE: 7   FULL NAME: OTTO, MELISA   GRADE: 7
COUNSELOR: JOHNSON                       COUNSELOR: SMITH
TEACHER/ROOM: PETERS/111                 TEACHER/ROOM: FRANKS/102
LOCKER#/LOCK#: 444/121                   LOCKER#/LOCK#: 321/776
COMBINATION: 21-31-12                    COMBINATION: 01-05-29

FULL NAME: KLUMB HEIDI   GRADE: 7
COUNSELOR: JOHNSON
TEACHER/ROOM: PETERS/111
LOCKER#/LOCK#: 542/511
COMBINATION: 22-31-01
```

STUDENT/PARENT INFORMATION

STUDENT	PARENT(S)	ADDRESS	CITY/ST	ZIP	CONTACT1/TEL	CONTACT2/TEL
ANDERSON LAURA	ARTHUR ANDERSON	16 MAPLE BLUFF RD.	SUNNYTOWN, WI	54701	FATHER/832-9856	MOTHER/832-6548
BROWN STEPHEN	HARRY L. BROWN	4741 LAFAYETTE DRIVE	SUNNYTOWN WI	54701	FATHER/832-6665	JIM BROWN/832-9955
CARDOZA WILLIAM	MANUEL CARDOZA	3435 ELM ST.	SUNNYTOWN WI	54701	MOTHER/832-6612	
GUSTAFSON RICHARD	DAVID GUSTAFSON	5 NOLOP HILL RD.	SUNNYTOWN WI	54701	FATHER/832-6578	MOTHER/832-4512
KLUMB HEIDI	ROGER KLUMB	21 SHAWNO ST.	SUNNYTOWN WI	54701	FATHER/822-5476	MOTHER/834-2226
LI KIM	JOHN LI	1 CRESENT DRIVE	SUNNYTOWN WI	54701	MOTHER/833-6541	
OEHLKERS ANN	WILLIAM OEHLKERS	60 ROGERS AVE.	SUNNYTOWN WI	54701	MOTHER/831-2154	
OTTO, MELISA	JENNIFER OTTO	2431 WAYCROSS LANE	SUNNYTOWN WI	54701	MOTHER/832-9678	
WISEMAN ERIC	EZRA WISEMAN	2225 ROY ST.	SUNNYTOWN WI	54701	MOTHER/831-7854	

FIGURE 6.14 Student/Parent Information from *PFS: School Recordkeeper* (PFS® is a registered trademark of Software Publishing Corp.)

```
                              TEACHER CLASS REPORT
TEACHER/ROOM        STUDENT        M   F      PARENT(S)        CONTACT1/TEL       CONTACT2/TEL
------------     ----------------  -   -   ----------------   ---------------   ------------------
FRANKS/102       ANDERSON LAURA        F   ARTHUR ANDERSON    FATHER/832-9856   MOTHER/832-6548
                 LI KIM                F   JOHN LI            MOTHER/833-6541
                 OTTO, MELISA          F   JENNIFER OTTO      MOTHER/832-9678

        COUNT:                    3   0   3


                              TEACHER CLASS REPORT
TEACHER/ROOM        STUDENT        M   F      PARENT(S)        CONTACT1/TEL       CONTACT2/TEL
------------     ----------------  -   -   ----------------   ---------------   ------------------
PETERS/111       BROWN STEPHEN     M       HARRY L. BROWN     FATHER/832-6665   JIM BROWN/832-9955
                 CARDOZA WILLIAM   M       MANUEL CARDOZA     MOTHER/832-6612
                 GUSTAFSON RICHARD M       DAVID GUSTAFSON    FATHER/832-6578   MOTHER/832-4512
                 KLUMB HEIDI           F   ROGER KLUMB        FATHER/822-5476   MOTHER/834-2226
                 OEHLKERS ANN          F   WILLIAM OEHLKERS   MOTHER/831-2154
                 WISEMAN ERIC      M       EZRA WISEMAN       MOTHER/831-7854

        COUNT:                    6   4   2

                              TEACHER CLASS REPORT
TEACHER/ROOM        STUDENT        M   F      PARENT(S)        CONTACT1/TEL       CONTACT2/TEL
------------     ----------------  -   -   ----------------   ---------------   ------------------

                 ----------------  -   -
        COUNT:                    9   4   5
                 ----------------  -   -
```

FIGURE 6.15 Teacher Class Report from *PFS: School Recordkeeper* (PFS® is a registered trademark of Software Publishing Corp.)

```
                DOMINANT LANGUAGE REPORT
DOMINANT LANGUAGE          STUDENT        M   F
-----------------       ----------------  -   -
ENGLISH                 ANDERSON LAURA        F
                        BROWN STEPHEN     M
                        GUSTAFSON RICHARD M
                        KLUMB HEIDI           F
                        OTTO, MELISA          F

          COUNT:                       5   2   3

ENGLISH/GERMAN          OEHLKERS ANN          F

          COUNT:                       1   0   1

HEBREW/ENGLISH          WISEMAN ERIC      M

          COUNT:                       1   1   0

KOREAN                  LI KIM                F

          COUNT:                       1   0   1

PORTUGUESE              CARDOZA WILLIAM   M

          COUNT:                       1   1   0
          ----------------------------  -   -
COUNT:          5                      9   4   5
          ----------------------------  -   -
```

FIGURE 6.16
Dominant Language Report from *PFS: School Recordkeeper* (PFS® is a registered trademark of Software Publishing Corp.)

```
REQUISITION#:
REQUISITION DATE:
ACCOUNT#:    DEPT:
ITEM DESCRIPTION:
QUANTITY:
ESTIMATED COST:
DELIVERY DATE:
REQUESTED BY:
SUGGESTED VENDOR:
PO#:    PO DATE:
DATE RECEIVED:
ACTUAL COST (DELETE ESTIMATE):
DATE RETURNED (DELETE COST):
REMARKS:
BUDGET:
```

FIGURE 6.17
Budget Form from *PFS: School Recordkeeper*
(PFS® is a registered trademark of Software
Publishing Corp.)

```
SCHOOL PROPERTY#:
DISTRICT PROPERTY#:
ITEM DESCRIPTION:
MANUFACTURER/MODEL#:
SERIAL#:
CATEGORY CODE:
LOCATION:
SCHOOL DEPARTMENT:
PURCHASE DATE:
PO#:    COST:
FUNDING SOURCE:
SUPPLIER:
ITEM CHECKED OUT TO:
ROOM#:
DUE DATE:
SERVICE VENDOR:
TEL#:
DATE FIRST REPAIRED:
DATE THIS REPAIR:
REPAIR COST1:
REPAIR COST2:
REPAIR COST3:
REPAIR COST4:
REPAIR COST5:
REPAIR COST6:
DATE NEXT MAINTENANCE:
MAINTENANCE COST1:
MAINTENANCE COST2:
MAINTENANCE COST3:
MAINTENANCE COST4:
MAINTENANCE COST5:
MAINTENANCE COST6:
REMARKS:
```

FIGURE 6.18
Property Management Form from *PFS: School Recordkeeper*
(PFS® is a registered trademark of Software Publishing Corp.)

understanding of how students learn.

Two readability programs were reviewed. Suggestions describing how these programs may be used were offered, and the advantages and limitations of this type of program were discussed. Readers were cautioned that readability is more complex than many readability formulas make it out to be.

The introduction of microcomputers into schools has brought about the reintroduction of speed-reading programs. Whereas pacing devices have been used for well over twenty years, microcomputers offer a new vehicle by which

```
BLDG/ROOM:     INTERCOM#:
CLASS:
TEACHER:     PERIOD:
EVENT:
SCHOOL/PUBLIC EVENT (S/P):
DATE:     DAY:
START TIME:     END TIME:
SPONSOR:
SPEAKER:
AV EQUIP:
STAFFING:
CUSTODIAL INSTRUCTIONS:
AV/STAFF/ROOM RENTAL FEE:
DEPOSIT/PAYMENT:
RECEIPTS:
ROOM TYPE:
ROOM RENTAL:
MAX SEATING:
ROOM FIXTURES:
```

FIGURE 6.19
Room and Even Scheduling Form from *PFS:*
School Recordkeeper (PFS® is a registered trademark of
Software Publishing Corp.)

this "old wine" may be introduced. Of crucial importance is the fact that these programs are based on symptoms of reading difficulty and not on the cause. As such, the reader was warned of their use.

Authoring systems and languages were described and a number of different examples were offered. Authoring systems range in complexity from the simple to the intricate. The intent of these systems and languages is to permit educators to design their own instructional material. While this is indeed a noble goal, several impediments to this task were highlighted.

Utility programs are also designed to make the teacher's job easier. Several examples of programs were given and specific programs that accomplish specified tasks were identified.

Each day, more and more software companies are advertising new microcomputer spelling programs. The pros and cons of using software to teach spelling were presented, and four popular spelling programs were discussed. At issue is the question of whether spelling software actually increases the spelling accuracy of students.

Finally, uses of administrative software were discussed. An example of one program, *PFS: School Recordkeeper,* was used to describe how a reading teacher, supervisor, or administrator could use this program to reduce paperwork and keep records on a variety of topics.

RELATED READINGS

BURKE, ROBERT L. *CAI Sourcebook.* Englewood Cliffs, N.J.: Prentice-Hall, Inc., 1982.

DAVISON, ALICE. "Readability Formulas and Comprehension." In *Comprehension Instruction: Perspectives and Suggestions.* Gerald Duffy, Laura R. Roehler, and Jana Mason, eds. New York: Longman, Inc. (1984) 128–144.

MOORE, DAVID W. "What Research Did Not Say to the Reading Teacher: A Case Study," *The Reading Teacher,* Vol. 37, no. 1 (October 1983), 14–19.

WALKER, DECKER F., and ROBERT D. HESS. *Instructional Software: Principles and Perspectives for Design and Use.* Belmont, Calif.: Wadsworth Publishing Company, 1984.

REFERENCES

BENNETT, RANDY ELLIOT, "Applications of Microcomputer Technology to Special Education," *Exceptional Children,* Vol. 49, no. 2 (October 1982), 106–113.

BOCKMAN, FRED, "Creating Your Own Software with Mini-Authoring Systems," *Electronic Learning,* Vol. 2, no. 6 (March 1983), 72–75.

COHEN, VICKI BLUM, "Criteria for the Evaluation of Microcomputer Courseware," *Educational Technology,* Vol. 23, no. 1 (January 1983), 9–14.

DAVISON, ALICE, "Readability Formulas and Comprehension," in *Comprehension Instruction: Perspectives and Suggestions,* Gerald Duffy, Laura R. Roehler, and Jana Mason, eds. New York: Longman, Inc. (1984) 128–144.

DURKIN, DOLORES, "What Is the Value of the New Interest in Reading Comprehension?" *Language Arts,* Vol. 58, no. 1 (January 1981), 23–43.

HODGES, RICHARD E., "On the Development of Spelling Ability," *Language Arts,* Vol. 59, no. 3 (March 1982), 284–290.

HOLMES, GLYN, "Computer-Assisted Instruction: A Discussion of Some Issues for Would-be Implementors," *Educational Technology,* Vol. 22, no. 9 (September 1982), 7–13.

JONES, KENNETH, and THOMAS DUKES, "Microcomputers in School Administrative Management," *Educational Technology,* Vol. 23, no. 3 (March 1983), 38–39.

LATHROP, ANN, and BOBBY GOODSON, *Courseware in the Classroom,* Menlo Park, Calif.: Addison-Wesley Publishing Company, 1983.

MERRILL, PAUL F, "The Case Against PILOT: The Pros and Cons of Computer-Assisted Instruction on Languages and Authoring Systems," *Creative Computing,* Vol. 8, no. 6 (July 1982), 75–77.

MOORE, DAVID W., "What Research Did Not Say to the Reading Teacher: A Case Study," *The Reading Teacher,* Vol. 37, no. 1 (October 1983), 14–19.

MORRIS, DARRELL, "Concept of Word: A Developmental Phenomenon in the Beginning Reading and Writing Process," *Language Arts,* Vol. 58, no. 6 (September 1981), 659–668.

ROBLYER, M. D., "The Case For and Against Teacher-Developed Microcomputer Courseware," *Educational Technology,* Vol. 23, no. 1 (January 1983), 14–17.

RULE, REBECCA, "The Spelling Process: A Look at Strategies," *Language Arts,* Vol. 59, no. 4 (April 1982), 379–384.

SCANDURA, JOSEPH M., "Microcomputer Systems for Authoring, Diagnosis, and Instruction in Rule-Based Subject Matter," *Educational Technology,* Vol. 21, no. 1 (January 1981), 13–19.

STEINBERG, ESTHER, R., "Reviewing the Instructional Effectiveness of Computer Courseware," *Educational Technology,* Vol. 23, no. 1 (January 1983), 17–19.

WILLIAMS, WARREN S., ROBERT SMITH, and WAYNE ESCH, "Using New Computer Software Products to Manage and Report Educational Data," *Educational Technology,* Vol. 21, no. 2 (February 1981), 46–51.

SEVEN

SELECTING SOFTWARE

Upon completing this chapter, you will be able to

— 1. Explain the differences between software and courseware.

— 2. Identify the procedures to follow when reviewing reading software.

— 3. Define what is meant by the term "pedagogical adequacy."

— 4. Evaluate reading software using the Microcomputer Reading Software Review Form.

The earliest attempts to offer instruction via the computer were quite different from the computer-assisted instruction (CAI) we know today. Initial offerings relied on large mainframe computers connected to school-located terminals via telephone lines (Budoff and Hutten, 1982). The number of instructional programs available for these large computers was limited in comparison to today's standards. Relatively few programs were available to run on these expensive behemoths. Another difference is that whereas large, mainframe computers used curriculum materials developed by teams of programmers, content area specialists, psychologists, and other experts, much of the microcomputer software of the 1980s has been prepared by programmers and educators entering the software business for the first time. These small-scale operations have been referred to as "cottage industries." The emergence of this cottage industry has resulted in a wide disparity of software quality. Some (Thomas and Gustafson, 1983) feel that the electronics industry in particular does not understand the needs of the classroom. Moreover, even if they did, this would not guarantee that a company would be able to market a high-quality educational package. Compounding the problem further are the developmental costs of producing and marketing educational software. These expenses are so great that many companies are unable to field test the materials adequately before releasing them for public consumption. One estimate of the cost to produce a high-quality software program is $10,000 per instructional hour (Gleason, 1981).

Despite the high costs to produce good materials, the publication of educational software has roughly paralleled the microcomputer explosion. In the 1980-81 school year, sales of educational software totaled approximately $10.7 million. While this appears to be a lucrative market, projected annual sales for 1985 are $75 million (Hofmeister, 1982)! As more and more individuals attempt to capitalize on this burgeoning market, the quality of software will continue to vary, from programs lacking in technical and informational aspects to those that maximize the full capabilities of the microcomputer. This chapter is designed to alert the reader to the pitfalls that await the unwary user.

AN OVERVIEW OF EDUCATIONAL SOFTWARE

Programs for school microcomputers are categorized as either software or courseware. Software refers to the computer program—usually available on floppy disk, cassette tape, or plug-in cartridge—and the instructions or documentation describing the operation of the program. Courseware connotes a more complete educational package. The documentation, for example, is usually more comprehensive. In addition to the operating instructions, course-ware also may include supplemental worksheets, background information describing how to use the software, and suggested follow-up activities.

The application of CAI to content areas is still in a shakeout period. Initially, many individuals in school districts purchased microcomputer hard-ware before examining the availability of software. Unfortunately, this led to some situations where teachers had access to microcomputers but found only a few usable programs. Availability of programs, however, does not guarantee that effective CAI will automatically ensue. According to Holmes (1982), some programs are inappropriate either because of breadth of coverage or a method-ological bias. Fortunately, as microcomputers become more prevalent in schools, the quantity and quality of educational software should improve and these problems will be overcome.

The use of microcomputers to supplement instruction has several advan-tages. For one thing, most software allows students to progress at their own rate, skipping unneeded instruction and focusing instead on those facets that are most relevant (Spencer and Baskin, 1983). Another desirable feature is that computers can serve as tireless tutors for students who need practice on particular skills. Reading teachers remark over and over again that this capability provides the added drill that many remedial students need but that they are unable to provide. A third feature is the continual feedback that computers provide. Students seem to thrive on knowing—almost immediately— how they are doing on a particular lesson. Finally, many programs are designed with a built-in management component that automatically tabulates students' responses. These management systems allow teachers to monitor student progress and tailor instruction to students' needs (Huntington, 1981).

Even with these advantages, educators should remember several facts. First, the computer does not replace traditional instruction but supplements it. Most software programs can, at best, cover only a small portion of any curriculum; hence, they are best suited to complement instruction provided by the teacher. Most software is not designed actually to instruct students but, instead, to drill them on previously presented materials. Second, software should be selected to complement classroom instruction and the existing curriculum. If a unit on affixes, for example, is to be taught, a teacher might consider using software packages that also cover this skill. When educators overlook the need to integrate software, the result is that programs become used in isolation, with no apparent link to day-to-day classroom activities or student needs. The computer is used, in other words, simply because it is available, not because students need specific skill instruction. Perhaps most important is the fact that CAI in the hands of a mediocre teacher will probably result in ineffective instruction. As Holmes (1982) states, "a good machine cannot replace a bad teacher" (p. 10). In the end, the software selected, along with an appropriate understanding of the values and limitations of CAI, will determine whether microcomputers reach the potential that many foresee. Indeed, the next decade should prove interesting as educators attempt to integrate the theoretical aspects of CAI with the realities of the classroom.

AVAILABILITY OF READING SOFTWARE

The dynamic nature of the software publishing industry makes it impossible to determine the exact number of software packages available for teachers of reading. Wedman (Judd, 1983), however, after reviewing reading software from 32 publishers' catalogs, sheds some light on what reading teachers can expect to find in the way of software. According to Wedman, during the early 1980s, 253 microcomputer programs were available to help teach reading skills. Most of the programs—143, or 57 percent—were designed to teach decoding skills. Of this group, 50 percent focused on phonic skills, 20 percent taught structural analysis skills, 20 percent taught dictionary skills, 5 percent covered sight vocabulary words, and 6 percent attempted to teach use of contextual analysis.

Ninety-five programs, or 38 percent, were categorized as attempting to teach comprehension skills. Of this group, 72 percent covered vocabulary-building exercises, 20 percent attempted to reinforce literal comprehension, and 8 percent focused on interpretive comprehension.

Wedman's final category, study skills, accounted for only 15 (6 percent) of the 253 programs. These programs covered such areas as organizing skills, reading maps, charts, and graphs, using resource materials, and improving reading rate.

If we were to extrapolate these data to today's reading software market, we could conclude the following:

1. Most reading software is designed to teach decoding skills.
2. Most of the decoding software focuses on phonic analysis skills.
3. Only a small percentage of existing software attempts to provide assistance in using contextual analysis (i.e., the syntactic and semantic cueing systems).
4. Most materials designed to reinforce comprehension skills do so through vocabulary expansion exercises.
5. Few programs provide instruction in higher-level comprehension activities.
6. There is a dearth of study skills software.

Published Software Reviews

While microcomputers have the potential for increasing teacher effectiveness, instructional effectiveness is determined by both the quality of the teacher and the instructional materials available. Assuming that all of us are first-rate reading teachers, how can we be sure of selecting software that is of high quality? One fairly painless way to find appropriate software is by reading microcomputer magazines that examine software through a reviewing process.

A number of *educational* computing magazines regularly carry reviews of microcomputer software. Some of the more popular publications, along with their addresses, are

Classroom Computer News
Box 266
Cambridge, Mass. 02138

Educational Computer
Box 535
Cupertino, Calif. 95015

Electronic Education
Suite 220
1311 Executive Center Drive
Tallahassee, Fla. 32301

Electronic Learning
902 Sylvan Ave.
Englewood Cliffs, N.J. 07632

The Computing Teacher
Department of Computer and Information Science
University of Oregon
Eugene, Ore. 97403

Recently, a plethora of *general* computing publications have also appeared on the market. Most of these contain reviews of educational as well as noneducational microcomputer software. While it is impractical to list all these magazines, a few of the more popular ones are

Byte
70 Main Street
Petersborough, N.H. 03458

Creative Computing
Box 789-M
Morristown, N.J. 07690

80 Microcomputing
80 Pine Street
Peterborough, N.H. 03458

Info World
375 Cochituate Rd.
Framingham, Mass. 01701

PC
Ziff-Davis Publishing Company
One Park Ave.
New York, N.Y. 10016

In addition to these, more and more national, regional, and state journals published by reading and language arts professional groups are including columns devoted to microcomputers and software reviews. *The Reading Teacher*, published monthly by the International Reading Association, for example, instituted a regular column entitled "The Printout" in the fall of 1983. *The Journal of the New England Reading Association* also carries regular reviews of popular microcomputer software that can be used to teach reading and the language arts. Both of these journals, along with *Language Arts*, published by the National Council of Teachers of English, frequently have articles that discuss microcomputers and language arts software. There is even a quarterly publication for educators entitled *Computers, Reading and Language Arts* that provides articles on practical applications of classroom computers, reviews of courseware and books, information on new curriculum materials, and guest editorials.

Published reviews are not without their limitations, however. Kurland (1983) contends that the focus on individual programs tends to perpetuate the tradition of a narrow educational focus. Software, he believes, needs to be evaluated in the context in which it will be used if a complete analysis of its worth is to be studied. Individually published reviews tend to examine the programs out of context and, hence, may not explore all facets of use that a teacher may need to understand.

Another shortcoming is that reviews are sometimes written by individuals without sufficient knowledge of the reading process. Typically, these reviews are done by staff writers for educational or computer magazines. Usually, these authors possess excellent credentials for making technical software evaluations, but they frequently lack knowledge about how children learn to read and, as a result, may believe a program is better than it actually is. The author can recall reading one review of a speed-reading program that received an outstanding review in a nationally published computer magazine. Reviewing the program from a reading professional's perspective, however, revealed that it was based on questionable theoretical grounds that had twenty years earlier been demonstrated to have an insignificant impact on the reading rate of students. Here was an example of outdated pedagogy wrapped with high-technology trimmings.

Published reviews, therefore, must be read with caution. Whenever possible, it is preferable to compare two or more reviews on the same software package. This tends to reduce the risk of purchasing programs that may be inappropriate for the intended purpose.

In this author's opinon, some of the best reviews of reading and language arts software are those available from the Educational Products Information Exchange (EPIE). EPIE, in collaboration with the Microcomputer Resource Center at Teachers College, Columbia University, the Consumers Union of the U.S., and a consortium of large school districts, began evaluating educational software and printing reviews of tested materials in 1982. These reviews are available under the name PRO/FILES (Figure 7.1). The 1984 price of this set of reviews was $265.00 including shipping. While not inexpensive, when one considers that most educational software retails for $30.00 and higher, several inappropriate software purchases can quickly pay for the price of the PRO/

FIGURE 7.1   EPIE PRO/FILES Kit (Educational Products Information Exchange (EPIE) Institute.)

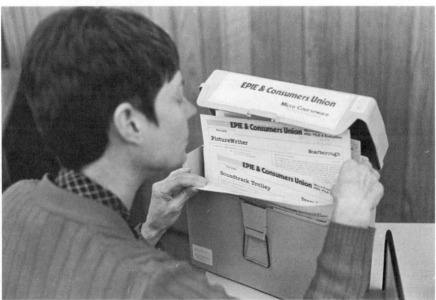

FILES. The complete set of reviews included in the PRO/FILES kit can be ordered from

EPIE Institute
P.O. Box 839
Watermill, N.Y. 11976
(516) 283-4922

The advantage of the PRO/FILES reviews over many other published reviews is that the EPIE materials are the combined efforts of many individuals. Steinberg (1983) contends that software reviewers should have content matter knowledge, teaching experience, and knowledge of the computer-assisted instruction. Furthermore, she states that a thorough review should include input from individuals from each area. The EPIE reviews appear to meet these criteria (Figure 7.2).

Typical PRO/FILES reviews include information about the hardware needed to run the program; the components of the courseware; an overall rating of instructional as well as software design; analysts' summaries; general program structure; a description of how the teacher can use the program; the instructional-educational value of the program; summaries of what other reviewers have said about the program; observational reports on student users; statements about the objectives, contents, methods and approach; and remarks on the evaluation and management capabilities of the program.

Reviewing Your Own Reading Software

While an increasing number of publishers are including software reviews in their magazines, only 20 percent of the existing software has been reviewed (Lathrop, 1981; Merton, 1983). That means that users must assume responsibility for evaluating much of what exists in today's marketplace.

A variety of evaluation forms have been proposed throughout the literature. The length and quality of these forms vary greatly. On one hand, some are amazingly short and simply require placing check marks under identified categories. Typically, a statement such as "Content is clear and logical" is offered. The reviewer then places a check mark in one of the following columns: Strongly Agree, Agree, Disagree, Strongly Disagree, or Not Applicable. Other forms are more open ended and require the reviewer to respond in a narrative fashion to statements such as "Briefly describe the program mentioning any strengths or weaknesses." Still other types of forms require reviewers to use a Likert Rating Scale, whereby a numbering system is used to denote educational quality. The numeral 2, for instance, may indicate complete agreement with a statement such as "Uses Correct Grammar and Spelling," a numeral 1 partial agreement, and a 0, no agreement.

After using several varieties of forms, consumers are often struck by two facts. First, evaluating the educational quality of software is exceedingly difficult when a quantitative (i.e., numbering) system is used. Second, few if

Language Arts

Word Attack

Davidson & Associates

HARDWARE CONFIGURATION (*used for analysis)

Apple II, II Plus*, IIe   64K
IBM Personal Computer   64K IBM DOS

COMPONENTS

	PRICE
2 Disks, 43-page User's Guide	$49.95
Backup Disk	$10.00

PRODUCER

Davidson & Associates
6069 Groveoak Place No. 12
Rancho Palos Verdes, CA 90274
213-378-3995

USERS SPECIFIED BY PRODUCER

Grades 4-12
Ages 8-adult
Individuals

CONTENT TOPICS

9-level vocabulary building
27 sets of 25 words

Teacher- or student-created
content possible

CURRICULUM ROLE

Language Arts
Supplemental
Drill & Practice
Educational Gaming

COPYRIGHT

1983

AUTHORS

Janice G. Davidson
Richard K. Eckert, Jr.

OVERALL RATING OF INSTRUCTIONAL DESIGN   9/10

OVERALL RATING OF SOFTWARE DESIGN   8/10

ANALYSIS SUMMARY   May 1983

WORD ATTACK is a very well designed program for practicing and improving vocabulary. Learning is effectively reinforced with four separate activities for each set of vocabulary words, and the words are grouped into nine levels of difficulty. The variations in difficulty between levels is not great enough to support the wide target audience; able fifth graders could use the first levels of the program while students preparing for the S.A.T. would benefit from, but might not be sufficiently challenged by, the more difficult levels. The excellent editing feature that is part of the program allows the teacher to customize the program, however, by adding word lists. The program is quite interactive, allowing the student to call on "help" and to recycle missed items as well as choose the level of difficulty and whether to practice adjectives, nouns, or verbs. The arcade-style game is motivating and can only be played well by students who have succeeded at the more mundane activities in the program. There is no management system or permanent recordkeeping to facilitate classroom use.

After determining the lesson to be run, the student selects one of the four activities: word display, multiple-choice quiz, sentence completion, or the word attack game. The only tedious part of the program is the introduction of the vocabulary: word display. A word is displayed (without pronunciation guides), then a brief definition is displayed under it, and then the word is used in a sentence. For class use of the program, study sheets make more sense. The next suggested activity is the multiple-choice quiz. An elapsed time clock adds interest to the drill, which can be played with either vocabulary words or definitions as the given. Sentence completion requires the student to remember and spell the appropriate word from the set. The student can call on "help" for a list of four options. In the word attack activity, a brief definition appears on the screen and the student positions a small attacker beneath the correct answer, of the four vocabulary words displayed, and shoots it. Three keys are used for these screen manipulations. The game can be played at one of three speeds, and the faster the student answers, the more points are scored. Bonus points are scored by hitting an occasional interloper that travels across the screen. Sound effects in the word attack activity are optional.

RECOMMENDATIONS TO THE PRODUCER

1. Include a management system for classroom use.
2. Include pronunciation guides in the word display activity.

INSTRUCTIONAL & SOFTWARE DESIGN

Goals & Objectives	Contents	Methods & Approach	Evaluation & Management
• Goals and objectives are supported by the content	• 4 activities for each of 27 lists of 25 words	• Presentation enhances the content	No evaluation of student mastery of content other than activity scores
Developer's Rationale "Designed to teach you new words, their meanings and their usages in an interesting and exciting way."	**User Appropriateness** Content is appropriate for grades 6–8 through 12 Level differences are not distinct but difficulty does increase	**Technical Quality/Warranty** Both disks must be loaded before activities can be used 1-year replacement of defective or damaged disks	**Tests** User's guide has suggestions for using activities for placement No tests
Development Evidence Upward Bound students with whom the program was field tested are described as having "significantly improved their reading vocabularies."	**Accuracy and Fairness** No problems noted	**Documentation/Teacher's Guide** Operating instructions are clear Word lists and placement suggestions are helpful	**Branching** None
Learner Objectives "...recall, use, and spell the word(s) correctly."	Editing feature can be used to expand the program scope	**User Control** Menus list skill levels, activity choices, and content (adjectives, verbs, or nouns) Student chooses from 3 rates in word display and word attack	**Records/Management** No management system No permanent recordkeeping
SAMPLE VOCABULARY	**Clarity** Directions are clearly stated	Student chooses whether to recycle missed words in multiple-choice and sentence completion activities	Student sees records of number of items and percent correct at the end or exit point of sentence completion: at the end or/or exit point of multiple-choice, student also
Level 1 Adjectives abundant - more than enough nimble - quick moving vast - very large	A demonstration is available Frame formatting contributes to clarity	"Help" is available in sentence completion activity	sees number of seconds used; word attack score is based on correct answers, speed of answering, and any bonus
Level 3 Adjectives august - dignified bland - mild exhausted - tired out	**Graphics** Easy-to-read upper and lower case alphabet	Student can exit at will and receive an activity score New word files can be created	points scored for skillful shooting of graphic interloper
Level 5 Nouns morale - a mental attitude passion - a strong feeling tariff - a tax on imports	Word attack activity graphics are simple but appealing	**Feedback** Correct: "Keep it up, Joe" or similar phrase in multiple-choice and sentence completion; points accumulate in word attack activity depending on speed of answering	
Level 7 Verbs dilate - to expand eschew - to avoid flay - to whip	**Audio** Optional in word attack activity	Incorrect: "Try again"; the answer is given after 2 tries in multiple-choice and sentence completion	
Level 9 Verbs abase - to humiliate caulk - to make watertight ratify - to approve		**Random Generation** Vocabulary words are "shuffled"; used for feedback phrases	

FIGURE 7.2 Sample Review from EPIE PRO/FILES Kits (Educational Information Exchange (EPIE) Institute.)

any, of the forms specifically address issues that reading teachers need to be concerned about. It is for this reason that the *Microcomputer Reading Software Review Form* was developed (Figure 7.3).

MICROCOMPUTER READING SOFTWARE REVIEW FORM

Dr. Robert T. Rude
School of Education and Human Development
Rhode Island College
Providence, Rhode Island 02908

Title of Program:

Publisher:

Hardware Configuration and Peripherals Needed:

Copyright Date: Price:

Skill Area(s) Covered (eg. Decoding, Comprehension, Study Skills,
    etc.):

Brief Description of the Program:

Appropriate Grade Level(s):

Instructional Grouping (eg. individual, small group, etc.):

Type of Program (circle):

              Game   Tutorial   Drill and Practice

        Problem Solving   Simulation   Other

Primary Use (circle):

        Developmental   Remedial   Enrichment   Diagnostic   Management

Prerequisite Skills Needed:

Time (in minutes) Needed to use Program:

CONTENT

  Accurate:
  _____
  _____
  _____

  Pedagogically Sound and Consistent with Current Reading Theory:

    A. Does program require encoding or decoding student
        responses?
        _____
        _____

    B. Are decoding skills taught within the context of words?

        _____
        _____

    C. Does the program allow students to respond correctly
        without actually "reading" the words?

        _____
        _____

    D. Is the text material sufficiently meaningful to allow
        the application of phonological, syntactic, and semantic
        cues?
        _____
        _____
        _____
        _____

    E. Does the program encourage the integrated application of
        skills whereby decoding and comprehension skills
        interact with each other?
        _____
        _____
        _____
        _____

    F. Other Pedagogical Concerns:
        _____
        _____
        _____
        _____
        _____

  Instructional Objectives Specified:
  _____
  _____
  _____

  Free of Race, Ethnic, and Social Stereotypes:
  _____
  _____
  _____

INSTRUCTIONAL QUALITY

  Clear and Logical Presentation:
  _____
  _____
  _____

Level of Difficulty Appropriate for Intended Audience:

_____
_____
_____

Clear Directions (for students and teachers):

_____
_____
_____

Motivational Impact:

_____
_____
_____

Use of Appropriate Feedback:

_____
_____
_____

Appropriate Graphics/Color/Sound:

_____
_____
_____

Appropriate Use of Computer Technology:

_____
_____
_____
_____

Opportunities Provided for Transfer of Learning:

_____
_____
_____

Support Materials and Documentation are Comprehensive and
Understandable:

_____
_____
_____
_____
_____

On the basis of this review, summarize your feelings about this
software and decide whether you would recommend it for purchase.

_____
_____
_____
_____
_____
_____

```
----------------------------------------------------------------
----------------------------------------------------------------
----------------------------------------------------------------
----------------------------------------------------------------
----------------------------------------------------------------
----------------------------------------------------------------
----------------------------------------------------------------
----------------------------------------------------------------

                    Reviewer:
                    ----------------------------------------
```

FIGURE 7.3   A Software Review Form for Reading Software

The Microcomputer Reading Software Review Form

The *Microcomputer Reading Software Review Form* is intended to guide teachers of reading as they select courseware for their students. Unlike some commercially available forms, this form requires the reviewer to respond with written statements rather than check marks. As a result, it takes more time to complete than some evaluation systems, but its advantage is that once a software product has been reviewed, it is easy to go back and recall the content and quality of the program, something that is virtually impossible to do with a check-off system.

Another advantage is that it requires considerable thought to complete the form. As a result, the reviewer tends to conduct a more in-depth analysis of the material. Thus, there is greater opportunity to uncover program shortcomings.

A final advantage of the form is that it is especially designed for evaluating reading software. A special section of the form focuses on the pedagogical soundness of the program as it relates to current reading theory. This is important, for if a program is technically well designed but is found wanting because of pedagogical or theoretical limitations, it may not be worth using.

Keeping these general comments in mind, let us examine each of the subsections of the form.

Title of Program.   While this is self-explanatory, one word of caution is warranted. Some programs are available in mutliple versions. Revisions are sometimes indicated by a decimal system such as XYZ 1.1. Or sometimes a revision is simply designated by a roman numeral such as *ScreenWriter II.* Specifying the correct title avoids confusion between earlier and later editions or similarly named programs.

Publisher.   Always record the complete address, including zip code. If a telephone number is provided in the documentation, record it on the review form. Sometimes it is necessary to telephone the company to get answers to technical questions that your local computer store salesperson may be unable to answer (e.g., Will this program load onto a hard disk?).

Hardware Configuration Needed.   This section refers to the specific hardware necessary to run a program. List not only the brand and model of computer but also such things as amount of RAM needed, number of disk drives required, and any other miscellaneous materials required such as color adaptor board, color monitor, printer, or modem.

Copyright Date.   Again, look for revision updates. Revisions of programs are usually noted by different copyright dates. Sometimes a title may not reflect a revision update, but the copyright date almost always alerts the user to this update.

Price.   Some educational software is discounted through mail-order outlets. Make note of this. Remember, though, that some mail-order houses will not process school purchase orders. Highlighting the price the school system will need to pay for the material may ease the eventual ordering process.

Skill Area(s) Covered.   Specify what facet of reading is addressed: decoding, comprehension, study skills, rate, and so on. Some software covers more than one skill area. If so, make note of it. Also, consumers shouldn't totally rely on publishers' claims. Some software vendors believe their programs reinforce decoding or word identification skills when in fact they really stress encoding or spelling. And some spelling programs are really reading programs.

Brief Description of the Program.   Catalog descriptions or other advertising claims usually reflect the program purpose. It is a good idea for reviewers, however, to add insights if there is a discrepancy between the advertising claims and impressions of the software.

Appropriate Grade Level(s).   It is virtually impossible to pinpoint one specific grade level at which a program should be used. It is, however, possible to determine a band of grade-level appropriateness. Preschool, kindergarten, primary, intermediate, junior high school, or high school are the most common categories. Remember, though, what might be appropriate for use at the intermediate school level in one building may be inappropriate in another. The academic capabilities of students determine, to a degree, the appropriateness of any type of instructional material. (How often have you heard a teacher bemoan the fact that a particular basal reader is inappropriate for one group when another teacher feels the material is ideally suited?)

Instructional Grouping.   Microcomputer software can be used in a variety of settings. Some programs that purport to teach comprehension on an individual basis are more appropriately used when a small group of students congregate around a single machine. Collaborative learning can broaden students' understanding of events. Nonetheless, some software is designed to be used individually. This is especially true of materials that automatically keep records of students' progress via a management system. When appropriate, note this feature on the form.

Type of Grouping.   Microcomputer software designed to teach reading skills is generally categorized as one of five or six types of programs: games, tutorial, drill and practice, problem solving, and simulation. Sometimes teacher utility programs are also included as a category. Only a short review of each category will be presented here since a more in-depth analysis with examples was already presented in Chapter 3.

Games are self-explanatory. A number of software publishers have taken advantage of children's interest in arcade games to stimulate interest in learning reading skills. A tic-tac-toe game, for instance, could provide the template for learning vocabulary words.

Tutorial programs are informational sequences followed by questions. Many reading software comprehension activities follow this format. Typically, a paragraph of information is presented followed by multiple-choice questions.

Drill-and-practice activities comprise a high percentage of reading software. More often than not, these programs resemble electronic workbook pages. Many programs that reinforce decoding skills utilize a drill-and-practice format.

Problem-solving programs present information that the student is required to integrate to answer a problem. A story in which one of three answers to a question might help solve a mystery is an example of problem-solving software.

Simulations are the most sophisticated types of educational programs. Simulations used to teach reading are generally not reading programs, per se, but science and social studies programs that require students to read connected discourse. One popular simulation places children as fur traders attempting to increase their wealth by trapping furs and selling them at one of three forts. Reading ability as well as strategy and luck are needed to outwit the program.

Utility programs permit the computer to be used to perform special functions such as preparing worksheets, word search games, crossword puzzles, banners, and so on. These programs are designed primarily for teacher use rather than student use.

Readers are reminded that it is often difficult to categorize programs, since they may actually be "hybrids" of two or more types of software (such as a game as well as a simulation). Identifying categories is only a means to help comprehend program underpinnings and should not be viewed as a cut-and-dried affair.

Primary Use.   Reading software may be designed to be used in developmental, remedial, or enrichment settings. Furthermore, some programs provide diagnostic profiles of student performance or automatically record student responses. An experienced reading teacher can quickly match print materials with an appropriate audience. The same general principles apply to computer software. Interest level, conceptual understanding necessary, and vocabulary load are just three factors that may make a program appropriate for developmental readers but inappropriate for remedial students.

Prerequisite Skills Needed.   All software used to teach reading requires some prerequisite abilities. Programs designed to teach letter recognition, for example, usually require familiarity with the computer keyboard—especially the Enter or Return key and the space bar. At a more advanced level, students may need sophisticated decoding skills to read the text found in adventure game programs. A child unable to apply the principles of syllabication, for instance, may be unable to unlock the word "cryogenic." In fact, preteaching of vocabulary may be necessary to understand the meaning of the word.

Time Needed to Use Program.   The time needed to use programs varies tremendously. At one extreme, many drill-and-practice activities can be completed in five or ten minutes. On the other hand, some interactive novels require considerable student input and can last for hours or even days. It's important to determine time requirements so computer activities can be scheduled in the time allocations available. Educators shouldn't overlook the fact that it takes time to load and save some programs. This fact should be considered when filling out the review form.

Content.   Content is perhaps the most important aspect of software review. Unless a program possesses intellectually honest and well-presented content, the technical adequacy of the software is of little consequence. Kurland (1983), Lathrop and Goodson (1983), and Steinberg (1983) warn about the lack of quality software in today's marketplace. As mentioned earlier, this problem is due in part to the fact that some reading software has been designed by individuals who possess considerable knowledge about computers and programming but know little about reading theory or pedagogy. In order to be useful, educational software must be pedagogically adequate. As reading professionals, we know that some practices lead to improvement in reading while other practices are left wanting. Here are a few important characteristics that teachers should look for when examining reading software.

Many noncomputer activities that teach decoding skills require verbal responses from students. Reading software, however, usually requires the student to type a response (word) on the keyboard. The difference between these two activities is that the former requirement demands decoding (reading) while the latter requires encoding (spelling). One way this limitation can be overcome, though, is by having pairs of students work at the computer. The more accomplished reader can then check the reading accuracy of the less able child. This also increases the number of students who can use the computers at any one time.

Decoding skills should also be taught by having students read words in connected discourse. This permits them to use all of the cueing systems available: phonological, semantic, and syntactic. Words presented in isolation, more often than not, only permit use of the phonological system.

Some programs permit students simply to strike keys at random until the correct response is found. This is hardly the type of help they need to become independent readers. A good software program should reduce the chances of a correct response being entered by guessing.

To encourage comprehension, text material should be meaningful. Nonsense words flashed on the screen do little to encourage appropriate reading strategies. Ideally, the material should be of high interest and written at a student's instructional level. Just as teachers shouldn't prescribe conventional print materials written at a child's frustration level, so too should they avoid assigning computer software that is written at one's frustration level.

The instructional objectives of a program should always be identified by the program developer. These objectives need not be displayed on the screen, but they should at least be available in the support materials that accompany software. Objectives provide a number of benefits. First, they permit teachers to determine if the software is appropriate for the intended use. Next, objectives permit educators to select or develop tests to determine whether the content has been learned. Finally, objectives assist teachers in determining if the software is suitable for the intended audience. Without having specific objectives identified, multiple reviews of the software may be needed to determine the content. This may require many hours—something most teachers can ill afford. Objectives provide a quick overview of the program.

Finally, educational software should meet the same standards that are used to judge print material appropriateness. There is no place, therefore, for software that perpetuates race, ethnic, or social stereotypes.

Instructional Quality. According to Roblyer (1981), instructional materials used with microcomputers should meet the same mechanical demands as those used for noncomputerized media. That means that misspellings and grammatical errors are unpardonable. Materials with these shortcomings should be discarded or returned to the publisher, since using them with students may send an implicit message to students: pride in work is unimportant.

Teachers should also demand materials that are clearly and logically presented. This is especially true of comprehensive software packages that attempt to cover a variety of reading skills. Programs that present multiple decoding or study skills, for example, should have them laid out in a logical hierarchy. Alphabetization skills could be organized from correctly arranging single letters in words to two-letter words and then proceed on to three or more letter words.

It is important that the software take advantage of typical age-group knowledge and maturation. Learners must have the prerequisite background of experiences if they are expected to complete some assignments. Furthermore, the instructional pace must be commensurate with the ability level of the target group.

Ideally, programs should be so easy to use that they are self-prompting. Such programs are sometimes referred to as "menu driven" or "user friendly." Many programs, however, lack this ease of use. Instead, students (and teachers) must labor over the documentation that accompanies the program. It is imperative, therefore, that the documentation be clearly written and easy to understand. Conceivably, it could be so difficult to comprehend that the user would be unable to decipher the instructions and would refuse to use the program. Directions for program use should be examined from two perspectives: the teacher's and the student's. Software that doesn't meet the clarity criteria for both groups should be avoided.

Use of Appropriate Feedback.   According to Roblyer (1981), studies investigating the use of feedback in computer-assisted instruction have revealed that students are not always interested in receiving feedback for correct answers. Instead, they are more interested in feedback when an inappropriate response is given, since the feedback may enable them to select the right answer the second time. Programs should always provide useful corrective information when incorrect answers are given by students (Steinberg, 1983). Correct feedback may, in part, be one reason why computer-assisted instruction is viewed by children in such a positive light. It is in our interest as educators, then, to select programs that provide this type of meaningful feedback.

The nature of feedback might vary from group to group. Young children may be delighted to see a blinking clown appear whenever they correctly match two letters. Older students, however, would frown on such feedback. Instead, they might find statements such as "Great job, Fred," or "No, but you are very close. Try again." to be more meaningful. The impersonal feedback of some programs leaves much to be desired. Whenever a child correctly answered a question in one program reviewed by the author, the computer responded "Good job, student." By simply using the student's name instead of the impersonal word "student," a friendlier, more personal tone would have been imparted.

Appropriate Graphics/Color/Sound.   The necessity of using graphics, color, and sound varies from program to program. Each of these attributes influences the quality of the software. Adventure-type reading games for young children are so dependent on graphics that without it the programs would be totally uninteresting. Arguments can be made for and against the use of sound to enhance a program. Some teachers prefer programs that provide the user with the option of toggling the sound off or on. While many educators find the roar of laser beams and the shrill of bells and whistles distracting, the author met one remedial reading teacher who commented that she loved this din. It was when the computer stopped making noise that she knew her students were experiencing problems or were up to no good!

Appropriate Use of Computer Technology.   Simply put, software programs should have features not contained in conventional instructional material. Immediate feedback, record-keeping capability, and a high degree of interaction are three features frequently not available from other materials. As mentioned earlier, using the computer as an electronic workbook is not a cost-effective practice.

Opportunities Provided for Transfer of Learning.   There are several ways in which transfer of learning can be enhanced. When learning vocabulary words, for example, make sure that the words are presented in phrase, sentence, or paragraph settings. Since this is how students usually encounter words outside of school settings, it only makes good sense to provide opportunities to use the words in realistic settings. A second way in which transfer of learning can be enhanced is through the supplementary materials that are sometimes included with computer software. These materials might be stories that require students to use the skills learned earlier on the computer. As a rule of thumb, the closer the match between the material to be learned and the setting in which the skill or information to be used is found, the greater the chance for transfer of learning to take place.

Support Materials Are Comprehensive and Understandable.   Some of the most exemplary support materials are those issued with Minnesota Educational Computing Consortium (MECC) programs. Each diskette is accompanied by extensive documentation that includes (1) objectives of the lesson; (2) illustrations of selected screen information; (3) maps, charts, or graphs; (4) worksheets; and (5) suggested follow-up activities.

On the other hand, some educational software is accompanied only by a single sheet of paper listing the program title, credits, the hardware configuration needed to run the program, and a copyright statement. Choosing between these two sets of support materials should be easy for most reviewers.

Summary.   It is a good idea to draft a summary statement regarding your overall feelings about the program once it has been reviewed. At this point, some individuals prefer to assign a quality point rating. A frequently used scale is one where 1 represents a program of low quality and a 10 indicates a program of merit. Many reviewers also make a recommendation regarding purchase of the software. This procedure enables an individual to go back at a later time and determine whether the program should be included in a school's software collection.

SOME CLOSING THOUGHTS ABOUT MICROCOMPUTER SOFTWARE

Conducting personal reviews of reading software is a time-consuming task that takes considerably longer than simply reading a review of the program in an educational computing journal. Some authorities (Gleason, 1981) have suggested that a thorough software review of a typical software program takes approximately forty hours. Using the *Microcomputer Reading Software Review Form* as a guide reduces this time to between two and four hours, excluding time needed to observe the program actually being used by students.

While it might be quicker to use a ten-item checklist, such lists invariably come up short. Checklists and simple rating scales don't require the qualitative analysis that a written review form demands. So, while it requires more time to complete a formal, written review, the time is well spent, since the level of analysis exceeds that of a checklist.

Each reviewer ultimately needs to develop standards that are workable and permit reviewing of a wide variety of software materials. Conceivably, no single form can fulfill all needs. Nevertheless, it is important to have a jumping-off point whereby materials can begin to be reviewed. The purpose of the *Microcomputer Reading Software Review Form* is to serve as an initial screening device in discovering instructionally effective materials. As such, it is a means to an end. Don't permit the form to become an end in itself. If necessary, users should modify the form to fit their particular needs.

SUMMARY

Overall, computer-assisted instruction can result in a number of positive benefits. These benefits cannot occur, however, unless educational software of sufficiently high value is used. While more and more reading software packages appear on the market, teachers of reading need to become critical consumers of this software. The quality of software can be determined in a number of ways: by reading published reviews in trade magazines, by reading the journals of the profession, and finally, by reviewing the software independently. This chapter has suggested the benefits and limitations of each of these processes. One thing is for sure. Selecting high-quality reading software is a personal matter that varies from individual to individual. It is hoped that this chapter and the text generally have enumerated the opening steps that teachers must take to move into the educational computing arena gracefully and with confidence.

RELATED READINGS

JONES, NANCY BAKER, and LARRY VAUGHAN (eds.). *Evaluation of Educational Software: A Guide to Guides*. Chelmsford, Mass.: Northeast Regional Exchange, 1983.
NATIONAL COUNCIL OF TEACHERS OF MATHEMATICS. *Guidelines for Evaluating Computerized Instructional Materials*. Reston, Va.: National Council of Teachers of Mathematics, 1981.
WALKER, DECKER F., and ROBERT D. HESS (eds.). *Instructional Software: Principles and Perspectives for Design and Use*. Belmont, Calif.: Wadsworth Publishing Company, 1984.

REFERENCES

BUDOFF, MILTON, and LEAH R. HUTTEN, "Microcomputers in Special Education: Promises and Pitfalls," *Exceptional Children*, Vol. 49, no. 2 (October 1982), 123–128.

GLEASON, GERALD T., "Microcomputers in Education: The State of the Art," *Educational Technology*, Vol. 21, no. 3 (March 1981), 7–18.

HOFMEISTER, ALAN M., "Microcomputers in Perspective," *Exceptional Children*, Vol. 49, no. 2 (October 1982), 115–121.

HOLMES, GLYN, "Computer-Assisted Instruction: A Discussion of Some of the Issues for Would-be Implementors," *Educational Technology*, Vol. 22, no. 9 (September 1982), 7–13.

HUNTINGTON, JOHN, "The Impact of Changing Computer Resources on Educational Institutions and Computer-Based Educational Training Programs," *Educational Technology*, Vol. 21, no. 10 (October 1981), 55–59.

JUDD, DOROTHY H., "Learning to Read and Write Using the Computer," *Educational Computer*, Vol. 3, no. 6 (October 1983), 22, 24.

KURLAND, D. MIDIAN, "Educational Software Tools: The Rationale Behind the Development of the Bank Street Writer," *Teaching Writing Through Technology*, Chelmsford, Mass.: Northeast Regional Exchange (1983), 112–123.

LATHROP, ANN, "Software ... Previewing and Reviewing," *Educational Computer Magazine* (September–October 1981).

LATHROP, ANN, and BOBBY GOODSON, *Courseware in the Classroom*, Menlo Park, Calif.: Addison-Wesley Publishing Company, 1983.

MERTON, ANDREW, "Computers in the Classroom," *Technology in the Classroom*, Vol. 3, no. 9 (September 1983), 39–42, 44, 46.

ROBLYER, M. D., "When Is It 'Good Courseware'? Problems in Developing Standards for Microcomputer Courseware," *Educational Technology*, Vol. 21, no. 10 (October 1981), 47–54.

SPENCER, MIMA, and LINDA BASKIN, "Computers in the Classroom," *Childhood Education*, Vol. 59, no. 4 (March–April 1983), 293–296.

STEINBERG, ESTER R., "Reviewing the Instructional Effectiveness of Computer Courseware," *Educational Technology*, Vol. 23, no. 1, (January 1983), 17–19.

THOMAS, REX, and BRIAN GUSTAFSON, "The Design, Development and Evaluation of a Low-Cost Computer-Managed Spelling System," *Association for Educational Data Systems*, Vol. 16, no. 3 (Spring 1983), 168–176.

APPENDIX A

SELECTED COMPUTER BOOKS FOR STUDENTS

BASIC Fun: Computer Games, Puzzles, and Problems Children Can Write by SUSAN LIPSCOMB and MARGARET ZUANICH (Avon, 1982).
BASIC Programming for Kids by ROSALIE SAIN (Houghton Mifflin, 1983).
Chip Mitchell: The Case of the Stolen Computer Brains by FRED D'IGNAZIO (Dutton, 1983).
Computer by IAN GRAHAM (Watts, 1983).
Computer Anatomy for Beginners by MARLIN OUVERSON (Reston, 1982).
Computer Basics by HAL HELLMAN (Prentice-Hall, 1983).
Computers by LINDA O'BRIEN (Watts, 1978).
Computers by NEIL ARDLEY (Watts, 1983).
Computers: How They Work by NIGEL HAWKES (Watts, 1983).
Computers in Your Life by MELVIN BERGER (Crowell, 1981).
The Computer That Said Steal Me by ELIZABETH LEVY (Four Winds, 1983).
The Computer Caper by MILTON DANK and GLORIA DANK (Dell, 1983).
The Creative Kid's Guide to Home Computers by FRED D'IGNAZIO (Doubleday, 1981).
Cupid Computer by MARJORIE MILCSIK (Atheneum, 1981).
From Baker Street to Binary: An Introduction to Computers and Computer Programming with Sherlock Holmes by HENRY LEDGARD, E. PATRICK McQUAID, and ANDREW SINGER (McGraw-Hill, 1983).
Home Computers—A Simple and Informative Guide by SCOTT CORBETT (Little, Brown, 1980).
The Human Side of Computers by DANIEL COHEN (McGraw-Hill, 1975).
Inside Your Computer by I. R. SINCLAIRE (Wayne Green, 1983).
Katie and the Computer by FRED D'IGNAZIO (Creative Computing Press, 1979).
The Kid's Guide to Home Computers by DANIEL and SUSAN COHEN (Pocket, 1983).
Miracle Chip: The Microelectronic Revolution by STANLEY ENGLEBARDT (Lothrop, Lee, and Shepard, 1979).
Programmed for Love by JUDITH ENDERLE (Berkley, 1983).
What Can She Be? A Computer Scientist by GLORIA GOLDREICH and ESTER GOLDREICH (Lothrop, Lee and Shepard, 1979).

APPENDIX B

SOFTWARE DISCUSSED IN THIS BOOK

Antonyms and Synonyms (Hartley Publishing Company)
The Apple Gradebook (Creative Computing Software)
Bank Street Writer (Scholastic Publishing Company)
Banner (Sam Wilson & Associates)
The Battle of Shiloh (Strategic Simulations, Inc.)
The Benchmark Spelling Checker (MetaSoft Publishing Company)
The Benchmark Word Processing System (MetaSoft Publishing Company)
Cloze Plus (Milliken Publishing Company)
Comprehension Power (Milliken Publishing Company)
Contractions (Educational Activities, Inc.)
Courseware Development System I (CDS) (Bell and Howell)
Computer Air Combat (Strategic Simulations, Inc.)
Computer Baseball (Strategic Simulations, Inc.)
Computer Quarterback (Strategic Simulations, Inc.)
Create—Vocabulary (Hartley Publishing Company)
Dragon's Keep (Sierra On-Line)
DragonWare: Spelling Bee Games (Edu-Ware, Inc.)
Enchanter (Infocom, Inc.)
Fighter Command (Strategic Simulations, Inc.)
The Game Show (Computer Advanced Ideas)
Geopolitique (Strategic Simulations, Inc.)
Getting Ready to Read and Add—Elementary, Volume 7 (MECC)
Ginn Computer Management System (Ginn and Company)
Homonyms (Hartley Publishing Company)
Homonyms (Milliken Publishing Company)
Homonyms in Context (Random House School Division)
The Learning System (Micro Lab Learning Center)
Letter Recognition (Hartley Publishing Company)
Lexicheck IIe (Quark, Inc.)
Magic Window II (Artsci, Inc.)
Magic Words (Artsci, Inc.)
Mastertype (Scarborough Systems)
Matchmaker (Counterpoint Software, Inc.)
MECC—Elementary—Mathematics, Volume 1 (MECC)
MECC—Elementary—Language Arts, Volume 2 (MECC)
Peachtext 5000 (Peachtree Software, Inc.)
PFS: File (Software Publishing Corporation)

PFS: Graph (Software Publishing Corporation)
PFS: School Recordkeeper (Software Publishing Corporation)
PFS: Write (Software Publishing Corporation)
Prefixes—Elementary, Volume 5 (MECC)
Quill (D. C. Heath)
Readability Analysis Program (Random House School Division)
Reading Level Analysis (Bertamax, Inc.)
The Road to Gettysburg (Strategic Simulations, Inc.)
SAT Word Attack Skills (Edu-Ware, Inc.)
*School Utilities—*Volume 2 (MECC)
The Sensible Speller (Sensible Software, Inc.)
Sentence Combining (Milliken Publishing Company)
Spellagraph (DesignWare)
Spellakazam (DesignWare)
Spellicopter (DesignWare)
The Spelling System (Milliken Publishing Company)
Story Machine (Spinnaker Software)
Story Maker (Bolt, Beranek, and Newman, Inc.)
Study Skills: Alphabetization Sequence (Milliken Publishing Company)
Suspended (Infocom, Inc.)
Tennis Anyone—Plurals (Data Command)
Tic Tac Show (Computer Advanced Ideas)
Troll's Tale (Sierra On-Line)
Type Attack (Sirius Software)
Typing Tutor III (Microsoft Corporation)
Vocabulary—Dolch (Hartley Publishing Company)
Vocabulary—Elementary (Hartley Publishing Company)
VisiCalc (Personal Software Inc.)
VisiPlot/VisiTrend (Personal Software Inc.)
Vowels (Hartley Publishing Company)
Wisconsin Design Computer Management System (Learning Multi-Systems, Inc.)
The Witness (Infocom, Inc.)
Word Attack (Davidson & Associates)
Word Juggler (Quark, Inc.)
Word Master (Developmental Learning Materials)
Wordsearch (Hartley Publishing Company)

APPENDIX C

PUBLISHERS' ADDRESSES

Artsci, Inc.
5547 Satsuma Ave.
North Hollywood, Calif. 91601

Bell and Howell
7100 N. McCormick
Chicago, Ill. 60645

Bertamax, Inc.
101 Nickerson St., Suite #550
Seattle, Wash. 98109

Bolt, Beranek, and Newman, Inc.
50 Moulton St.
Cambridge, Mass. 02138

Computer Advanced Ideas
1442A Walnut Street, Suite 341
Berkeley, Calif. 94709

Counterpoint Software, Inc.
4005 West Sixty-fifth St.
Minneapolis, Minn. 55435

Creative Computing Software
39 East Hanover Ave.
Morris Plains, N.J. 07950

D. C. Heath Software
D. C. Heath and Company
Lexington, Mass. 02173

Data Command
670 Broadway
Bradley, Ill. 60915

Davidson & Associates
6069 Groveoak Place, #12
Rancho Palos Verdes, Calif. 90274

DesignWare
185 Berry St., Building Three, Suite 158
San Francisco, Calif. 94107

Developmental Learning Materials
1 DLM Park
Allen, Tex. 75002

Edu-Ware, Inc.
3445 Peachtree Road, N.E.
8th Floor
Atlanta, Ga. 30326

Ginn and Company
P.O. Box 2649
Columbus, Ohio 43216

Hartley Publishing Company
P.O. Box 431
Dimondale, Mich. 48821

Holt, Rhinehart & Winston
School Marketing Dept.
383 Madison Ave.
New York, N.Y. 10017

Infocom, Inc.
P.O. Box 855
Garden City, N.Y. 11530

Learning Multi-Systems, Inc.
340 Coyier Lane
Madison, Wisc. 53713

Lightning Software
Box 11725
Palo Alto, Calif. 95014

MetaSoft Publishing Company
6509 West Frye Road, Suite 12
Chandler, Ariz. 85224

Micro Lab Learning Center
2310 Skokie Valley Rd.
Highland Park, Ill. 60035

Microsoft, Inc.
10700 Northup Way
Bellevue, Wash. 98004

Milliken Publishing Company
1100 Research Blvd.
St. Louis, Mo. 63132

Minnesota Educational Computing Consortium
2520 Broadway Drive
St. Paul, Minn. 55113

Peachtree Software Incorporated
3445 Peachtree Road, N.E.
8th Floor
Atlanta, Ga. 30326

Personal Software, Inc.
1330 Bordeaux Drive
Sunnyvale, Calif. 94086

Quark, Inc.
2525 West Evans, Suite 220
Denver, Colo. 80219

Random House School Division
400 Hahn Rd.
Westminster, Md. 21157

Sam Wilson & Associates
NBC Building, Suite 420
7500 Bellaire Blvd.
Houston, Tex. 77036

Scarborough Systems, Inc.
25 N. Broadway
Tarrytown, N.Y. 10591

Scholastic Publishing Company
730 Broadway
New York, N.Y. 10016

Sensible Software
6619 Perham Drive
West Bloomfield, Mich. 48033

Sirius Software
10364 Rockingham Drive
Sacramento, Calif. 95827

Sierra On-Line
Sierra On-Line Building
Coarsegold, Calif. 93614

Software Publishing Corporation
1901 Landings Drive
Mountain View, Calif. 94043

Spinnaker Software
215 First Street
Cambridge, Mass. 02142

Strategic Simulations, Inc.
883 Stierlin Road, Bldg. A-200
Mountain View, Calif. 94043-1983

Author Index

Subject Index